D0373922

Clive James was born in Sydney in 1939, and educated at Sydney University and at Cambridge, where he was President of Footlights. He has published four mock-epic poems, *Peregrine Prykke's Pilgrimage*, *The Fate of Felicity Fark*, *Britannia Bright's Bewilderment* and *Charles Charming's Challenges*; a book of verse letters, *Fan-Mail*; three books of literary criticism, *The Metropolitan Critic*, *At the Pillars of Hercules* and *From the Land of Shadows* (which is available in Picador); and the autobiography *Unreliable Memoirs* (also available in Picador). He was television critic of the *Observer* between 1972 and 1982, and has published three selections from his column, *Visions Before Midnight*, *The Crystal Bucket* and *Glued to the Box* (all available in Picador). He himself has made frequent appearances on television, most notably in 'Saturday Night People'. 'The Clive James Paris Fashion Show' was nominated for an Emmy and 'Clive James at the Movies' for a *BAFTA* award.

Also by Clive James in Picador

Unreliable Memoirs
Visions Before Midnight
The Crystal Bucket
Glued to the Box
From the Land of Shadows

Clive James

BRILLIANT CREATURES

published by Pan Books

First published 1983 by Jonathan Cape Ltd
This Picador edition published 1984 by Pan Books Ltd,
Cavaye Place, London SW10 9PG
© Clive James 1983
ISBN 0 330 28343 X
Printed and bound in Great Britain by
Cox & Wyman Ltd, Reading

This book is sold subject to the condition that it
shall not, by way of trade or otherwise, be lent, re-sold,
hired out or otherwise circulated without the publisher's prior
consent in any form of binding or cover other than that in which
it is published and without a similar condition including this
condition being imposed on the subsequent purchaser

to Prue Shaw

Mi trasse Beatrice, e disse: 'Mira
Quanto è il convento delle bianche stole!
Vedi nostra città quanto ella gira!'

Paradiso **XXX**, 128–30

I have looked upon those brilliant creatures,
And now my heart is sore.

Yeats, *The Wild Swans at Coole*

But when Queen Guenever wist that Sir Launcelot bare the red sleeve of the fair maiden of Astolat she was nigh out of her mind for wrath. And then she sent for Sir Bors de Ganis in all the haste that might be. So when Sir Bors was come tofore the queen, then she said: Ah, Sir Bors, have ye heard say how falsely Sir Launcelot hath betrayed me? Alas madam, said Sir Bors, I am afeared he hath betrayed himself and us all.

Malory, *Le Morte d'Arthur*, XVIII, 15

~ INTRODUCTION ~

This book is my second attempt to avoid writing a novel. The first, called *Unreliable Memoirs*, I got away with by labelling as an autobiography, but the same trick will not work twice. So this book will have to be called a novel, even though it is patently not a novel in the accepted sense. For the novel in the accepted sense I have nothing but respect. Hundreds of them come out each year and the few that I manage to absorb rarely fail to astonish me by the author's capacity to take a genuine interest in the world and put his own personality in the back seat. I have made all the usual cracks about there being too many novels. I believe I was the first to suggest that there should be an Arts Council grant for not writing a novel. The candidate would submit an outline of the novel he proposed not to write. If he proposed not to write a whole sequence of novels, the grant would be renewed annually.

But such jokes were defensive. I had long since become impressed, not to say depressed, by the high state of development the modern novel had reached, especially among my acquaintances. Some of these latter I knew to be personally ambitious beyond the point of mania, yet their novels were miracles of detached limpidity. All the lessons ever taught by my illustrious ancestor Henry (this is a rare acknowledgment of consanguinity, since the Australian branch of the family seldom mentions the American connection) had been thoroughly assimilated. Not even the first-person narrator, if the novel had one, could remotely be identified with the writer. If a man were writing, it would be a woman's viewpoint. If a woman were writing, it would be a child's. If a child, a dog's. Everything was distanced, poised, gravid with implication. What room could there possibly be for a would-be novelist who wrote directly from the self, could create no characters that were not elements of the self, and had no real area of interest beyond what Gide, talking about Montaigne, called the mutability of the self? Not a lot.

Not a lot, but some. Because although the novel proper has always tended towards an autonomous naturalism in which everything must pass the test of credibility, there has also always been, tending in the opposite direction, the novel improper. The relationship of the novel improper to the novel proper is nothing like so grand as the relationship of antimatter to matter. There is no antagonism: they do not explode when they meet. Indeed there is no real equivalence: the novel proper is in the main line of human achievement and the novel improper is, at best, what used to be called a sport. But in the English language the novel improper has its own interesting heritage from Sterne down through Peacock to Firbank and beyond, and in addition there has always been a gratifyingly high incidence of respectable novelists who show signs of wanting to kick over the traces. Trollope often got sick of thinking up realistic names, for example, and employed facetious ones instead, to the pious anguish of my aforementioned great namesake thrice removed.

Whether *Finnegans Wake* is the one thing or the other is a question that a sensible critic will dodge answering, even if he has read it. All I mean to say is that for the writer who hasn't got what it takes to write an adequate novel, there are precedents to suggest that the inadequate novel is a worthwhile category of its own. Peacock's *Nightmare Abbey* hasn't got much character development, but think of its high good humour. Firbank's *Vainglory* hasn't got much political commitment, but think of its distilled elegance. It will be pointed out that these men had genius. But often, in the arts, that is what genius does for the rest of us – it shows the way by taking childish liberties. Peacock wanted to goose his friends while unloading some of his curious erudition, so he did it. Firbank wanted to call a stuffed shirt Sir Somebody Something, so he did it.

We are all thankful for the way contemporary poetry explores the depths, but most thankful is the poet who scratches the surface, because he can go on working with a clear conscience. By the same token, with so many gifted, dedicated novelists pushing their medium to its limits, there is some warrant for reactionary frivolity. The worst that can happen is that nobody will notice. So in this book, with my sense of duty taken care of by a hundred seriously toiling contemporaries, I have undertaken to do nothing except indulge myself, although I hope it has not been done at anybody's expense except my own. The character called the world's most famous young female film star might possibly recognise herself. There is a notoriously clever playwright who might just pick himself out of the crowd. Otherwise those who think that every *roman* must have a *clef* will speculate in vain. Everyone in the book is a fabrication, either fulfilling the author's wish for virtue or placating his regret for vice. Saints and monsters may identify if they wish, but no normal person looks like any of these people, talks in their measured sentences, or has so much free time in the day. Everyone I know works for a living if he is lucky. There are no bright and beautiful television girls who drive Porsche 928 sports cars. Most of the bright ones aren't beautiful, most of the beautiful ones aren't bright, and of the two that are both, one can't drive and the other owns a second-hand Audi with the back bumper crumpled from a shunt.

These are the creatures of my mind, such as it is. Perhaps I invent them only to prove that solipsism, in its next to final stage, is at least capable of diagnosing itself. 'I am all the daughters of my father's house,' says Viola in *Twelfth Night*, 'and all the brothers too.' There are no prizes for feeling like that. But there should yet be space on a bookshop shelf for the kind of novel that can never win the Booker Prize. And there is no telling that I will not get a grant to write another. In Australia a novelist got a grant for a book called *I Strapped a Mirror to My Brain*.

Which could almost be the subtitle of this book, if I stopped to think about it. But why think about it when I have a trained scholar to think about it for me? Ably providing the critical notes at the end of the text, Peter C. Bartelski (of Sydney, Sussex and Sidney Sussex College, Cambridge) is a living legend who, if he did not exist, I would scarcely dare to invent. To fabricate my polymath compatriot would have been to ape Nabokov's *Pale Fire*, an example of the novel improper with which only a fool would try to compete. Besides, as a part-time critic myself I am slow to mock the full-time don who can go on seeing significance when the rest of us have been forced by pressure of time to abandon the quest. Most readers will call it a night at the end of the last chapter if they get that far, but in the unlikely event of My First Novel making its mark in the academic world, Peter C. Bartelski's efforts will at least help ensure that any critical discussion, even if condemnatory, takes place at a suitably informed level. He knows everything. If I have ever read half the books he says I have, I long ago forgot what was in them. It is good to be told that their contents have been incorporated into my innermost being. Only one objection to his line of argument can I find. He seems to suggest that this book rehearses the imminent collapse of civilisation as we know it. I don't think we'll get out of it that easily.

This book is so full of other books, old pictures and remembered music, is such a box of borrowed clothes which the characters put on themselves and on each other, that it might seem at first like an echo of what Nietzsche once said about how only an aesthetic attitude can justify the world. But it will emerge, if the reader perseveres, that my own belief is to the contrary. The world justifies itself and would still be worth living in if there were no art. Only on that assumption does art provide solace. Art can't be escaped to. It isn't Switzerland.

This is the story of a man who thought it was. He mistook his weak moments for sensitivity, gave himself up to the allure of the beautiful, and almost vanished. One knows him well, although one can never know him well enough. In the year 658 BC a certain Chinese individual, important then but forgotten now, was described in the official annals as having been robbed by Heaven of his mirror. They meant that he had become blind to his own faults.

Brilliant Creatures

~ one ~

'Hark!' cried Lancelot Windhover, waking up in his usual frenzy of hyperventilation, or whatever you call it when you can't remember how to breathe. 'Whelk! Faugh! Noah! Quark!' He gave himself artificial respiration. After a while it worked. When the panic was over the despair started. With heaving chest he mentally reviewed his troubles and could see no real reason for continuing to live. Elegantly he tottered to the window, his body, with the possible exception of a pair of small motorcycle-style panniers at the waist, looking like the corporeal manifestation of a fit man half his age – which would have been, should you have made it, a pretty fair assessment of his true emotional development, since nobody so old can look so young without a certain deficiency in the gift for self-criticism. Or so, at any rate, Lancelot thought, giving himself points for the critical insight but taking them away again because of the revealed proneness to soul-searching, which he regarded as self-obsession. Not quite the same thing as self-criticism, but more than enough to reduce him to desperation all by itself, even without the aid of the joke panorama visible when he dragged aside the heavy curtains.

Rain fell as if an expensive postal address gave you no privileges at all. Members of the Royal Family lived not far away. Were they getting rained on to this extent? Lancelot flaked crusts of yellow sleep out of his eyes. As a physical satisfaction this activity ranked somewhere below nosepicking but sometimes it takes only the tiniest success to bring a waverer back from the brink. He formed the intention not to commit suicide after all. It was his first big mistake of the day.

Elsewhere in the large house, his wife and children were no doubt up and about by now, if not gone shopping or to school or whatever it was they did. Although Lancelot still made love to his wife he drew the line at sleeping with her, and thus tended to get out of touch with her plans. Charlotte he had married for an automatic entrée to the less interesting but, he had presumed, more deeply satisfying world which lay beyond and above the Bohemia he had already conquered. In his then role as the stylesetter of his Oxbridge generation he had found many doors open, thereby gaining a perspective of further doors which only a judicious marriage could get him through. Charlotte was a particularly beautiful, particularly clever daughter of the academic establishment. Her family had been professorial since well before Darwin left for Tierra del Fuego. Lancelot, not wholly blinded by love, had seen a chance for the kind of respectability that mere brilliance finds it difficult to attain. Perhaps he should have realised that the pleasure Charlotte took in his company was a token of how the studious network in which she had grown up bored her to distraction. She wanted from him the excitement of primal creation, he from her the secure base of enrolment in a secular clergy. So each of them had in time found that the new door led into an empty room. But at least for him it was a safe place, where he had been at first surprised, and then saddened, to discover that his proposed exploitation of his wife's connections had turned to an actual dependence on her stable personality. Nowadays he never fell in love without dreading the possibility of being forced to leave home. He was like that Chinese firework called a plate-spinner. It must have a plate or it won't spin.

Nine in the morning in London meant that it was well before dawn in New York, so it would be foolish to telephone Samantha. Disturbed at that hour she would be spiteful even if alone. Not that there was any doubt about alone being the way that she would be. That she would be alone was so inevitable there was no point checking up. Also the question was moot whether being subject to a stream of abuse would necessarily be all that much better than not hearing her voice at all. Certain sections of her body came into his mind, inducing a rush of aching sweetness which he guessed must be what heroin felt like when injected – he was too old to know. Samantha probably knew, just as she knew everything else that was not worth knowing. She touched herself while making love but then all the girls in her age-group did that nowadays, just as they all had

14

the same cursive handwriting. He supposed his daughters did it too. Telephoning her would be a mistake, no question of it.

'You woke me up.'

'It doesn't sound like it. Have you got somebody with you?'

'That's difficult to say.'

'Is he on the job at this actual moment or are you just lying beside each other radiating a soft glow of well-being?'

'It's impossible to tell at this stage. Why don't you ask me when I've had a chance to go through the documents?'

'Go to buggery.'

'That would be marvellous. I'll ring you at work.'

Feeling sick, Lancelot headed for the nearest bathroom. What he saw Feydeau doing on the stairhead landing made him feel sicker. Youngest of the dogs, Feydeau was trying to screw his expensive behind into the weft of the carpet. Presumably this had something to do with an irritated sphincter, although whether the condition was being exacerbated or ameliorated by the treatment was hard to tell, since the resulting whimpers were open to either interpretation. Lancelot tried to take solace from his ability to do that sort of thing in a specially designed room. There was something to being human even when you were brought face to face with your inadequacies.

Not that what he saw in the mirror showed any particular signs of anguish long endured. Nor would it have done even to, say, Colette, who when analysing her hero Chéri's physiognomy had been able to tell so much from the texture of his eyelids. In Lancelot's case there was simply not a great deal to analyse beyond a pleasant regularity of features, the lower planes of which he now shaved, sealing the open skin with a liquid which boasted in Spanish that it had been created especially for men. His plenitude of straight blond hair felt itchy at the roots but he decided to postpone washing either it or the body which held it a slightly greater than average distance off the ground. Tonight would do. It was the second such procrastination in two days: Lancelot felt no compulsion towards a diurnal bath. If challenged he would invoke the threat it posed to the natural oils, over which he now drew various items of plain, well chosen and expensive clothing.

'Feydeau's doing something unspeakable on the landing,' said

Lancelot when he reached the kitchen, in which their cook, called something like Mrs Hermesetas, was currently ferrying bacon and eggs from the stove to the stripped pine table. At the window end of the table sat Lancelot's wife. At the other end was his younger daughter Tessa, who was dressed in jet-black jodhpurs and a sequinned bomber jacket, as well as being painted and decorated like an extraterrestrial doll. Her hair was arranged in spikes, each a separate colour of Italian ice-cream and terminating in a tinsel star. Also present were two more dogs, Scribe and Sardou, snuffling in counterpoint as they sucked up separate platefuls, left over from the previous evening, of a chopped food which was supposed to contain so much meat that there was really small point in the dog-owner's not sitting down to join the animal for an intimate supper by candlelight.

'Did you walk him?' Charlotte asked Tessa, who shrugged her puffed shoulders by way of reply and left the room with a tinkling of little bells. An independent observer might have supposed that she was absenting herself in order to compensate for her error by dealing with the result, but her mother knew that such a chain of cause and effect could be brought into being only with the kind and intensity of struggle which was not worth initiating until her husband was out of the way.

'Will they let her into the school looking like that?' asked Lancelot, adding hot water to the grains of a species of decaffeinated coffee whose name sounded like a man being tortured.

'She isn't *at* school, for God's sake. Have you been ringing the inspirational Samantha?'

'Just checking up on something at work.'

'With the night watchman, I suppose.'

'No, the secretaries have to get in early. Some of them do, anyway. Victor's very strict in that respect.'

Charlotte looked around the racks of carefully displayed ceramics as if wondering what it all added up to, beyond an elaborate homage, brightened with half an acre of stripped pine, to the history of British crockery in the pre-modern period. Lancelot was pleased that what he had said was sufficiently up to snuff so as not to provoke outright contempt, belief having long since been out of the question. Scribe and Sardou had by now absorbed their morning ration of diced filet mignon. Sardou sniffed Scribe's behind and looked away in vague discontent, as Pierre Balmain might perhaps have done before belatedly deciding that an early prototype of Jolie Madame verged on the unsubtle.

'Are you gracing us with your presence tonight?' asked Charlotte.

'Only to change. Reception at Victor's for Hildegarde's book about India.' Lancelot wondered how Charlotte managed to make her clothes look so staid. To the extent that he still paid her any attention at all he was prepared to admit that her smocks and so on suited her unassertive beauty. But only the unclad bits of her, it seemed to him, could plausibly be regarded as flesh. The bits that were covered up could not be said to exist. She was like a fashion sketch from a knitting magazine. Actually he felt about her body the way she felt about his personality, but he had fewer resources for guessing this fact than she had. The image of Samantha once more burst into his mind, this time holding one of its breasts in one hand while the other hand anointed the shadow between its thighs with baby oil.

'Must go,' he said through a mouthful of grains. 'I'll just try that call again quickly first.'

'Secretaries weren't there after all?'

But Lancelot was already half way up the stairs. Being far more willing to embrace tragedy than farce, he adroitly hurdled the still gruesomely preoccupied Feydeau, but did not hesitate to dial the same fourteen-figure number which had cost him so much anguish a few minutes previously. This time it did not answer at all. He redialled in case of a mis-dial and went on standing there for a long time while unacceptable imaginings attacked. He could picture the completeness with which, if suitably distracted, she would ignore the telephone. She would be capable of enjoying herself immeasurably even if the apartment house were under siege by black commandos with flame-throwers. On the other hand she might have gone for an early morning run. After all, she was on the east side of the Park and the buildings on Central Park South form an even more beautiful skyline in the first flush of dawn than they do after dark. Samantha, however, despite her scintillating academic record, could not be said to have any aesthetic interests apart from those she mugged up *ad hoc* as background for the feature articles she contributed to glossy magazines. What interested her chiefly was social adventure combined with highly concentrated erotic experience. He hung up, rang again, and found the number engaged. It was engaged a second time and a third.

On one of the shelves in front of him were twenty-five or so copies of *Special Pleading.* He had bought the surplus stock of his early and only collection of verse rather than see it go to remainder. Once the shelf had held two hundred copies but some of them at various times had made convenient gifts for business acquaintances and he had conferred one each on his successive mistresses as part of the initiation process. The collection had made a considerable impact when it came out. He had shared the political irascibility of his literary generation and indeed still did, to the extent at any rate of espousing socialist principles and voting Labour, or at any rate not voting Conservative. But unlike his contemporaries he had never climbed into a roll-neck sweater which did not emanate from Sulka at the very least. While his friends were proclaiming the advanced tooth decay and gingivitis of the social system, Lancelot was assembling an Adrian Stokes archive which soon included Adrian Stokes himself, who found him brilliant. Maurice Bowra also found him brilliant. Isaiah Berlin had not found him brilliant but had found him charming. He spent a lot of time being found either brilliant or charming even before his book emerged. While being sufficiently combative to earn him a place among the dissatisfied, its constituent verses assuagingly reproduced, in soap and wax, the enamels and cameos of his French models.

From that day his name stood for a tasteful eclecticism contained within an apparently rigorous formal symmetry. In the following decade his reputation deteriorated into fame. He graduated from writing poetry to writing articles, from writing articles to editing, and from editing to being a consultant. The Sixties he had spent being a celebrity. The Seventies he had spent profitably enough with harking back to the Sixties and helping pump oxygen into the guttering idea of flair. As half the board of Style Consultants – his Keble contemporary Anthony Easement constituted the other half – he was a keeper of the flame. One of the large firms most importunate for advice had been Victor Ludorum, owned and managed by Victor Ludlow. While retaining his interest in Style Consultants, Lancelot had joined Victor Ludorum the year before last as Senior Special Projects Adviser. It was one of those steps forward that feels like a step back before your foot has even finished travelling through the air. But Style Consultants was no longer doing well. If he were to go on bringing home any bacon at all he needed to do great things for Victor Ludorum. To do that he needed to please Victor, and the moment Lancelot needed to do something he lost his facility for doing it. It was like trying to walk while thinking about how to walk. It was like remembering how to breathe. The overseas operator said he had no means of checking the line. The operator in the US said she had but wouldn't. Maybe he should just assoom, she suggested, that his party was tied up.

Burst tears thinly coating the whole area of his eyes, Lancelot strode out of his study in a commendably dignified manner and trod with his full weight on Feydeau's tail, which was thus compressed, for the width of a shoe, to the thickness of a beer coaster. Since Feydeau was already in the blast-off position, with his legs splayed and his pampered fundament screwed well down into the carpet, he lost no time in becoming airborne, leaving nothing behind him except some roughly parallel dark smears and a brimming sonic reservoir of protest. Lancelot, standing against the wall with one hand over his eyes and the other on his fibrillating heart, was yet able to hear, if not see, that the dog had gone to the kitchen in order to swear out a complaint in front of the other dogs and enlist their vociferous aid as witnesses. Charlotte left them to it and opened the front door for him.

'I might go to the country a day early,' she said, 'and leave you to get on with it. You're miserable, aren't you?'

'A bit. Work, mainly. It's all too awful.'

'Did you get through to her?'

'That was work, honestly.'

'By the time she gets back I'll be out of the road. She can have jet-lag on your shoulder. But tomorrow I have to be here because those people from *Prestige* are coming to photograph my Ideal Academic Table. Shouldn't you have wellies on or something?'

'It'll probably ease off.' He darted a kiss at her temple, raising a small puff of talcum, or at any rate the whiff of it. Under the columnated portico he hesitated long enough to notice all over again that the masonry was showing some ominous cracks. Between the puddles in the gravel forecourt he zigzagged to his unassumingly smart foreign car, the rain speckling his light-weight trench coat to give an effect he quite liked. Of course he should have been wearing Wellingtons – at his age he should have been wearing waders and a sou'wester – but vanity, he told himself, would not allow it. He knew about his vanity and thought that that made it less. He knew he thought that and thought that that made it all right.

The spring rain sluiced down, differing from the winter rain in that you could see it for longer each day. Heading out into the traffic, he was reminded by his wet skin of Biarritz the year before last. The tide had been out far enough to leave room for a good-sized frisbee-throwing circle on the gently shelving *sable d'or*. Lancelot was just getting set to field a long-distance fizzer from his son Toby, when he noticed Samantha walking towards them from the direction of the southern beach. Samantha was the daughter of one of Charlotte's academic colleagues, an eminent if irascible philologist who always holidayed at a big house down there, a tumbledown crenellated nonsense about a kilometre back from the cliffs. Once she had been a very pretty girl. Then for several years she had not been present, a fact noted with regret by the children, and especially by Toby, who had a crush on her even though she was several years older and notoriously cruel. Now, when she appeared again, she was a beautiful young woman. Her delectable body attracted the sunlight so powerfully that Lancelot could practically see the photons speeding up on their way towards her. While the frisbee was still in mid-air, the role that he might play in her life became clear to him all at once, like a clairvoyance. Absorbing these two revelations, the look of her and the thought of what he must do, he turned with elaborate casualness to catch the speeding frisbee behind his back. It hit him in the kidneys like a discus. There was a good deal of uninhibited laughter from the assembled golden youth, abetted by a discreet but visible giggle from Charlotte, lazily guarding her pale skin under a driftwood shelter while she got on with her self-imposed task of keeping up with the serious new writers. The whole holiday arrangement was a flagrant example of everything that Lancelot believed needed changing. He was proud that his *gauchiste* convictions had never altered. That they had never been tested was a separate issue. What was the point of a bourgeois funk-hole beside a foreign sea? Only London was real. London, whose gritty actuality was turned by your windscreen wipers into grisaille fans on which no Mallarmé would ever write a poem or Conder paint a pink Arcadia. And about time too. Give the people a chance, thought Lancelot, driving past a long wall comprehensively decorated with such rubrics as DEATH TO NIGGER SLIME and YID FILTH OUT.

Having completed the journey from the extremely fashionable postal district in which he lived to the extremely unfashionable postal district in which he worked, he found the car-park behind the Victor Ludorum building full, which gave him a chance to circle several of the surrounding blocks in search of a space, find one in a side street, and then run on tip-toe in his mandatorily minimal shoes for several hundred yards through the rain. As Senior Special Projects Adviser he was entitled to parking space but he was so senior that there was no one above him to complain to and as an Adviser he had no department below him through which to enforce an order. He reported directly to Victor, which effectively made him powerless while Victor wasn't around, and Victor, for whom book publishing was only a minor part of an undercapitalised empire which also embraced at least two national newspapers and four magazines, spent as little time in the office as possible, running his enterprises either from his large house in Hampstead or from any one of a constantly fluctuating aggregate of other dwellings throughout the world. Consequently the only thing Lancelot could immediately make happen was the expulsion of his secretary from the office while he telephoned.

The rear view of his retreating secretary was not pleasant. Her name was Janice and he was convinced that even an independent observer would be able to guess the loudness of her voice from one glance at the size of her bottom, which at the moment was converting the normally parallel vertical lines of a pair of corduroy jeans into a spaciously curved magnetic field pattern. Swinging away from that grim spectacle as he dialled, he found himself regaled with an equally depressing outlook seemingly assembled for the specific purpose of characterising a fractionating society. Apart from getting wet, what were those three Arab women doing in front of the Indian cinema? Her telephone was still engaged. He hung up, folded his arms on the desk, and rested his head on them, like a child in school during an enforced period of quiet.

~ two ~

Y ou don't take sugar, do you?' shouted Janice, not so
much asking a question as stating a fact – as well she
might, because she had been making Lancelot cups of coffee for
many months. Her excuse for forgetting such things was that he
wasn't normally supposed to be there. Actually nowadays he
was usually there all the time, having discovered that to take up
his privilege of staying away was tantamount to removing his
finger from the dike. Not for the first time he pondered the easy,
imperceptibly divided stages by which he had progressed from
valued counsellor, meeting Victor over lunch at the Garrick, or at
carefully planned planning meetings complete with agenda, to
hapless dogsbody moving one step ahead of catastrophe, with
nowhere to park and haunted by a secretary whose fog-horn
voice was a warning that something enormous was travelling
just behind it.

'This came,' yelled Janice, vaguely waving a manila folder
before putting it down in front of him. 'From that chap in Los
Angeles. You said you wanted to see it.'

Focusing on the front of the manila folder helped blur the
image of Janice going away, so that she looked merely like a
hessian-wrapped bale of sponge rubber floating out of the room
under its own power. A typed label said: 'A World History of the
Short, by Ian Cuthbert'. Just under that it said 'An Expanded
Synopsis'. Lancelot did not want to see that word 'synopsis'. At
the very least he wanted to see a label saying 'A First Draft'.
Lancelot had already seen a synopsis of this book and did not
really want to see another, however heavily revised. Ian
Cuthbert had been given an advance of several thousands of
pounds for this book during the initial flurry of activity when
Lancelot had joined the firm. One of several old friends from
whom Lancelot had made the capital error of commissioning
books, Ian Cuthbert was a particularly flagrant proof that in

23

such circumstances the possessor of a wayward temperament, far from nerving himself to behave more predictably for friendship's sake, will actually become less pindownable than ever.

'In *A World History of the Short*', Lancelot read for what seemed the hundredth time, 'the course of history is traced in terms of what has been achieved, attained, distorted and destroyed by one type of man – the short man. At first seeming to be the kind of humorous *tour de force* that would ordinarily be expected from so irreverent and variously erudite an author, the book will quickly reveal itself to be as deeply serious as its tone is gay . . .'

An unfortunate word in Ian's case, thought Lancelot: a book so shamelessly devoted to its author's physiologically based obsession should not be an indulgence of his psychosexual quirks as well. Lancelot skipped the rest of the blurb cum preamble – which occupied two, or more like one and a half, A4 pages – and sampled the synopsis proper. There was scarcely a phrase he did not recognise at a glance.

' . . . that Keats and Pope were not the only short poets . . . Horace, too, was of small stature . . . arising in the case of Alexander of Macedon . . . Pippin the Short. Would Napoleon have invaded Russia if he . . . Orde Wingate . . . Lord Nelson . . . Babyface Nelson . . . in Andrei Bely's great novel *Petersburg* the hero's father, Apollon Apollonovitch Ableukhov, is specified as being 56 inches high . . . Mozart, Wagner, Stravinsky . . .'

'Irreverent,' said Lancelot to himself. '*God* what an out-of-date word.' He added half a cup of caffeinated low-quality coffee to the cup of decaffeinated high-quality coffee already in his system. Nowadays he did not drink alcohol in the mornings, with the result that during the period before lunch he was no longer able to identify interior disquiet as anything else except interior disquiet. Unless he missed his guess, this revised synopsis was actually shorter, if he could use that adjective without nausea, than the previous version. Skipping like a flat stone over smooth water, he read on.

' . . . can thus be regarded as a sign of Franco's success in coming to terms with his psychological make-up . . . from Lenin to Yezhov . . . Stalin, on the other hand, not only appeared as a tall man in the official portraiture – which would probably have been careful to represent him in that manner even without direct intervention from the Kremlin – but stood on a box behind the parapet of the Lenin mausoleum when taking the salute in Red Square . . . in the early years of his popularity Alan Ladd stood on a box but there is some evidence that as his power increased, the heroine was obliged to stand in a hole . . . the obvious relish Montherlant takes from describing Saint-Simon as *unusually* small . . . Balzac, Claudel, Péguy . . . Caruso, Bjoerling . . . Bernard Berenson . . . the horizontal direction taken by Frank Lloyd Wright's prairie architecture was one of the two possible reactions to his physical stature, the other being, of course, the projected mile-high skyscraper . . . classic paper by Ernest Jones on the chess-player Paul Morphy shows the danger of an exclusively Freudian approach in a case where surely Adler's emphasis should be paramount even if not exclusive . . . Beerbohm, Kipling, T. E. Lawrence, Lawrence Durrell . . .'

Lancelot closed the folder and shifted it to one side. Plainly at this rate Ian's manuscript would never be forthcoming. As well as almost wholly lacking the brilliance for which its author was supposed to be famous, the synopsis, under its doggedly frolicsome tone, had the unmistakable dead ring of lost conviction. Lancelot remembered tales of a famous author-about-town whose last book, published incomplete after his death, had been coaxed from him chapter by chapter, one payment at a time. But in that case the payments were fractions of a hypothetical advance which had never been given in the first place. Ian's advance had been enormous. *A World History of the Short* was a standing reproach to Victor Ludorum, a blatant reversal of the sound business principle by which authors must deliver a manuscript now in order to be paid with inflated currency later.

Lancelot, who had read modern languages at Oxford, could remember the day when Ian Cuthbert had been the most promising talent in a Cambridge so full of promise that it had made Oxford feel provincial. Ian's contemporaries had plotted to take over the British theatre and in a remarkably short time they had actually done so. But their mental energy had seemed like indolence when you looked at Ian. He had worn his overcoat like a cape and talked about what Gide had said to Roger Martin du Gard as if he had been there to overhear it. He had published in the *Cambridge Review* an article on Empson that not even Empson could fully understand. Balthus had given him a small drawing. Yet for some reason the whole frostily coruscating galaxy of Ian's creative intellect had remained locked in its closet. While less gifted deviants came out and conquered, Ian went further in. At the height of his influence as a literary taste-maker he was already notoriously difficult to deal with. He was responsible for the most nearly successful attempt to revive the reputation of Denton Welch, but his own book on Welch materialised only as a pamphlet. Officially appointed by the relevant public agency to edit a comprehensive magazine of the arts, he was like a general with a million tons of equipment pinned down on the beach by nothing except an excess of opportunity. The magazine used up the budget for a dozen issues without appearing once. Similarly his thrice-renewed three-year contract with one of the fashion magazines engendered little except legends about the size of his emolument, which was increased from generosity to extravagance in an attempt to make him produce more, and then from extravagance to munificence in an attempt to make him produce anything. At the editorial working breakfasts – there were always at least two of the titled photographers present to capture the scene for posterity – Ian spat witty venom through clenched teeth, poured nitric acid on other people's ideas and died of love for a young painter called Monty Forbes, whom he wooed by telling obscure stories about Cocteau and Radiguet. Ten years later he was still in love, still unrequited, and could scarcely be depended on to turn up for his own funeral. Lancelot was on the verge of admitting to himself that *A World History of the Short* had been a mistake from its inception. Ian's sense of humour, though real, was anything but genial, and only a comprehensively forgiving spirit could begin to get away with an idea in such bad taste. Probably it wasn't even much of an idea, though they had laughed heartily enough while hatching it, and three different television comedy teams had since endorsed their judgment by mounting sketches based on the same notion. Now Ian was sitting in Los Angeles, the huge advance long spent. The time in Los Angeles was three hours behind New York. Lancelot didn't want to think about New York. In his room at the Casa Perdida Motel on Santa Monica Boulevard, Ian would be staring now at the pasteboard wall, while no doubt the stabbed corpse of some forgotten young actor floated outside in the swimming pool, whose surface would be thinly rippled by the drip of water from a green plastic hose uncoiled arbitrarily across the neon-lit concrete.

The telephone rang on Janice's desk. Temporarily putting down the kind of housebrick-thick paperback novel which records how the rape of a Choctaw squaw eventually leads to the foundation of a vast industrial empire, she picked up the receiver and bellowed into its mouthpiece as if it were a cave in whose depths children missing for several days might possibly have taken shelter. 'If you don't mind waiting just a moment, I'll see if he's available.' Draping her free hand loosely across the mouthpiece, instead of plunging the whole apparatus into the bucket of kapok which would have been the minimum required to dampen the clamour, she yelled intimately: 'It's that Brian Hutchings person you were supposed to see this morning.'

Lancelot was indeed meant to be seeing Brian Hutchings that morning, but was not at all surprised to hear that Brian Hutchings would not be turning up until about lunchtime, which meant that Brian Hutchings would be putting in an appearance somewhere around the middle of the afternoon, if he showed up at all. But this time he was almost bound to make it, the number of postponements and cancellations having grown to the point where even Brian showed signs of being shamefaced. Not in his face, of course: like all literary men who erect sloth into a moral stance, he made sure that his features conveyed little beyond a sneer of contempt for the petty workings of the quotidian world. One of Lancelot's best ideas, an iconography of modern literary London, had been made dependent on Brian's producing a set of captions and some kind of loose narrative to link the visual material. For an averagely industrious writer it would have taken two weeks. Brian, with his prestige as an untrammelled literatus on the line, had stretched the business out into a second year.

'You *will* try to make it no later than three, won't you?' pleaded Lancelot. 'Because we'll need some time to look at what you've done and give some thought to what still needs doing.'

'Yeah. I'll be there. Don't go on about it.'

'I'm not really going on about it, just pointing out that there's an element of time.'

'You can always forget the whole thing. I don't like being badgered, OK?'

After several apologies Lancelot managed to secure what sounded like a measure of forgiveness. He got the phone back into its cradle with the same air of relief that one feels when a large fly finally uses the open part of the window as an exit instead of the closed part as a sounding board. The time he had set aside for coping with the threatened Brian interview he reluctantly decided to spend on yet another tentative investigation of the virtually terminal damage which circumstances seemed to have inflicted on the Gillian Jackson project and beyond that on himself. The whole affair was waiting for him in a large box-file on the top shelf of a low, special set of shelves, crammed with almost nothing but bad news, which crouched to his left and demanded attention with such insistence that the uproar had become self-defeating. The Gillian Jackson box-file had everything in it except something you could publish. It had an outline, lists of chapter headings, photographs of the potential interviewees, magazine tear-sheets of variously sumptuous lay-outs evoking the splendour in which the interviewees lived, a sheaf of memos from Victor telling him to get on with it, and an apple core. This last item was withered and shrivelled in a way that Lancelot was tempted to feel should be regarded as symbolic of the whole undertaking. He removed it without even bothering to wonder how it had got there. He had been leaving things lying around lately. Luckily he did not smoke.

The idea, otherwise known as the concept, was simple, or at any rate had been meant to be. Gillian Jackson, star agony columnist and the most famously intelligent beauty of the day, would interview all the other famously intelligent beauties of the day on the subject of the way they led their lives. Lancelot tried to avoid using the term 'lifestyle' in conversation but had little doubt that it would eventually be prominent in the book's attendant publicity material and perhaps even the title. Yet the idea was strong enough to survive the inevitable hazards. If it turned out that the celebrated ex-wife of the multi-millionaire pop singer led no life at all beyond the effort involved in picking up the telephone to order room-service, that would not especially matter, since any conversation involving Gillian, provided it was long enough, would be automatically marketable. If, on the other hand, the interviewee was someone like Elena Fiabesco, the relatively impoverished aristocrat who managed to live like an empress through sheer improvisational ingenuity, then to that extent the book would be genuinely instructive. It would be a picture book with substance. Failing that, it would be a picture book with style. At the moment it was a picture book with nothing. Victor had agreed with alacrity to the suggestion that Gillian Jackson should write a book. Indeed it had been Victor's idea that the advance should be so large. Several months went by before it became clear that Gillian Jackson was constitutionally incapable of asking anybody a question. All she could do was answer letters. Unfortunately the approximate target date for publication was by then irrevocable. The book had to be ready for press in the early autumn after the imminent summer, and already it was spring. A manuscript of some kind thus became an indispensable requirement. Since Gillian Jackson could not be expected to supply it, her share of the work would have to be ghosted.

Shopping through the list of available female ghost writers who would also be socially acceptable among the upper-crust and media-star interviewees, Lancelot had quickly realised that effectively there was no such list. The socially acceptable ones were short of reportorial experience and the ones who knew how a tape-recorder worked would have small chance of coaxing from a nuance-conscious interlocutor anything resembling an air of complicity. Really the only suitable candidate was Serena Blake. At one time briefly Lancelot's mistress, Serena was a recognised adornment in the grander drawing-rooms. She wore clothes well, could talk polite rubbish endlessly at the dinner table, and managed the difficult trick of generating a certain air of originality while being so short of negotiable attainments that she had to scratch for a living. By now in her middle thirties and still intermittently subsidised by a succession of short-suffering lovers, she had tried various things from writing fashion features to running a patisserie, but the thing she tried most often was suicide. She had wrists like a World War I battlefield. She had looked, however, very pretty as she lay back in the heaped pillows of the private hospital room where Lancelot went to see her.

'Darling, I just couldn't *do* it. I'd be terrible. I'd utterly muck up all your deadlines and probably wouldn't get anything out of them.'

'All you have to do is get them talking and out it will all spill. You're one of them, you see. Whereas Gillian isn't really. She's Got No Background.' Lancelot made a mouth with this last sentence to show that it wasn't his opinion. It was his instinct, but not his opinion.

'I haven't either.'

'Yes, but you're not worried about it. That's why they're all so relaxed while you're around.'

'Even though I'm slashing my wrists all the time.'

'At least they know that while you're doing that you won't have time to stab them in the back.' Lancelot was rather pleased with himself for this and was even more pleased when Serena said she'd give it a try. She extended her bandaged arms to him. As he kissed her and breathed among her short strawberry blonde curls, Lancelot wondered why their affair had lasted only a week.

It was not long before he was reminded of the reason. Serena was so completely disorganised that things which had already been done came undone when she was in the vicinity. How had she ever managed to write those fashion features? Time after time he sat with her to plan interviewing forays and to draw up lists of questions to be asked. Time after time she had come back with notes she could not read or tapes in which well-bred banalities were interrupted by nervous giggles or separated by a long hiss.

For the rest of the morning and most of lunchtime Lancelot shuffled the transcripts of Serena's touchingly thin interviews into various permutations and combinations. Whichever way he organised them they gave the same effect as an access television programme put on by a consumer group of deaf-mutes staging a protest against dishonest plumbers. It was high time to start admitting to himself that Serena would have to be taken off the case. Doubtless there was some other task she could be given: he didn't want to be responsible for dumping her altogether. Perhaps she could help with the research for Lady Hildegarde Plomley's projected book about famous poets and novelists who could draw. This was an idea with everything, except that Lady Hildegarde, the actual writer, had no time to do the actual writing, being far too busy with an extensive television series about Victorian prime ministers. She wasn't writing that either, but her co-writer had first call on her services. The only drawback with regard to Serena's taking over the research was that Serena knew next to nothing about literature. As he scooped away at a pot of cottage cheese with chives he decided the difficulty could be overcome by supplying her with lists. That left only the question of who should draw up the lists.

At this point the arrival of Brian Hutchings was announced. The announcement was made by Janice, who had just received the information on the telephone. Lancelot was still recovering from the blast when Brian walked in, but he had the presence of mind, before ushering his guest into seclusion for what could easily be an embarrassing colloquy, to instruct Janice not to disturb him with any phone calls unless they emanated from New York, a large city on the eastern seaboard of the United States. He decided once again not to specify Samantha's name, in case Janice should at some time repeat it within earshot of his wife – i.e., anywhere in the metropolitan area. As usual Brian was impressive for his air of lean fitness, an effect which became doubly striking when you found out that he made up with a surplus of alcohol for a deficiency of solid food and took no exercise beyond random fornication. He was very good-looking if you didn't mind the built-in sneer. Very few women minded it at all. Lancelot disapproved of him on all levels and from every viewpoint, but admired his knack for remaining apparently, and probably really, untroubled in the midst of catastrophe – a reversal of the usual liberal tendency to panic about the unimportant.

'Heard your girl telling you I was here,' said Brian, when they had withdrawn into the adjacent conference room and spread the meagre contents of the relevant box-file on the big table. 'How do you stand the row she makes?'

'She's quietened down considerably,' said Lancelot defensively. 'I took her into a field and we had a little talk.'

'Hasn't made her bum any smaller. Is this all the stuff?'

'Yes,' said Lancelot, 'but what we want are the captions to go with it. What have you brought?'

From a limp Indian leather briefcase Brian produced a few sheets of paper, some of them typed and the rest handwritten. Lancelot got the sense that an intention to turn all the handwritten pages into typewritten ones had been hastily put into practice and only partly fulfilled. Some of the sheets of paper had circular stains on them, which when handwriting was involved seemed to entail an always noticeable and often radical redistribution of ink. But at least there were signs of some kind of writing having taken place. After excavating a valley full of sand it is better to unearth an isolated shard than nothing at all.

The Egyptian analogy kept coming back to Lancelot on those occasions, frequent in the next hour, when Brian had trouble deciphering his own hieroglyphics. But there were whole stretches of time, often extending as long as four or even five minutes, when the process of matching what had been written to what had already been decided ought to be illustrated seemed almost orderly. Brian really did know a lot. Group photographs of poets leaning together outside pubs in Soho and Fitzrovia had evoked from Brian some bitter samples of his famously sardonic running commentary on the vanity of bardic ambition. It was a rule in these precious items of iconography that first-rate literary figures were rarely seen together. Each first-rate literary figure was to be seen only with second-rate literary figures. Thus Dylan Thomas was supported by obscure BBC radio producers and various Welsh camp-followers who had come up to London for the weekend and stayed to go broke along with their hero. 'It is not entirely certain,' ran one of Brian's captions, 'whether the Ewan Gareth Davies who later claimed ownership of the dishevelled locks second from left was a minor academic or an academic miner.' Lancelot laughed dutifully at this, while tacitly deciding that for libel reasons it would have to be struck out. The same applied to some scathing résumés of what had gone on long ago during visits by ageing, now almost ancient, American beatnik poets to the Albert Hall. Brian had not been present but he had the knack of making you glad that you hadn't either. He was especially unforgiving about Allen Ginsberg's beard, much to the fore in photographs otherwise featuring British avant garde poets with such meta-American names as Horowitz. The whole ambience was irredeemably dated – much more so than any preceding period – and Brian knew exactly how to pile critical contempt on top of fate's decree. It would be a pity to lose any of that but the lawyers would be hovering and these particular photographs were essential if the book were to appeal to anyone at all under forty. Somehow Brian would have to be persuaded to take a rather more yielding view. The trouble was that Brian, who openly despised almost every poet of the modern era, secretly despised the few exceptions.

'You don't seem to have actually written much about Tambimuttu,' said Lancelot tentatively, congratulating himself on being so direct. In fact Brian had obviously written nothing whatsoever about Tambimuttu, but by making the statement conjectural Lancelot had left the possibility open that something relevant might yet be lurking among the papers and had thus put the onus on Brian to be fully explicit.

'Wasn't sure that the pictures of him were quite absurd enough,' said Brian with quiet defiance. 'We only need one of him wearing the suit and then in the others he should be in that national dress thing that they get themselves up in, what's it called, a scrotum?'

'A dhoti.' Lancelot was impressed, for the nth time, with the way Brian made dereliction sound purposeful, as if what looked to the casual eye like total inefficiency were really part of some long plan. He remembered, better than if it had been yesterday, an occasion some ten years back when a diaphanous pamphlet of Brian's short stories, published under Brian's personal imprint, had been recommended among the current artistic events in an arts round-up column of a magazine to which Lancelot had been adviser. Lancelot could still recall the name of the magazine but could not, strive as he might, remember what the column had been called. Something monosyllabically spondaic. What's In? Up Now? And the pamphlet's title, what had that been? Anyway, it was felt at editorial level that Brian should be given assistance in the task of making sure that those few people who wrote to him at the Perihelion Press requesting a copy of the pamphlet – *The Day*, that was it – should actually receive the advertised item in return for their money. It was called a Credibility Operation. The mere offer of assistance had been enough to arouse Brian's witheringly expressed defensiveness, but what impressed Lancelot was not the pitch of invective so much as the sheer amount of time Brian had been able to expend on the logistics. With three unpaid but enslaved girl assistants on tap, it took two days to acquire envelopes slightly bigger than the pamphlet. Envelopes slightly smaller than the pamphlet had materialised promptly enough. In fact if Lancelot had not providentially arrived the pamphlet would probably have been trimmed to fit them. But it had taken a further stage – in which a hundred envelopes large enough to hold framed wall paintings by Paolo Veronese had been duly purchased, brought to the office and compared wonderingly with the object meant to go in them – before envelopes roughly the right size were finally acquired. All available cash having thus been exhausted, it was another day before an expedition was ready to leave the office in search of postage stamps. The post office was just around the corner but unfortunately the corner took the form of a public house. A second expedition had to be fitted out in order to find the first. Remembering all this, Lancelot became abstracted, giggled when he came to himself, and said: 'We've made some progress.'

'What's that supposed to mean?'

'I mean I'm delighted with what you've done, honestly. It's really terrifically funny and brilliantly interesting. But we do need to close those gaps quite soon or we'll miss the revised publication date.'

'Would that matter so much? What's the hurry?'

'It's already been in the catalogue twice. You get libraries budgeting for these things and if they don't turn up the firm's credibility sags.'

'Not much of a reason to get *your* knickers in a twist.'

Lancelot could either agree and half-make his point or disagree and see his point forgotten in the resulting argument, so he agreed. Having established between them that all was going well in spite of the world's folly, they packed up the work, Lancelot having first, by way of Janice, ensured that Brian's scraps of paper were photocopied and the copies placed carefully in the box-file, which thus became one of the few box-files on Lancelot's disaster shelf to have gained weight through any other reason except memos from Victor. It was a small plus but at least it was not a clear minus. That made it a large plus. Lancelot was still palely aglow from it when, having shown Brian out, he returned to his office and was informed by Janice that someone calling herself Samantha had telephoned but that she, Janice, had put her, the said Samantha, off, on the grounds that he, Lancelot, had left instructions that he did not want to be distracted, hadn't he? And no, there hadn't been any mention that she, this Samantha person, had been telephoning from New York, although come to think of it there *had* been a sort of international effect on the line. Yes, she, Janice, was ready to concede that she, Samantha, had telephoned him, Lancelot, several times in the past, but she, Janice, could scarcely be expected to remember one name among a stream of others, and anyway he, Lancelot, had said nothing about making an exception for a familiar name, only about a possible call from New York. Which hadn't, Janice reminded him in the voice of a toast-master talking to a crop-duster, been mentioned.

~ three ~

I t was perhaps only the shock effect of hearing all this at close range that stopped Lancelot felling his secretary with a flying kick to the throat. He wondered how she would look staked out face down naked on an ant-hill, with the ants drawing up plans for the huge task of consuming her posterior. For the ants it would be a public works project dwarfing the Tennessee Valley Authority in its awesome scope. They would have to build roads and set up base camps. They would need oxygen. There would have to be Sherpa ants to hump the equipment. He imagined a softer voice, the voice that he had been denied and which suitably prompted would have said it loved him. But no sooner had the storm of Lancelot's anger gathered than it circled back into his own soul and vented its wrath there. He cursed himself for having given his bomb-voiced, Hottentot-bottomed secretary insufficiently explicit instructions. He cursed himself again for cursing himself instead of her, all unaware that his reluctance deliberately to cause pain was one of his charms, or would have been if it were not a leading ingredient in his capacity to cause pain inadvertently.

Nevertheless Lancelot was in the early stages of a melt-down. The gamma radiation might have damaged Janice's large mass of organic tissue irreversibly if Frank Strain had not walked in and suggested, at a length wholly incommensurate with the simplicity of the message, that he had some figures upstairs Lancelot might like to see. In cold truth, the only figures Frank Strain might have had which Lancelot could conceivably have liked to see would have been an actuarial table establishing the statistical certainty of people who looked and talked like Frank boring themselves to death at an early date – tomorrow, for example. Frank was one of the firm's four chief editors. The four chief editors were the editors who chiefly did the editing that Victor was not interested in or, after having momentarily become interested, did not have time for. Of the four chief editors, three actually edited, leaving Frank free to consider the business side of the business and thus check up on how much Lancelot's projects cost relative to what they earned, i.e., increasingly a lot compared with a little. Frank's would have been a dull job even if he had dressed and conversed like the Count Robert de Montesquiou. But a dull job had found an even duller man. He wore large black brogues with short laces tied in small bows that looked like dead flies; baggy suits that would have suggested the existence of a special press to render trousers creaseless if it had not been for a rich network of transverse wrinkles radiating from the low crotch; and shirts that served no other function except to obviate the necessity of knotting his tie around his bare neck. This week's tie, Lancelot noticed, before Frank turned to lead him very slowly down the corridor and up a flight of stairs so narrow that one bumped a wall if one coughed, was patterned after a colony of parasitic organisms stained and sectioned for microscopic examination. Last week's tie had looked like the molecular structure of mud. The tie of the week before last had looked like this week's tie, which meant that next week's tie would look like last week's. Frank's office looked so like the office of a man like Frank that you felt it had been decorated by Julia Trevelyan Oman or some designer similarly renowned for being fanatical about detail. There were a lot of books to denote publishing, and several group photographs of Selwyn College Junior Common Room committees with Frank in the back row, these latter to hint at his dynamism and charisma. There being a varnished oak veneer door in each side of the office, Lancelot saw no reason why they should not make their respective exits and finish dressing for the coming scene. Lancelot could come back on with high horned wig, knee breeches, buckled shoes, lace stock, silk coat, white make-up, a beauty spot and a quizzing glass. Throwing one foot forward and bowing low, he could cry, 'La, Sir! I see you have me!' Frank could come shambling forward in gaping shoes, matted hair, a tattered suit lined with newspapers, a scraggled beard, forehead shiny with dirt, and toting a bindle.

As things were, the encounter was perhaps a trifle under-directed, especially considering the amount of dramatic content which it relatively promptly, and for Lancelot entirely unexpectedly, proved to have.

'It's about tax,' said Frank with obvious relish. 'Tax is what it's really about. There's what's sometimes known, it's not my phrase for it but it's a phrase they often, and I suppose it conveys the sense as well as any other, and I wouldn't say a crisis because that would be putting it, so perhaps it's better to just bend with the prevailing, and call it what everybody else calls it.'

'What do they call it?'

'Mm? Oh, didn't I say? A tax problem.'

'What tax problem? To do with me?'

'Yes, of course.'

Frank went on to elucidate, choosing words which would have affected Lancelot like a public recital of Motley's *Rise of the Dutch Republic* if their cumulative import had not been so acutely and painfully relevant to himself. It seemed that the Internal Revenue Service saw no reason why he should not be reclassified from Schedule D to PAYE. Admittedly he had several sources of income and his arrangement with Victor Ludorum purported to be a freelance contract. Nevertheless he was, in the IRS's considered view, effectively an employee of Victor Ludorum. The fact that he had signed the contract in the belief that it was a freelance contract was irrelevant. So was the fact that he had asked for no pension provisions. So was the fact that for all previous contracts, no matter with which employer, he had always been classified as Schedule D. There was no suggestion of fraud on his part. The rules had merely been changed retroactively. What was more they might well be changed retroactively all the way back to the beginning and with regard to his participation in Style Consultants as well, so that he would have to repay about a decade of expenses deducted against tax. He would have a chance to appeal, but meanwhile tax would be deducted at source. Frank showed him the first notification of payment under the new arrangement. The money had already been sent to Lancelot's bank, and was not even half the usual amount. In fact the sum deducted exceeded the top rate of tax, apparently because a double National Insurance contribution had been taken away too, almost as if he were not already paying a double National Insurance contribu-

38

tion as a matter of course.

To an uninformed glance, Lancelot when leaving Frank's office would have looked no more stunned than he or anybody else ever did when leaving Frank's office. He was still upright and the glaze on his eyes did not exceed in thickness that on the average domestic pot dating from the Sung dynasty. Privately, however, he felt as if he had been sandbagged, stripped naked and left to crawl home across a large desert he could not name. Back in his own office he fell weakly into Janice's swivel chair, a feat of coordination made considerably easier by the fact that Janice had gone home. The electric clock always gave a soft click when the minute hand was exactly vertical. At five o'clock that click would not have been over before Janice was out of the starting blocks and barrelling down the street towards the tube station, with unwary subcontinentals bowled off their feet and unrolling out of their saris. By now she must be halfway towards whichever gymnasium she went to in the evenings in order to build up the muscles in her behind, before moving on to night school for her lessons in voice projection and how to write slowly. It was remarkable how secretaries had widened their range in his time. Once they could only not do shorthand. Now they could also not do longhand. Lancelot was spinning back and forth in a half circle, knocking his kneecaps without noticing. He caught himself. He was being obsessive. Compulsive behaviour declares itself through repetition and can thus be identified, he told himself, reaching for the telephone. At the office where the magazine Samantha worked for was published – it was called *Courage in Profiles* and consisted mainly of illiterate minor celebrities interviewing each other – they said she had already gone to lunch. An early lunch, he thought, putting on his coat and arranging the collar. An early lunch finishing late. He imagined her sitting in Morton's, or Joe Allen's, or somewhere even more terrible such as the Palm Court at the Plaza, while some old young publishing executive with an Astroturf hair transplant told her she was talented. He could hear her rather piercing laugh momentarily drowning the resident quartet as they got on with the job of ritually eviscerating Schubert. Well, two could play at that game. In twenty minutes, after a quick drive through the romantic

London rain in his unostentatious but satisfactorily elegant conveyance, he would join his young friend Nicholas over a couple of well-judged Bellinis behind the wooden louvred windows of the Carambar in Covent Garden. The Girl Fridays and personal assistants of communications executives by whom they were just ceasing to be impressed would be perched on velvet stools and ready to vouchsafe him the sidelong glance befitting his residual measure of fame. Obsession did not stop you looking and could even be said to take the sting out of it. Anticipating novelty if not adventure, Lancelot felt marginally less unhappy as, head down against the fitfully spitting rain, he hopped and jumped rapidly between the puddles to his car, which at first looked as if it had almost nothing wrong with it.

Several long scratches down the driver's side, forming a stave on which the paired lightning flashes of the SS looked like some sort of musical signature, were the only external signs of damage apart from the deflated front tyre. The door, whose lock had been forced, opened after a brief struggle, to reveal that the chunkily named Krooklok had done its work. Indeed the Krooklok was the only piece of equipment inside the car which could be said to have remained intact, because although the rear-view mirror had for some reason been left unbroken it was nevertheless lying on the back seat. A festoon of variously coloured wires hung out from under the dashboard. The radio and cassette-player assembly might or might not have been harmed. There was no way of telling, because it was missing entirely, along with all of its attendant cassettes. The window in the door he was holding open with his hip had appeared at first to be wound down but now proved to have been redistributed around the car's interior in the form of many-faceted opaque fragments, like lacklustre ice. The reason why the window had been removed was easily deduced. To soak the front seat with urine while sitting inside the car would have been difficult even if not degrading. The prospective thieves, their main intention thwarted, had obviously taken their revenge by removing the window and relieving themselves into the car from the outside. That there had been more than one of them was a conclusion impossible to avoid. No single human body, unless suffering from terminal beri-beri, could contain so much waste fluid. Lancelot found it hard to believe that any of the local Pakistanis, Punjabis, Sikhs, Sepoys or Gurkhas could have been responsible. Justifiably paranoid, most of them either never let their children out of the house or else sent them to school through a tunnel. Likelier candidates were one or more of the groups of white teenage neo-Nazis who, singing an impressionistic version of the Horst Wessel song, regularly marched through the area on their way from the Employment Office to one of those shops where for the cost of a week's dole money you can buy yourself a pair of jack-boots, a ceremonial dagger or an old copy of *Signal* with Sepp Dietrich on the cover. What Lancelot could not understand was why the surrounding population of Satyajit Ray extras had done nothing to interfere with an atrocity which must have gone on for at least half an hour in broad daylight and part of whose aftermath was an expensively dressed man holding his face in his hands and having a mid-life crisis in their midst.

Snapping out of it, Lancelot strode purposefully into the nearest shop to ask the proprietors what they had seen. Finding that it sold incense, he changed his mind and strode purposefully out again. He thought of offering violence to a smiling onlooker but reluctantly decided against it on the grounds that she was probably Gandhi's mother. He hailed a passing taxi with his right arm, thinking that he had better bag it and keep it waiting because it was the only taxi he would be likely to find. He hailed a policeman with his left arm on a similar principle. Neither the taxi driver nor the policeman seemed to see him, even though they were looking straight at him. Lancelot wondered, as he wondered often, whether he really existed.

'A pity, isn't it?' said a man with the turbaned head of a maharaja, a double-breasted pin-striped suit over a Fair Isle sweater, and socks under his sandals. 'This sort of thing is happening far too much nowadays. We say *kerab*. Accent on the second syllable. It means bad.' Lancelot thought he could perhaps make a start on repairing the car by dropping to his knees and blowing into the valve in order to reflate the tyre. Then he saw that the tyre had been stabbed, and besides, the footpath was too wet.

~ four ~

In the populated half-light of the Carambar, Nicholas Crane, the successful young author of novels so horrifying that juries gave them prizes to get out of reading them, had good cause to be glad that Lancelot was late. From a concealed public address system an old Xavier Cugat record spoke of bad movies set in Acapulco. The ghost of Abbe Lane rattled the maracas while Nicholas gazed deep into the sea-green eyes of Sally Draycott, a girl he had been besieging for what seemed like centuries. Feeling he was not going to attain his object was for him such an unusual sensation that he had begun to savour it. Sally was so beautiful, so intelligent, so original, so mysterious and so incomparably the most exciting woman he had ever encountered that he had almost reconciled himself to going on giving her a few minutes of his precious time even after it had become established seemingly irrevocably that they would not be lovers. At this brief meeting today, which was meant to end with Lancelot's arrival, the chief aim was to have been the generating of a moral climate in which the close friendship obtaining between Nicholas and Sally could continue without longing on his part and constant wariness on hers. When they met later that night at Victor's, they would be enviable chums, enjoying each other's company without anxiety and seeking other intimacies without recrimination. But just when Nicholas was congratulating himself on this further step towards maturity, something in Sally's manner told him that the sincerity of his renunciation had tipped the balance. An overtone of complicity in her voice, a discreet but not wholly necessary licking of the lower lip, an extra degree of heat off her silken skin – these signs working in an unanalysable combination told him that he was like a man who gives the slot machine one last defeated crank of the handle as he turns away and then hears the air fill with the sound of cascading silver.

He was in like Flynn.

'You know what's wrong with these Platonic relationships, don't you?' Nicholas pretended to ask.

'No sex,' said Sally, nodding with mock agreement.

'That's it. You don't get to take your clothes off and lie down together.'

'And that's essential, is it?'

'No, not essential. Just fantastically desirable and good even when you merely like each other. Fabulously good when you more than like each other. Inexhaustibly and transcendentally fabulous when you like each other very much indeed.' The most prominent young novelist in his generation of young novelists, Nicholas favoured cumulative verbal effects. As in a Verdi aria, the same melodic figure kept on coming back with ever more elaborate orchestration. Ideas exfoliated into rococo curlicues.

'What *about*,' asked Sally, with deliberately crushing emphasis, as if she were the kind of television interviewer who tries to make difficult concepts palatable by sounding like a kindergarten teacher, 'the *way* that the *fabulous passion* tends to *burn* itself *out* in the *gentleman's* case and leave the *lady* watching the *telephone?*' Actually Sally was the other kind of television interviewer, the kind who tries to sound normal, and was thus only half as far ahead in her career as she might have been.

'Which lady is this?' asked Nicholas. 'Most of the women I've known so far, familiarity bred contempt because contempt was the only possible emotion you could experience once familiarity had been established.'

'So gallant. Will I get talked about like this?'

Striving to conceal his profound glee at her concessive use of the future tense, Nicholas pretended to consider. He looked at her while tilting his head to various angles. He sat back, held up his thumb, and measured the proportions of her face, a process which, even while he was making a joke of it, struck him as an act of necessary aesthetic homage. Women with eyes half that big got around without bumping into anything. So why all the superfluous material? In order to be lovely. An end in itself.

'No,' he said finally. 'In the event that you granted me what I've obviously been seeking, I'd consider it highly unlikely that my sense of gratitude for being so deeply involved in your life could do anything except increase dramatically. Escalate exponentially. Hypertrophy to the most stag . . . '

'Right. Got it.'

'What we're postulating here is the attainment of the ultimate intimacy with the person loved. If the person loved regarded letting a man go through the contents of her handbag as the ultimate intimacy, that's what this man would be after.'

'Like Flaubert.'

'Was that his number? Trust the frogs. I was thinking of the Birdman of Alcatraz, actually. Anyway you can see what I mean.'

'I can indeed, and I think it's rubbish.'

'So do I. What I've been after from you is just sex. But what's so *just* about just sex? I mean in the sense of what's so *mere* about mere physical passion? It includes everything. It includes a complete appreciation of the adored one in all her qualities, or what you suppose her qualities to be. If it uses itself up quickly then you've picked the wrong person. But you weren't wrong about the passion, only about the person.'

'*You* weren't wrong. You always say you when you mean I. And you think that your appreciation of me is a true one, do you?'

'What do you think?'

'I think that when you look at me or at anyone else you see yourself. What you don't realise, thank God, is that it's really quite a disarming self. No wonder we all roll over and kick our heels in the air.'

Nicholas smiled at this in a winning way, adding the touch of self-mockery that he supposed made it more winning still. He was not to know that she took his charm for granted and liked him for his energy. The day might come when he would be capable of such a reflection and so be a more formidable seducer than ever, although with perhaps less chance to achieve a woman like her. At this precise point, when matters were being settled in mid-air along their eye-line, there was a rustle in the shrubbery beside them.

In the Carambar the waiters behave as if they own the place and the people who own the place behave like waiters, so it is not always easy to tell employer and employee apart. Such outbreaks of industrial democracy are rare in Britain and soon cure themselves if left alone, but at the Carambar, even though it had been open now for three years, you still often heard your first name when being served a drink. 'Message for you, Nicholas,' said a handsome young man called Crispin as he leaned through a potted palm to deliver a fresh brace of carefully titrated Bellinis. 'Lancelot can't make it. Trouble with his car. Says he'll see you tonight.

'Perhaps Samantha's back,' said Sally.

'Not for a day or two yet,' said Nicholas, shrugging off disappointment with an emphatic negative. He always enjoyed showing Sally off to his older friend and rival, knowing that her steadiness led Lancelot at least momentarily to regret Samantha's theoretically desirable volatility. 'The poor bastard is in a perfect frenzy of jealous anguish. He's got visions of her taking a header into every bed in New York. I console him by saying that it won't be *every* bed in New York. Just the beds of the really famous blokes. The really successful blokes with the antique cocaine spoons worn as personal jewellery and tufts of pubic hair plugged into their foreheads like an uncut carpet. Only the ones who are younger, richer, more virile than him. Only those. That's what I tell him.'

'You'd be a lot less frightening getting each other down than you are bucking each other up.'

'Is that what you think happens?'

'I know that's what happens. You and he make it funny. Funnier in your case because you're stronger. He's just older. But take away the mutual hysteria and that's what you're all up to. Staging a conspiracy.'

'It isn't really like that.'

'Then tell me what it's really like.'

'You tell him something so he'll tell you something,' Nicholas explained. 'But you each say the bare minimum because neither of you wants to give the other the idea that he could do better. At the outside you might subtly hint that the girl had succumbed to your blandishments. But you wouldn't say she turned purple in your arms, had convulsions for half an hour and then spent the rest of the night at the foot of your bed saying prayers of thanks.'

'Why not?'

'Because he might be thinking: only *purple*? Only half an *hour*? Only *saying* prayers?'

'I don't believe any of that. But if we waited to meet men who weren't vain and didn't boast, we'd wait for ever.'

'Because the kind of men you want to sleep with are vain and boast.'

'Don't be smug about it. Some of us can perfectly well do without. As it happens I *am* going to let you sleep with me tonight but I don't want you to tell anybody and least of all Lancelot. People already assume that we're doing it anyway just because that's your reputation. But an assumption on their part and an open admission on ours are different things.'

'I promise.'

'And those other women you've been pretending you've given up. You'll give them up?'

'I promise that too.'

'Don't promise what you can't deliver or you'll be lying now as well as later. I just don't want your crowd dragging me down to its level. It's bad enough you let them do it to you.'

'Which level is this?'

'Oh, I don't know. The level of unfeeling disguised as sophistication, I suppose. That level.'

'I never thought you'd sound like advice to the lovelorn,' said Nicholas, believing that he was stung on behalf of his friends rather than on behalf of himself.

'Quite a lot of true things get said that way. You can't imagine how I hate it when the joke's supposed to be on Charlotte. It's *with* Lancelot but it's *on* Charlotte, isn't it? He can tell the story against himself because the story's *for* him really, because even if he's a randy old middle-aged trendy diving around with a pretty girl at least he's got the girl. What's Charlotte got?'

'Her career. The house. The children. Him. For a long time up to now and for a long time to come. While all around them the perfect marriages are coming apart like wet paper bags.'

'You might be right.' Sally's gift was for setting herself high standards without thinking herself unique. She knew it could all happen to her and wondered what it would be like living for a long time with a man you loved and who was not faithful.

Luckily she did not love Nicholas, whom she felt was being unfaithful to her already even as he sat there. Lapsing for once into the kind of married-lady fantasy she disapproved of, she imagined him as old as Lancelot, opening the front door after a bad day and looking right through her when he met her in the hall.

~ five ~

Opening the front door after a bad day, Lancelot looked right through Charlotte as he met her in the hall.

'You look as if you've seen a ghost,' she said, but what he had mainly seen was the taxi meter. It had been some time since he had watched one of these in action, so he had received a painfully sharp indication of how the financial structure of British society had changed in ways not necessarily to his benefit. Coming on top of his duet with Frank Strain, the revelation had been traumatic. When he had finally got through talking to the police and had made arrangements for the car to be accepted at a nearby garage whose personnel looked like the United Nations in blue overalls, he hailed the only other taxi in existence apart from the one that had ignored him earlier. Perhaps it was the same one coming around again. Anyway, he nominated his destination and climbed in, to be greeted by the sight of a new kind of meter which looked like a Japanese digital radio alarm clock, or digital alarm clock radio. Clock alarm radio digital. Lancelot assumed that the decimalised sum of money formed by the illuminated green diodes represented the fare charged to the previous passenger and had been left on display by mistake. He slid open the glass panel to inform the driver of this fact and discovered that it was not a fact. The large sum of money, which was already growing larger as he watched, was the price it cost to start the journey. Then he found that by referring to a chart stuck on the partition the passenger could convert the large sum shown on the meter to a sum very much larger still, provided he was quick. If he was slow, the calculation would be obsolete before it was finished. The green luminous figures changed in a continuous rush, as if a cyclometer had been attached to a coffee-grinder. The total fare cost Lancelot everything he had on him. He stepped out into the rain like a man in a trance. The ghost he had seen was his own.

'Trouble with the car,' he muttered. 'Vandalised. They tried to steal it. Took ages to find a garage and then it cost me everything to get home in a taxi. Everything. Nothing left.'

'Never mind. You can come with me in the Maxi.'

'Are you coming too?'

'Victor rang and said why didn't I? No doubt it's such a huge occasion that nobody'll notice we're both there, so your reputation will be quite safe.' In the ordinary way of things Lancelot would have detected the sarcasm, but his mind was full of green telephone numbers that did not answer, or else did but told you nothing.

'Are you going to change?' he asked, heading upstairs like a man to the scaffold.

'I'm already changed,' said Charlotte without rancour, deploying her pleated sleeves with a papal gesture. 'This is it.'

As if too tired to think of his own words, Lancelot said the same thing when they arrived at the gate of Victor's house in Hampstead. 'This is it.'

'I know,' said Charlotte patiently. 'I've been here too.' Years before she had seen a lot of Victor and had even, when asked, contemplated having a brief retaliatory affair with him, but neither he nor it would have been really her style. Nor she his, probably. By her husband she felt merely outshone. By Victor she felt obliterated. Or so she told herself, not to assuage injured pride – she had been too surprised that the possibility was there to be surprised when it evaporated – but to dull the pain of knowing that only her husband could touch her at the centre. Lancelot had been sincerely disappointed that her liaison with Victor had not flourished. Typically he had neither hidden his disappointment nor realised it would wound. In thrall to a permanent adolescent, Charlotte reflected that at least there would always be one child in the house. Provided, of course, that he did not leave.

She parked the car between a Rolls and something even bigger, which seemed to have no back wheels and was recognisable as a Daimler only when the light from the house struck the fluted grille. These and other large vehicles were patently the carriages of the very grand, but among them sports coupés of foreign provenance crouched knee high, suggesting that the gathering might be spiced by the presence of some of the successful young communications people. Lancelot, who was evidently not at his best, barked his shin against a lurking Ferrari. Nearer the inner gates there were more saloons and limousines, some of them with chauffeurs sitting in them already asleep, although away on the left there was a small group of men talking together whose peaked caps made their suits look vaguely like uniforms. Inside the inner gateway there was a swimming pool lit so brilliantly from within that you could barely notice how the surface was spotted by a light rain. If you bent down to touch the heated water you found it to be the exact temperature of the air, so that all you sensed was a change of texture. A good way past the far side of the pool the house began in the form of wide eaves, which even further away became glass walls, beyond which the house began all over again, and kept on going. Under the wide eaves there were people and beyond the glass walls behind them were other people. There must be a hundred people at least, thought Charlotte, with a fear that went back to childhood.

Lancelot wondered how soon he could get to a telephone. He had tried a quick call while dressing and had been connected to a laundry in New Jersey. Several wives of the rich and famous absorbed Charlotte into their number while Lancelot, like the rich and famous, circulated in search of the unexpected. Most of the faces were celebrated in one way or another and one of them, belonging to an American film actor, was so celebrated that for once Lancelot was glad Samantha was not beside him, because she would not have stayed beside him long. The actor, whose name was something like Brick Veneer, was smiling at a story being told to him by Lady Hildegarde, with whom Lancelot would at some stage of the evening have to raise the question of whether she would approve Serena as her chief researcher on the book about writers who could draw. He would have to raise the same question with Serena herself, which would raise the further question of what manner to adopt when telling her that she was relieved from the project about how glamorous women led their lives. At the moment Serena, wearing something in polka-dotted silk which above the waist consisted mainly of sleeves in order to conceal the wrists that looked like trench warfare, was half reclining on a muscatel velvet banquette while several prominent men, one of them the Shadow Foreign Secretary, paid homage. The challenge would be to break the news in such a way that she would retain that posture, instead of running outside to jump into the swimming pool or else heading for the master bathroom to sample one of Victor's wide selection of cut-throat razors.

Lancelot was asked what he wanted to drink by a man who looked like a cultural attaché. After a remarkably little while another cultural attaché simulacrum brought him the drink specified. Lancelot had often wondered how they worked that trick. The absurdity of generating books by artificial insemination, when there were already far too many books which had been brought into an increasingly ungrateful world by natural fecundity, was rubbed home by the spectacle of Victor's personal library, some of which could be seen filling the walls on three sides of this, the outer reception room, and which continued through the house on both main floors as the house itself continued up the hill. Victor, a South African Australian Jew educated in three internment camps and four universities, could read fluently in both the ancient languages and at least five of the modern ones. His Hebrew, however, was rumoured to be sketchy. Famously he had read every book in the world except those published by his own firm. The bookshelves, made of black glass slung between silver rails to produce an effect which reminded Lancelot of Tilly Losch's bathroom, contained rarities that would sometimes bring visiting scholars to their knees. The books gave way only to the paintings and pieces of sculpture, most of them collected during what Victor was fond of referring to as his Goering period. Portrait busts by Troubetzkoy and Golubkhina stood in niches of soft white light. The Nolan Ned Kellys were gifts from the painter. So, reputedly, were the Fairweathers, but the three Morandis had no doubt been obtained by other means. Hockney's 'An Even Bigger Splash' had the space of honour on the left wall of the withdrawing room, which Lancelot now entered, pausing briefly to greet Hockney himself. It was even larger than the outer reception room and except for the paintings and sculpture all four sides were filled with books. Here were many more people, including some of the loveliest women of the day. Lancelot's spirits, which seemed doomed never again to attain a reasonable level no matter how fast they rose, nevertheless went on rising. Even were he to be utterly deprived of libido, the presence of desirable women would at least reassure him that he was not in an undesirable place. Various well born and cared-for faces were tilted towards him in order to receive his formal kiss. Several of them he had seen transfigured by pleasure. What a pity you could not store those triumphs in a fund, to be drawn upon during lean times. But such reflections, he knew, were signs of weakness in themselves. You could not imagine Victor being thus bothered, any more than he was bothered by the eclectic voracity of his own taste. There he stood with his back to the long mantelpiece over which hung, to trick the eye and ravish the mind, a huge yet weightless Delacroix watercolour study for a Moroccan window. The whole room, and indeed the whole house, seemed to be pointed in that direction, but it wasn't just because of Delacroix. It was also because of Victor, who looked like a water polo forward run to fat and radiated proprietorial ease. At the moment the least popular female member of the Royal Family and the most popular female television newsreader were talking to each other across his chest. Lancelot received a small signal from Victor that now was not the time to approach, so he halted his forward drift, adroitly dodged various dangerously fissionable groups of bores, and threaded his way through into a sort of sit-down oasis in which, among other men of comparable age and stature, Nicholas was to be found comprehensively holding forth while young ladies sitting at various angles appreciated the results. It was evident that Nicholas was setting the pace, but as a sign of friendship he broke off from general conversation with only half his day's supply of witticisms duly imparted to the public, and made space at one side for Lancelot to sit down. Space at the other side was already taken by Sally, looking so at home that you could never have guessed she was here for the first time. So at home but not too at home. Lancelot was impressed all over again by her beauty. It made him want to run away and ring up. Deep black hair, simple black shift, fragile black sandals, clear skin – she looked as lustrous as a black and white photograph taken on colour film. Tall and looking all the taller for lying back, she watched the two of them being friends.

'What happend to your jalopy?' asked Nicholas.

'Everything. First thieves and then the police. They peed in it.'

'The cops peed in it?'

'No, the thieves.'

'Was this in broad daylight? Or were you parked down some alley?'

'It was practically in the main street. I was on a meter. There must have been half a dozen of them.'

'You mean they all lined up and hosed through the front window of your heap? Great.'

'I expect the chassis will more or less rust away in the course of time.' Lancelot switched his attention to Sally, patronising her ever so slightly, or what he thought was ever so slightly.

'How are you enjoying the high life?'

'It's certainly got more to offer than the summer ball at my university. Which was previously the smartest do I was ever at.'

'Did they have a *ball* at your university?' asked Nicholas with feigned surprise. 'I thought they had a *raffle* or something. Wasn't it more a sort of *sale of work*?'

'Who's that woman who's just come in?'

Even before he looked over his shoulder, Lancelot knew from the way the room had gone quiet whom Sally must mean. 'That,' he said, with an assumed tone of formality, as if christening a ship, 'is Elena.'

'Airliner?'

'Elena. Accent on the first syllable.' Lancelot sounded knowing, although not as knowing as he would have liked to sound. Elena would have looked statuesque if any statue had ever looked so alive. He had once called her Madame X dressed by Madame Gres, but it was a lasting regret to him that a single epigram was as close as he had ever come to being linked with her name.

'Holy smoke. What's her line of business?'

'She's a spy.'

'Who for?'

'The superpowers only,' said Lancelot, answering Elena's

smile as it flashed momentarily towards him like a traversing searchlight. 'She spies for all of them against each other. The most original woman in London by miles. Of a certain age, of course.'

'Oh, of course,' said Sally, wondering how anyone's body could give off so much illumination when three-quarters of it was covered in a black sheath dress. Was it true that you could be radiant by feeling radiant? Alas, not so. What you had to be was the focus of every male gaze in the room. What lit you up was being looked at. 'Suddenly I feel as if I've got a scarf tied around my head and I'm working at a lathe.'

'She's a wop dyke,' said Nicholas happily. 'Maybe she'll take you on. You're just the right height.'

'Tell me he's joking, Lancelot.'

'Not at all. Her husband died from jealousy. She's famously Sapphic.'

'Doesn't that just mean that she wouldn't go out with you?' Sally had quickly discovered that Lancelot enjoyed being taunted: it counted as intimacy.

'Go out with,' sneered Nicholas. 'Listen to it. The genteelness of it. *Go out with.*'

'She wouldn't, as a matter of fact,' Lancelot confessed largely. 'Although she does have a score of male admirers. But apart from her shall-we-say very close female companions her life centres on Victor, whose emotional career is definitely over, he being so much older and what have you. It's a sort of *mariage blanc*, all done on the social level. He never makes a move without her advice. She's where he gets what taste he has.'

'I should have thought his taste was perfect.'

'Oh God no. Forgive me, my dear, but this place is a bazaar. It's Playboy Mansion North.'

'What's wrong with a bazaar if everything in it's good?'

Lancelot started to tell her while Nicholas sat back to enjoy the argument. He was enjoying everything. Having Sally on his arm made him feel as if he had recently invented the universe. The thought of what was scheduled to happen later made him try to unthink it, on the childhood principle that if you refrain from dwelling on a forthcoming treat then it won't be taken away from you by circumstances. That day an articulated lorry had fallen sideways at a roundabout and crushed a panda car with two policemen inside it. Nicholas could easily imagine the same thing happening to him and Sally as they drove home. But it wouldn't, because he was not being presumptuous. He wasn't taking even his next breath for granted.

Charlotte was glad to see Elena arrive because the advent of the uncrowned queen of this little world meant that it would soon be the moment to approach the buffet tables, and she wanted to get away from the group of wives. They had all been talking married gossip non-stop and she owed them the chance to talk about her. Besides, she could see that one of Victor's most notoriously tedious factotums, Frank Strain, was inflicting unmerciful torture on a rather heartrendingly grotty young man whose inaccurately shaven face she thought she recognised.

'Frank, you've thrilled this young man long enough. Let me show him the way to the food.'

'Oh, you know each other!' asked Frank plaintively, but the words had the Doppler effect of a dying fall, the source from which they emanated having been left far in the distance.

'I can never thank you enough. Another few hours of that and I would have been dead. I'm David Bentley.'

'I thought you were. Your book of short stories was my bedside book just before Christmas. I can remember every bit of it except the title.'

'*Tactical Voting in the Eurovision Song Contest.*'

'Of course. Charlotte Windhover. I'm married to Lancelot Windhover, Victor's Special Projects Adviser. Do you come under that department? I suppose not.'

'I don't come under any department yet. I'm not actually published by Victor Ludorum. Charrap and Warbus did that book you read. Although I might be. He seems to be making moves in that direction. He's giving me lunch some time in the middle of the month after next and I suppose this invitation is a kind of preliminary ducking so I won't get all hot and bothered by his poshness. I'm talking too much.'

'Are you hot and bothered now? Don't miss out on those, they're usually pretty good.'

'What are they?'

'Pieces of pheasant.'

'I don't think I've actually ever eaten pheasant, unless they put it in the Wimpys without telling you. How many should I take?'

'One should be enough. We can circle back later if we want more. Come and sit over by the wall and then you can watch everybody.'

'I'm not hot and bothered but I disapprove like hell. This afternoon I was in Brighton talking to a lot of trained schoolteachers who can't find a job of any kind. It makes you angry, walking out of that into this.'

'I suppose it does.'

'And on top of the anger I feel out of place in this radical combat outfit. I should have changed into a suit. Not that I've got one.'

'What's uppermost, embarrassment or annoyance?'

'It's a cocktail. I've never seen so many women who look like jewellery advertisements talking to men who look as if they buy jewels to give to women who look like that. If I tried to talk to one of those females I'd drop my plate.'

'Thanks for the compliment.'

'Yes, but *you* talked to *me*. Otherwise I'd still be with that man hearing about loss leaders and warehouse costing.'

'All you have to do is relax, you know. You're dressed exactly the way the painters are, so if you pipe down everyone will think you're a painter too. There's old Lady Walsingham over there and she already thinks you're an abstract expressionist. Where did you get that jacket, incidentally?'

'My brother bought it off a wine waiter in Manila. It's got an invisibly mended bullet hole just here. I think my pheasant is a bit stringy.'

'All pheasants are a bit stringy. They're a wiry bird.'

'Have to be, I suppose. To have any chance of survival against the massed flak of the privileged orders. How do you defend all this?' he asked, waving a bone from which a fine diaspora of spiced gravy transferred itself to his cotton drill lapel.

'I expect you're right,' said Charlotte, dabbing the affected area with her napkin and wiping clean his CND badge. She shocked herself: even for someone not so shy it would have been a bold gesture. 'But if it could be defended, I suppose you'd do it by saying that in any free society there's always something like it. The rich and the secure create comfortable surroundings so that the gifted and the successful can seek each other out and make the rest of us feel nervous. Anyway, how long will it be before you belong with the successful a lot more than with us onlookers?'

'I don't think in those terms.'

'It won't matter much whether you think in those terms or not. The famous huddle together for protection.'

'I'll always be nervous.'

'You don't show it much except when you wave your food about and if you don't mention it nobody will know. I'm much more nervous than you are and I've had years more practice.'

'You, nervous? I don't believe it.'

'Oh yes. Trembling. Look. But the nice thing about social life, as opposed to real life, is that in social life you are what you seem. It cost me a terrific effort to come and get you.'

'So why did you?'

'I told you. I admired your book and I couldn't bear to see you being embittered at the outset by a tremendous bore. Listen, all this drives me practically batty with fright but it's got its good side, you know. You'll meet a lot of clever people here and clever people being clever together can be quite entertaining even when you don't admire them personally very much.'

'Isn't that Sally Draycott over there?'

'Which one?'

'The one growing on that table like a black orchid.'

'I don't know. She's very lovely.'

'She's just about the quickest thing on the box when they give her a chance.'

'She's all alone. Can't imagine she'll stay that way for long. Do you want to go and talk to her?'

'I think I'd rather stay where I am, if it's all right with you.'

Having eaten like a bird, Sally had left Nicholas holding forth to a suitably enthralled company and was now sitting alone at a small library table while she leafed slowly through a leather-bound volume containing a year's run of what clearly, even to the uninstructed eye, had a good claim towards being the most beautiful magazine ever published.

'Look at the Benois on the next page,' said Victor's voice from above. 'The countess standing in the pool was the mistress of one of my great-uncles. It was a huge scandal. Do you read the language?'

'Not a word,' said Sally. 'It's one of my great regrets. I did French and German and it's hard to find time even for those now. One of the good things about my university was the modern languages library. They had a reproduction of this but not the original. This is the first time I've ever seen what it really looks like.'

'That's the complete run, from 1898 right through until they had to pack it in. It belonged to my father. He brought some of his library out of Munich and got caught going back for the rest. He knew Diaghilev quite well. The really astonishing pictures are the little portrait heads by Somov. Look in the volume before that one, near the middle.'

'They're marvellous. Why isn't he famous?'

'Because he stayed in Petersburg. If he'd come to Paris with the ballet he'd be as well known now as Benois or Bakst. But he never came abroad except to study and when he finally emigrated it was too late. Now the Soviet critics tell lies about him and nobody in the West cares. It's very heartening that you should be interested in these things.'

'I don't see how it's possible not to be. Not that I know anything about it. If only we had nine lives.'

'Young Nicholas tells me that you're in television. I don't suppose that leaves you much time.'

'And it wastes a lot of the time it takes. That's probably why looking at something as lovely as this leaves me feeling a bit depressed.'

'No, it's just that everything you see there is touched by melancholy. Because it all got stopped.' Victor leaned down to a low shelf beside her, getting out a large-format edition of *The Queen of Spades* and spreading it open to show Sally the original Benois illustrations all tipped in by hand. From a long way away, Elena's gaze swung over them and moved on.

The evening was advancing. The celebrated American film actor was smiling at something being said to him by the second most popular newsreader, who was using her hands a lot, perhaps because on screen they were always tucked away out of sight.

'You don't think *she's* the quickest thing on the box?' asked Charlotte.

'God no,' said David. 'All aggression and nothing much behind it. Have you noticed how he never stops smiling?'

'Just being polite, I expect.'

'No, it's the coke.'

'Do you think that's what he's drinking? It isn't a very big glass.'

'The stuff I'm talking about is more of a powder, actually. The little spoon hanging around his neck is to tell you he can afford to snort it by the pound. He's been smiling like that in every movie he's made for the last ten years. It's because if his mouth relaxed the inside of his nose would fall out.'

'Good heavens. My husband has a friend who's reputed to do a bit of that sort of thing. I'm glad to say my children never have. Not that I know of. Isn't it supposed to be all over now, all of that?'

'So they say, but some of it's all right. Grass is all right. I grow my own.'

'You do? Don't the police come?'

'Where I live the police only come when the sky's red with flame.'

Later still, sitting at Serena's feet, Lancelot approximated his posture to that of the young man in the painting by Fragonard whose hand stretches out to shield his eyes from the radiance of the girl in the swing, while some cherub or other plunks a lute. Or did the cherub belong to Titian? No matter. He mooted to her the possibility of doing something about writers who could draw. Serena put two and two together but got only eight instead of her usual sixteen. She merely turned white. Tears of failure started down her cheeks, but at least she wasn't screaming. Suavely Lancelot presented the whole idea as natural, logical, and calculated to make best use of her talents. Perhaps slightly flown with wine by this time of the evening, she cheered up. Lancelot felt better too. At this rate he would soon be only gibbering.

The evening advanced volubly, into the relative time that stretches beyond the coffee. Head to head with her young man, Charlotte was not surprised to discover that various friends paid courtesy calls. One of them was the widow of a Prime Minister to whose policies David took particular exception, although the last of them had been carried out to its disastrous conclusion the year that he was born. The celebrated actor was outside floating, fully dressed, face upwards in the swimming pool, smiling at the occluded heavens. Lady Hildegarde's three beautiful daughters, their shoulders shawled against the chill, were arranged around the edge of the pool discussing philosophy with him and guarding him from harm, although he was apparently in possession of secret Eastern knowledge which would enable him, should the occasion arise, to remain underwater for some hours.

In what he liked to think of as Victor's boudoir, Lancelot sat on the edge of the bed and dialled the familiar fourteen-figure number with the effortless fluency of Ashkenazy playing a cluster of notes from the Chopin Opus 25 Etude No. 1 in A flat major. He was rewarded with the sound of the sea. The sound of the sea reminded him of the smell of the sea and that reminded him of her. The walls of Victor's bedroom were covered on three sides by a Gontcharova ballet backdrop with various doors let into it so that you could barely see their outlines. Lancelot could never decide whether this was brutality or inspiration. On the grey batik-covered fourth wall, facing the foot of the bed, hung three matched Boldinis of a fine lady getting out of her clothes. One of the Medici had had three Uccello battle scenes in a similar position, but everyone to his taste. Nowadays the Uccellos were in different cities. One day the Boldinis would be in different places too. After Victor's death, when his empire was broken up. But what if he were immortal?

This time the telephone uttered a long silence followed by the sound, heard from very far off, of locusts eating a packet of crisps. Boldini's fine lady was undressing after a heavy evening at the opera. There were so many layers of clothing that even after three canvases she was still not divested of them all, but you could see her long thighs. Boldini was supposed to exaggerate but Lancelot knew better. This time he heard the beginning of a connection and then a long howl. He matched it *mezza voce*. Victor's bed was like a raised tennis court covered in velvet the colour of a Raphael pope's cassock. The whole Borgia family could have climbed into it and still left room for a last-minute reconciliation with the Orsini. Samantha needed a large bed to do her justice. Quelling his imaginings, Lancelot was just reaching to dial again when Victor walked in. Lancelot dialled seven digits at random and then pretended to listen. He was disconcerted to hear the phone ringing at the other end and more disconcerted still when it was picked up and answered.

'What you want?'

'Could I speak to Mr Ashkenazy please?'

'We are Cypriot people.'

'I think I must have the wrong number.'

'You do this to us any more and we kill you. My wife no sleep. My children no sleep.'

'Sorry. Goodbye.' Lancelot put the phone down with a fair imitation of calm.

'You know Vladimir?' asked Victor.

'This is another Ashkenazy. He's doing some freelance research for us.'

Victor opened a door in the faded canvas, thereby revealing a bathroom which was not really all that much smaller than the bedroom, and briefly disappeared. When he came back, Lancelot gave him a concise run-down of the new plans, such as they were.

' . . . and Hildegarde quite likes the idea and thinks Serena would be ideal.'

Victor nodded all through this. In fact he had already been nodding before it started, a habit which made Lancelot feel like a chatterbox.

'And where does that leave the Gillian Jackson project? With no one doing it at all?'

This was the awkward question to which there was no smooth answer, so Lancelot tried honesty.

'Nobody, but it's better to face that and think again than to go on as at present.'

'All right. It's your pigeon.'

'And my neck.'

'Don't be silly,' said Victor, an exhortation so often on his lips that it counted as *politesse*. 'There's something else you might look into.' Victor explained that the world's most famous young female film star was about to walk into the house. She had already promised to write a book and publish it through Victor Ludorum in the first instance, instead of in America. To obviate the possibility of her agent talking her out of this admittedly quixotic course of action, she would have to be wooed. She came equipped with a husband but perhaps they would like to meet other couples in small-scale circumstances, large occasions being not to her taste. Soon she would be in the country for some time, starring in a big budget, prestige feminist epic called *The Woman Lieutenant's Frenchman*. Lancelot and Charlotte might care to cultivate her and her academic husband when she arrived in early summer. Serious little dinners, that would be the ticket. Emphasis more on brains than on glamour. Lancelot could make the initial acquaintance tonight. She would be coming here straight from dinner at the Palace.

Lancelot went away cursing Victor's habit of commissioning books from people instead of saying hello, but saw the advantages of such behaviour when the world's most famous young female film star duly arrived. There weren't many women who could make Victor's busy house fall silent. Certainly the royal lady with the elaborate hairstyle was unable to do so, a matter of enduring chagrin to her. Elena, when she chose, could do it by sheer aplomb, just by pausing before advancing. The world's most famous young female film star did it by transparency of expression. There was nothing special about her clothes: indeed she was notorious for purchasing the wardrobe of her last film and wearing it until she finished the next. She was neither very tall nor particularly shapely. But her face projected sensitivity. Thoughtfulness was turned outwards instead of in. She was so human that she made ordinary mortals look thick-skinned. It can be imagined, then, what she made her agent look like, when your gaze finally got far enough down to find him. So influential that he was a star in his own right, 'Zoom' Beispiel glowered past the right elbow of his client while eroding between his lipless jaws a cigar the size of a salami.

'I see she's brought a puppet with her,' said Elena, but the least popular royal female did not respond. Having long reconciled herself to not causing a sensation here, she was put out to see that someone else could. Elena leaned back so as to catch the ear of Lancelot, who was reclining between them, feeling like a faded manuscript between jewelled covers.

'Who is that extremely graceful young lady on the arm of your friend Nicholas?'

'Her name is Sally Draycott.'

'Drayhorse?'

'Draycott.'

'I don't think I know any Draycotts.'

'I thought she might take your fancy,' said Lancelot. He hadn't thought anything of the kind, but it seemed a good thing to be saying now. 'It's a big romance, that one.'

'She really is *too* beautiful. I imagine she must be very dumb.'

'On the contrary, she's highly intelligent. Too intelligent for her job, in fact.'

'Is she a hooker?'

'Television.'

'I knew it was *something* like that. You must bring them both to dinner.' The least popular royal female, who had been angling for another invitation from Elena for a long time, was put out all over again, but Elena drew the line at the British Royal Family in all its branches. She found it a bit recent.

'Is that who I think it is dangling from her wrist?' asked Sally.

'That's him,' said Nicholas. 'Or at any rate the ten per cent that shows above the surface. Clock the special choos. His feet are vertical in there. He gets lowered into them.'

'What do you think of her?'

'Great face. No tits to speak of.'

'I think I'd better get you out of here,' Sally said thoughtfully, but really she was talking about herself. She didn't want to catch Victor's eye. In a little niche of white light above the banquette on which they lay talking, a Troubetzkoy *grande dame* about two feet high sat surrounded by the fine accordion pleats, looking friable as biscuit, of a full-length Doucet ball gown. She had a bouquet in her lap and her head turned to one side. She belonged to Victor and would never get away.

~ six ~

Nicholas was in the passenger seat of Sally's Porsche 928 holding her high-heeled sandals in his lap while she drove in bare stockings. At the touch of a switch you could alter the angle of the squab so that you were either sitting up like a child at a kitchen counter or lying down as if in the care of an expensive dentist. The seat did everything except eject. He had it selected in the forward position so as to miss nothing of her profile in the light of the spaceship-style dashboard. Up until now, being driven by Sally in this wingless jet had been the best thing that had ever happened to him. He rather suspected that it was about to become the second best thing that had ever happened to him, but you could never tell.

'You realise,' she said, while looking for an opportunity to get out of third gear, 'that where we're going isn't much, don't you?' There was a sudden polite roar and the back of Nicholas's head sank about an inch into the soft top of the seat.

'I can't imagine why you never took me home before. Have you got your old mum living in the cupboard?'

'I just wanted to keep a few secrets.'

'So why now?'

'Because that pit you live in is full of writhing imagery. I can't breathe for ghosts in there even when I'm fully dressed. It would be like taking my clothes off in a hockey club shower room. Hooray girls, let's welcome Sally to the team.'

'Give us a break,' said Nicholas, pleased. As they came towards Knightsbridge a stretch of relatively clear road opened and Sally briefly got the projectile into top. It was like taking off from an aircraft carrier.

'What's the fastest you've ever been in this thing?'

'Only about a hundred and twenty.'

'Where was that, on the Autobahn?'

'On the M5.'

'Jesus Christ. Don't the police send the RAF after you?'

'There's a doodah under here that sort of burps when it smells radar. It's a bit illegal. But I'm a very safe driver.'

'I know. You like it, don't you?'

'It's what I would have done if I'd been a man. In fact I thought of trying it anyway. But I wouldn't have settled for anything except Formula One, and women just aren't strong enough physically to drive a proper racing car for any great distance. The g-forces are too powerful.'

'Have you been in one?'

'Not an F1. I've been in a Group 5 Porsche 935 K3/80 racing sports car on the Mulsanne straight at Le Mans.'

'How fast?'

'It's not the top speed that's important. It's how fast you brake and accelerate. About two hundred and ten, I suppose.'

'I don't see the attraction. I mean even where I'm concerned, let alone where you're concerned.'

'Beautiful machines, that's the attraction. They affect me exactly like works of art. More deeply, in most cases. I suppose I got it from my father. He was always staying on in the workshop to make model Javelins while the gentlemen who spent all day actually flying them were off at the picturesque country pub forgetting all about it. Tally ho, press on, pip-pip and all that palaver. I saw a Maserati with a Vignale body the other day that I'd love to own. I'd spend a lot of time just looking at it.'

'Posh address. You're practically a department of Harrods.'

'It's an address and nothing else. You'd better chew some barley sugar because you're in for a long climb. Shoes, please.'

'You weren't kidding,' said Nicholas as they neared the summit. 'Chris Bonnington gets sponsored for this sort of thing.'

'Walk in slowly or you'll hit the other side.'

'Is this all there is?'

'This is it.'

The flat was exceptionally neat, partly because there were so few things in it. One wall was covered with an intricate, fastidiously executed montage of magazine photographs and postcards featuring various interiors of houses, very few of them even vaguely contemporary. The effect was of the wall leading off into a hundred different imagined rooms. Apart from that and a workmanlike array of rather challenging books, there were two chairs, a table, a dressing table and a television set with two different kinds of VCR. The divan bed was big enough for one person to lie quietly. Two doors presumably led to a bathroom and a kitchenette, with the emphasis on the ette.

'All my money goes on the car,' Sally explained, taking off her small pearl earrings. 'It takes a week's salary to fill the tank. I'd rather have amazing things or nothing, you see. I've only got about four really good dresses. So for now I lie in bed, look at the wall, and choose the way I'd like to live if I ever strike it rich. Which will probably be never.'

'Would you care to show me how you lie in bed?'

She showed him with a generosity that made him feel all his Christmases were coming at once. At first he couldn't believe what he was seeing. Then, when he had started to believe it, he grew afraid that it would be taken away if he did not do all the right things. Experience helped him here, but not as much as she did, just by smiling at the right time, and in the right way. It had to be both, of course: if they smile at the right time but in the wrong way, or in the right way but at the wrong time, you might as well start looking for your socks.

'I was afraid I'd want to so much that I wouldn't be able to,' he said eventually.

'That's the advantage of getting on speaking terms first, mug. No anxiety.'

'Plenty of everything else but none of that.' He was glad. Sally, who wanted to be in love, was sorry, but not as sorry as she was glad. This hadn't happened for an age. Her body felt as if every atom had been taken out, polished, and put back. She looked it, too.

'You're lovely,' said Nicholas, balancing precariously.

'So are you.'

'I have to stick my hand on the floor to stay on the bed.'

'Already he's complaining. Try it this way.'

He looked into her transfigured face as if into a clear pool from which a nymph had suddenly surfaced and shattered his reflection. For once he enjoyed the actual moment, instead of enjoying the knowledge that he was enjoying the actual moment, or enjoying the knowledge that the actual moment would be remembered, however diminished, among the array of actual moments which would inform, shape and energise the way he wrote. His callow sophistication dissolved for a short while into innocence. He knew it, too. Which meant that it hadn't, quite. But let's give ourselves a break, eh? If only he could stay this way. Most people would give an arm for such happiness. Most people would give their happiness for such happiness, but only a few get the chance.

'I think we left before royalty did,' said Charlotte, making conversation as she drove Lancelot home in the Maxi. 'Victor might be offended.' Rain spotted the windscreen. Lancelot felt that it had been raining continuously since the fall of the Attlee government.

'She's not really present even when she's there, so it's no skin off our nose if we can't tell when she's gone. Who was that dishevelled person you got yourself stuck with?'

'Oh, he's *adorable*,' said Charlotte, surprised that Lancelot had noticed anything about her and doubly surprised to find herself defensive. 'He wants to ban the Bomb, democratise the Labour Party and help young blacks in his area learn to mend cars. His name's David Bentley and he writes short stories. Very good they are, too. I think you're going to be his publisher.'

'I certainly think we should go into children's books. Books *by* children is a bit steep. He looks about seven years old. Sounds very mature politically, though.'

'Oh no, he must be twenty-five. They look younger all the time nowadays. It's the muesli and the yoghurt.'

'Who wished him on you? Frank?'

'Sort of. I must say I like the style of that girl Nicholas brought. I think Victor did too. Is it a big affair?'

'Hasn't begun yet. She likes Nicholas very much but she's put off by his reputation.'

'That's refreshing to hear. Most of them are put on by it.'

'No, I don't think it's the *fact* of his being such a success with women that puts her off,' said Lancelot, who didn't think a serious woman could really be put off by something like that. 'It's the kind of attention that it could bring with it. She's got an irrational loathing for gossip columnists and all that sort of thing.'

'If she's got an irrational loathing for all that sort of thing,' said Charlotte, 'then she's certainly started keeping the wrong company.' But Lancelot's mind was elsewhere.

Later on it was still elsewhere, even though he felt so comfortable. Probably because he felt so comfortable. Charlotte would have given a great deal for her mind to be elsewhere. For a minute she even tried to think of young David but since she hardly knew him there was nothing much to go on. So she came back to being with Lancelot. Intense pleasure there always was; the grief of jealousy there always was; and while the grief spoiled the pleasure, the pleasure only made the grief more perfect. Perhaps she had always been too quiet for him. Replete and desolate, she could not cry for either reason. It would be so nice to be next to his body if only it were really there. As if to prove that it had been there, it went away.

Charlotte had the button down on the telephone beside the bed, but she could hear the downstairs telephone ping in sympathy, meaning that Lancelot had lifted the receiver behind the closed door of his study. A short while later there was another ping, meaning he had not got what he wanted. For Charlotte it was a relief, because sometimes those two small sounds could be half an hour apart and she never slept between them, even after a mouthful of pills. She almost felt sorry for him, but not quite.

'I'm alone at last,' said Victor on the telephone. 'The actors and the television stars got into a quiz about the movies. Endless, endless. It's the only thing they know anything about. Are you in bed?'

'Since ages. She's quite pretty, the actress,' said Elena. They were speaking in Italian, as they often did on the telephone at night. They always spoke on the telephone at night, but sometimes in English. 'Was the actor drugged or just stupid?'

'He almost drowned, in fact. Hildegarde's daughters took him away eventually.'

'They probably cut him up for souvenirs. What was his name again?'

'Block Wood or something.'

'And that awful so-charming young novelist of yours, the one who does the books full of disgusting words . . .'

'Nicholas Crane.'

'He seems to have acquired a presentable companion at last. After all those tramps. What is she called? That one in black and white. Something to do with horses.'

'Sally something.'

'She's mighty good-looking.'

'For men who like girls instead of women. She might turn into something one day.'

'Is that why you were showing her your etchings? So that she'll turn into something one day?'

'You forget that as a publisher I can't help being at least momentarily interested in any member of the younger generation who picks up a book without being forced to. I wouldn't want to lose a potential customer.'

'Why is Lancelot in such a panic?'

'He doesn't know what his girl's getting up to in New York.'

'He doesn't know what she gets up to when she's in London. There must be more reason than that. He told me some policemen went to the lavatory in his car. I don't think Her Highness was pleased to hear it.'

'I suppose he's worried about whether he's doing what I want. It's hard to convince him that's the only thing that worries me.'

'I'm lost.'

'The way he tries to guess my wishes instead of getting on and doing something unexpected. Which is what he's there for. That, and to amuse me.'

'A court jester.'

'Not at all. He has an enchanting comic imagination when he's not dying of nerves. I don't care how many ideas go haywire as long as he brings in the occasional unusual thing. Which he's eminently qualified to do. But he feels he's on trial.'

'That's you. People are bound to feel that way with you anyway, so with a big baby like him you can imagine. Did I see him making a rendezvous with the actress?'

'I told him to do that.'

'Has Charlotte been raising a love-child without telling

anybody?'

'Not to my knowledge.'

'She was looking after some young person from the Red Brigades.'

'He's going to be one of our new writers, if I can talk him into it. Very left wing. I thought he'd better get a glimpse of what he wants to blow up.'

'His eyes were everywhere. Charlotte would be a good Virgil for him, if you can have a female Virgil. A Beatrice. If she loved Lancelot less she would enjoy life. She would even enjoy Lancelot. Should I worry about her?'

'About Charlotte?'

'Fool. I meant Black and White. The one who might be something one day.'

'She comes from nowhere. No family, no nothing. Nothing has ever happened to her except a few A levels and a redbrick university. What's there for my imagination?'

'Everything. A thoroughbred without a pedigree. Think of the doors you could open for her. Quite apart from the door to your bedroom.'

'Speaking of which.'

'Speaking of which, perhaps tomorrow late. I'm going for dinner to the criminally boring Langweiles. Whom I've put off so long they've grown senile. She's completely cuckoo by now and he makes passes under the table. I'll be out of there like a shot. Eleven thirty at the latest.'

'Meaning twelve thirty at the earliest.'

'Will you come to me anyway?'

'Of course. Don't worry about Black and White.'

'Aha! You mention her again! You bring up her name! She intrigues you!'

'That's just what she doesn't do.'

'Do I still?'

'Always. Inexhaustibly.'

'There's my other phone. Will you hold on or shall I ring you back?'

Victor held on while Elena dealt briefly with the first of a string of admirers who checked in every night at about this hour from all parts of the world. Normally Victor would sign off so as not to block the traffic. He knew that by not breaking the connection he had tacitly admitted there was a speck of grit needing a few more layers of nacreous wrapping. He had surprised himself by protesting once too often. A twinge of guilt had unbalanced him. He had not even known the guilt was there until Elena had unerringly probed for it. The secret, consuming intimacy at the centre of their friendship had long ago reduced to ciphers all the men in her life and all the women in his. Both had sworn that it would do the same to anyone else either of them was likely to meet. Both of them had soon believed it where she was concerned. He had eventually come to believe it where he was concerned. But she had never quite believed it where he was concerned. She was too realistic.

'I'm back with you,' said Elena. 'And now tell me how much you adore me.'

'As if I needed to do that,' said Victor, knowing he did need to. So he did, while Elena asked him his catechism. They had armoured themselves against everything except time. Now that it had caught up with them, they had it to burn.

'Well, then,' thought Elena while they searched their memories for the first and best endearments. 'This is it.' In Italian the expression has no close equivalent, but you can still think it.

David Bentley walked home that night, pleased at having met the most attractive woman of his life. Several times he had to shelter from the rain, so it was already three in the morning before he even crossed the river. He was miles past the affected area when the bomb went off but he heard the thump, followed shortly by a lot of police and ambulance hooters yelling their two notes. See-saw, see-saw, see-saw. A white police Rover lit up like Blackpool went past him very quickly with the policeman in the passenger seat swivelling to take a look at him as he walked. David supposed it was terrorists they were looking out for and that he looked like a terrorist, or at any rate like what a policeman would expect a terrorist to look like who was walking casually away after igniting the fuse of an infernal machine. Actually, he found out next day, the bomb had been of the sophisticated variety that explodes in the lap of one kind of

Iranian who is just setting off to post it through the letterbox of another kind of Iranian. Either one group had been encouraged by the CIA to launch a holy war against another group or vice versa. Anyway, three men with bad shaves had climbed into a Ford Escort and promptly distributed themselves all over Marylebone. The police had already finished putting white tape around the area by the time David entered his own territory. A two-up two-down Georgian house shook to the rhythm of a reggae party. The whole place pulsed with light in time to the beat. They've plugged the mains into the bass, thought David appreciatively, keeping an eye out for muggers. In his district you could tell the muggers from the dossers a long way off. The muggers were the ones who set fire to the dossers. As he turned the second last corner he saw what looked like a small tribe of Mohawk Indians who had been painted white and drafted into the Parachute Regiment. They appeared to be relieving themselves in turn through the window of a Volkswagen Polo. He took another turn instead, approached his house from a different direction, and smoothly let himself in. Everyone was asleep.

~ seven ~

Next day, as a tribute to spring, the rain relaxed its tempo, sometimes stopping altogether for hours on end. Lancelot went to work in another ruinously expensive taxi and had his usual encounter with the cottage cheese, the cavernous box-files and Janice, the volume of whose voice had taken on, seemingly overnight, the sharp intonation of impatience betokening her bad time of the month. Janice's bad time of the month took up so much of the month that the few days remaining could with better reason be called her good time of the month. Only with difficulty could Lancelot establish a connection between Janice's menstrual cycle and such natural phenomena as human reproduction or the phases of the moon. On one occasion he had opened the bottom drawer of her desk and discovered a box of her jumbo tampons. Not so much a box as a crate, really. They had been called something like Tristar 747 DC-10 Super-Duper. Reflecting that he was not very fair to Janice in his thoughts, Lancelot would have thought even less of himself if it had been possible, but after finally getting through on the telephone to Samantha he had no self-confidence left to waste.

Her account of where she had been and what she had been up to struck Lancelot, who was keen to believe the best, as particularly unconvincing. But his fear swelled to terror when she told him that she would not, after all, be coming home straight away. Instead the magazine would be sending her to Los Angeles for three weeks or perhaps four, if not five. *Courage in Profiles*, which had already established itself in Lancelot's awareness as a publication of impressive flexibility as to its scheduling and work requirements, now seemed to have adopted an inexorable dynamic of its own, like an epic film about Napoleon. Who was in command, Abel Gance? She was supposed to be giving advice on English tone and social mores, not dedicating her life to a *chef d'oeuvre*. Lancelot found himself shouting and whining to fill in the gaps left by the voice at the other end. Then she had to go. She always had to go.

Lancelot had to go to Los Angeles. There was, after all, good reason. Ian Cuthbert was out there, probably already working on yet another synopsis of *A World History of the Short*. He could be encouraged to hurry up: also his brains might be – must be – picked for a list of famous writers who could draw. The world's most famous young female film star was back there by now, and would not be in London again for at least another month, so there was legitimate reason for thinking that some part of the necessary wooing would have to be done there. Also he could sound out some elegant ladies for possible interview by whoever would succeed Serena as Gillian Jackson's ghost on the lifestyles project. Bel Air was full of women with tales to tell of how they had once entertained JFK, Eisenhower, Roosevelt, Woodrow Wilson and Ulysses S. Grant. Besides, it would get him out of London long enough for his car to be repaired. Most of the trip could plausibly be charged to Victor Ludorum and even if he had to pay for it himself, hiring a personal Learjet in both directions and staying in the Khashoggi suite of the Beverly Wilshire, it could not possibly cost as much as another week of running around London by taxi. He started the long and ear-splitting job of leaving all the details to Janice, knowing that the expedition would take at least a week to set up even if everything went through without a hitch.

With all the dogs banished to the garden, Charlotte had her Ideal Academic Table ready by the appointed time of eleven in the morning, so she was not best pleased when the team from *Prestige* finally materialised at two in the afternoon. The photographer's assistant, who was the first to enter the hall and who was carrying what turned out to be the harbinger of a whole series of large, heavy silver boxes, was dressed up as if to attend a riot on the terrace of a football ground. His boots would have looked extravagantly aggressive if two members of the Rapid Deployment Force had been standing in them, and his hairstyle, razored to follicle level, resembled a peeled hard-boiled egg which had been dotted all over with a blue ball-point pen. What looked like the scar of a bungled tracheotomy proved on closer examination to be a dragonfly tattooed under his Adam's apple so that it wobbled when he swallowed. The photographer himself, who arrived next, was attired for jungle combat duty and had a three-day growth of beard plus eyes which had seen too much. As he went on to explain, in a succession of widely spaced expletives which gradually added up to a monologue, what he had seen too much of was Ideal Tables. He had seen the Ideal Media Table, the Ideal East End Playwright's Table and the Ideal Political Hostess's Table. He had seen tables, and died, ha ha. But he had to admit that Charlotte's Ideal Academic Table was unusually daring, especially in the positioning of the willow pattern sauce-boats.

The photographer's accompanying journalist wore green nail polish, a black satin bolero, a bisque crêpe-de-chine blouse, pistachio cheesecloth harem pants, thick opalescent grey eyeshadow and a shower of junk trinkets at the throat, but his gestures were comparatively restrained and after a while Charlotte ceased fearing for her crockery. What aroused her apprehension was the section editor who had tagged along unannounced. This was Delilah Ball-Hunt, and even Charlotte, who was not especially alert to the evil propensities in mankind, knew her to be an unusually perilous gossip. Dressed for World War II from her Veronica Lake peekaboo hairstyle down to the open-toed shoes through which her big toes pushed thin nylon membranes like twin herniae, the lumbering Delilah poked blowsily around in Charlotte's kitchen drawers while asking questions in counterpoint to the journalist. Charlotte, who when asked a question was more likely to answer it than fend it off, might just have coped with Delilah had they been tête-à-tête. But to answer the journalist's questions and to stonewall Delilah's demanded a wariness of which she was not capable.

'The embroidered napkins are wonderfully extravagant,' cooed the journalist, proffering a small tape-recorder as if it were a packet of black Balkan Sobranie cigarettes. 'Did you tat them yourself?'

'Oh yes,' said Charlotte.

'I suppose Lancelot's work keeps him away a good deal?' suggested Delilah sourly, folding her arms over her massive bosom and scanning the ceiling as if waiting for an overdue Lancaster to come home from the Ruhr.

'Oh yes,' said Charlotte. 'That is, not really. We're both very busy.'

'A lot of those plates are just *pretending* to be vermeille, aren't they? I mean you've very cleverly tarted them up with gilt.'

'That sort of thing, yes.'

'Does Lancelot go to the country with you on weekends?'

'Not always. Nearly always. Quite often he stays here to work, but hardly ever.'

'Ba-boom,' said the photographer, pressing his button as if it were connected to a bomb-release mechanism. 'Ka-pow. OK. Terrific. Put another gauze on that one,' he told his assistant, pointing to a light that looked like a hairdryer.

The gauze caught fire at just the time when Mrs Halitosis was serving the whipped cream wild strawberry pie that Charlotte was so worried about because the strawberries had to be Spanish. The assistant with the blue-speckled alopecia and the huge boots opened the back door and tossed the smouldering gauze into the garden, whereupon all the dogs entered the house and circled the Ideal Academic Table very loudly at high speed. By the time the fumes had cleared and the dogs had been removed with much skittering of radially extended claws on the terracotta floor tiles, the heat of the lamps had transformed the whipped cream to a rubbery scum. 'Pow,' said the photographer. 'Splosh. We've lost it.'

'Is Lancelot still helping Samantha Copperglaze with her writing?' asked Delilah sharply.

'I expect so,' said Charlotte, trying to make it clear that she resented, on general principle rather than because of a specific grievance, any interrogation along those lines. Even in the midst of her confusion she had time to wonder how Delilah could look so constantly embittered. She lived, Charlotte dimly remembered, mainly from feeding information to the tabloid gossip writers. Charlotte kept reviewing what she had let slip so far and decided that no cats had been alluded to which were not already long out of the bag. Ten years ago, Lancelot's infidelities might well have made a story for the kind of newspaper in which vengeful illiterates keep the conscience of the fortunate, but nowadays he was on the verge of being a forgotten man. Once again she almost felt sorry for him. Perhaps she ought to invent a spectacular affair for him – with the world's most famous young female film star, for instance – and give Delilah a taste of that. Or perhaps not.

'I think the whole idea of eating in the kitchen is just so adventurous,' said the journalist for the millionth time. 'Marvellous buzz. Nosh and dash. No-time to waste in the high-powered academic mealyou. Very Sixties aura about the whole thing. And yet with all this ravishing little-girl floral detail that you do. It's now and it's then. It's Thierry Mugler for the Laura Ashley people, if you get me.'

Charlotte, who not only didn't get him but didn't want him, nodded glumly at the exact moment when the photographer swung towards her, dropped to one knee as if he had been shot, and snapped a candid. Not long after that it was all over. Delilah was the last to leave, having lingered in the bathroom to go through the cabinets and the wet-bags. Obviously Delilah would have liked a drink or two, a square meal to follow, and an invitation to spend the night under the bed, but Charlotte finally managed to bundle her out. The Ideal Academic Table sat there in the comparative darkness of the unassisted afternoon light. Charlotte gathered what strength she had left and loaded the Maxi for a trip to the country. With the exception of the collapsed Spanish cream pie she packed all the food she had cooked for the Ideal Academic Table into a hamper and took that too. The remains of yesterday's steak and kidney pie would do for Lancelot. Those of her children who turned up in time were free to come along. They all declined, while retaining the option of coming up on Saturday by train. The dogs sat in the back on top of the hold-alls and the hampers. Popping and fizzing as it headed down the motorway in the slow lane, the ageing car looked, Charlotte was uneasily aware, like the poster for a Walt Disney film, but embarrassment mattered less and less as she drove further west along the valley of the Thames into an evening now lingering perceptibly longer than it would have done only a little while before, so that there was still some light left when she arrived.

The mill house was not very big. Nor were the lands around it very extensive. In fact they were a sort of yard. But a stream that fed the headwaters of the Thames flowed more or less under the living room and the setting in general seemed, especially in this silvered twilight, to have been concocted by Constable in a fit of romantic delirium. Everything was spongy underfoot from the recent rain. The cowslips were out but not yet the buttercups. Nothing you could see was out of place, except perhaps the concrete pill-box in the middle of the cow pasture on the other side of the river. Tramps sheltered there and used it as a toilet, so that the local children were forbidden to go in. The pill-box was a nuisance, but often the cows came between you and it, and anyway by now even the raw, brutalist cement of wartime was looking weathered and ready to be absorbed. Pockmarked by lichens, it was taking on the colour and texture of all the other stone in the district, whose houses and barns and boundary walls looked as if they had been made from chips and flakes knocked off St Paul's Cathedral, the materials for which had been quarried not far away. One day the ivy would pull everything down and possibly even the pill-box too.

The money Charlotte had brought to her marriage as a dowry, together with the earnings of Lancelot's first successes, had all gone into the London house, in the days when that much money got you a house freehold instead of a room for rent. What she earned as a lecturer was put into the mill house. Theoretically Lancelot put a portion of his earnings into its upkeep but in practice most of what he made went on their day-to-day living in London. Effectively the mill house belonged to her and the children. Since it was equipped with neither a disco nor an electronic games parlour they tended to boycott it nowadays. It was a while since any of them had been on a pony but perhaps it would happen again. Meanwhile the place was all hers. Here she could read, write, preserve fruit, coax the local freelance gardener to sterner effort, and visit neighbours. Many of the neighbours were quite grand. Three out of four of the most prominent London hostesses had their country houses in the area. Elena's house was scarcely half a mile away in a straight line, screened by oaks, chestnuts, yews, limes and an intricate system of tall boxwood hedges. You could walk to it easily around the river bend, while hearing through the trees the regular purr and gravelled squeal of large cars bringing guests and taking them away. Two miles over that way lived the nephew of the third or fourth most recent prime minister and his singing wife Dido, and just up the first hills into the Cotswolds was the village in which the Liberal choice for the leadership of the as yet embryonic Social Democratic Party listened to his advisers at the weekend. And then if you drew a circle of rather greater radius, say three-quarters of an hour each way by car, you would include those very large establishments with names like Castle This, That or The Other, whose lands were like little counties. Like a treasure map, the district was all joined up by winding paths and crooked roads. Somehow the power-line pylons which marched so inexorably everywhere else were hereabouts seldom visible. The calm was Augustan, Arcadian, idyllic. Nothing disturbed it except for the Tornado Multi-role Combat Aircraft being tested overhead, while every twenty minutes a Boeing KC-135 Stratotanker lifted out of the nearby USAF base to begin the long, eardrum-cracking climb up to its rendezvous with the atom bombers flying forever, day and night, to and from their failsafe points at the edge of Soviet airspace. The Stratotanker makes a noise on the limit of human endurance and for a while, when it was first assigned to the area, cows gave birth to calves with two heads and five legs, like portents in Livy. But soon even the animals settled down and got used to the inescapable facts of the Global Strategic Environment, the chief fact being that there is nowhere to hide, although there is no denying that some places are more comfortable to skulk in than others.

Skulking was largely what Lancelot did once he was alone. He had been looking forward to it but it unsettled him when it happened. On the first night Mrs Hermeneutics left him a piece of steak and kidney pie to heat up and went off somewhere, perhaps to a read-through of the *Iliad*. I GOINK AOUT, her note began. Lancelot put the piece of pie in the oven, preselected to gas mark seven, and went upstairs to do something sensible about his papers and bills. The smoke told him when the pie was ready but he was not prepared for the blast of heat when he opened the door. With singed eyebrows he donned the oven gloves and inserted them into the oven, groping for the pie dish.

It burned him even through the gloves, a clear indication that it needed rapid cooling down. He thought that to tilt it slightly and play the rubber teat of the cold water tap on it would cool it. Judging from the noise and steam it did, but the segment of pie, which must have already been loosened in the dish when the rest of it was eaten at lunchtime, flopped into the sink. Lancelot fetched a knife and fork and ate it from there, following it with a generous helping of some strange strawberry-studded creation coated with an edible form of white latex.

It was a bad start to a period of what had once been known as 'batching', meaning you looked after yourself until struck down by food poisoning. He would have got Nicholas over to play backgammon but Nicholas's telephone did not answer. He rather suspected that a call to Samantha's business number in New York would earn him a flea in the ear. He made it anyway, and was relieved to be told by someone else that she was not in the office, instead of being told by her that he was getting on her nerves. He made a resolution to call her less often and felt himself breaking it even as he made it, like the Hunchback of Notre Dame trying to construct a balsawood model aircraft. He had refused most invitations for the impending week so as to be free for her homecoming. Now he was alone with himself, and it had been a long time since he had much profited from his own company. When he turned on the television he found himself looking at Sally Draycott refereeing a verbal wrestling match between a militant trade union leader and a right-wing Labour MP. For men with diametrically opposed views they had remarkably similar hairstyles, in which the hair was grown long at the side and deployed very carefully across the scalp, an arrangement to which the trade union leader had added an effect of studied exuberance by having the whole confection blow-dried and sprayed with fixative, so that it floated just above his skull like a ginger beret of sugar-floss. Sitting between these two solemn zanies and marshalling their conflicting opinions with impressive fluency and competence, Sally looked paradigmatically beautiful, an ideal of healthy normality from which the two specimens sitting on each side of her could be regarded as the first, comparatively mild but irreversibly aberrant, deviations in an endless series of variants which ultimately left the human race looking nothing like her. Lancelot was sorry for himself that he was obsessed with someone even younger and so much less governable. He played all the steps from meeting Samantha onwards backwards in his head, and then imagined how he would have been with someone like Sally: opening doors, showing her things, being interesting because she was interested. Thus we dupe ourselves into thinking that our lives could have been so different if only a few things hadn't happened. Actually Lancelot had forfeited Sally twenty years ago, when he had lost the thrill of writing and when she was a little girl just learning to turn her nose up at cardboard-covered books with pictures and to ask for proper ones with all words.

Punching the 'off' button on the remote control before a strange man in a tweed kilt could tell him any more about dogs, Lancelot rang his business partner and was astounded to find him in. Catching Anthony at home was usually even harder than catching him at the office: embroiled in one glamorously doomed love affair after another, he spent most of his time crying on the shoulders of old mistresses while he asked them what he should do about new ones. Anthony agreed that it was certainly high time the accounts of Style Consultants were gone through, perhaps with a view to streamlining the cash flow structure. When Lancelot asked if that meant the company was in trouble, Anthony laughed reassuringly in a way Lancelot had long ago learned to associate with collapsing coal mines and the fate of Herculaneum. They fixed a meeting for next morning at their Bond Street office. That decided, Lancelot drank himself unconscious, and was asleep in his narrow bed before the first of the children came home.

~ eight ~

Thank God it's Friday, thought Lancelot next morning. He was thinking it along with several million other Londoners who unlike him were not alighting from a taxi in front of Sotheby's. What a perfect word for it the word 'alighting' was, carrying as it did the sense that whoever was debussing from the hired vehicle had first been stripped of all his assets. Even in the pit of depression, however, Lancelot still got the point of Bond Street on a mild day. From the shoe shop across the road a woman walked out and stood as if she was about to be photographed for pre-war French *Vogue* by George Hoyningen-Huene at his most fastidious. She was a poem in cashmere and silk. You could laugh at some old boiler in a mink but try laughing at a vision like that. A jersey vision you could pull through a plain gold ring and it would give off the smell of young lust. Under Socialism, thought Lancelot automatically, all the women will be beautiful and there will be no artificial fabrics. The warm air was quietly alive with the pampered sound of Rolls-Royce doors closing. Lancelot stood there, part of it all, the collar of his lightweight trench coat daringly pulled up behind his head, the complete *flambard*. Then he ducked around the corner, found the lift to be under repair as always, and climbed the six flights of stairs to Style Consultants' Bond Street office, which was tucked under the edge of a mansard roof so that you had to stand at an angle if you weren't sitting down with your head against the ceiling.

Anthony was sitting there amongst the cardboard boxes full of pacily designed brochures for exhibitions which had taken place at some time in the previous decade. The Style Consultants' clerical staff and accounting department was sitting at the typewriter against the partition. She was either erasing a typing error or else painting her nails white. Since she was good deal blacker than Egypt's night the latter course might have produced startling results and thereby helped to wake her up. Her famous tendency to nod off had nothing to do with lack of intelligence. She had plenty of that – certainly enough to know when she was on to a good thing. It was just that there was not a lot happening.

'You look hung over,' said Anthony, who didn't. Anthony paid the same sort of attention to his appearance as Lancelot but got even better results. His suits, hair and complexion all looked as if they were freshly sponged and pressed each hour. Anthony glowed. He was the swashbuckling, self-confident entrepreneur that prime ministers dream of.

'You see Habitat took over Mothercare?' asked Anthony. 'He's worth twenty-five million overnight.'

'How much are we worth?'

'Virginia, why don't you go down and get us some of that real coffee?'

'Yeah, why doan I? Cause iss miles, ass why.'

'Cut along, darling. And get one for yourself, too. Don't hurry. Pop along to the Royal Academy for a while and see the Japanese exhibition if you like. The *netsuke* are particularly charming.'

'Yeah, fanks. Whennay gunner fissat liff?' Virginia departed without removing her headphones, which judging from her syncopated gait were disgorging rhythmic music instead of the dictated letters and memos that Lancelot had at first imagined. When they were alone, Anthony's smile became more in-souciant than ever. He looked as happy as if he had just won the Queen's Award for Industry.

'We're ruined,' he said.

'How ruined?'

'Completely.'

'But how can we be? We've got no outgoings except this office and her salary. How much do we pay her?'

'Oh, only the standard rate for a secretary. About the same as the chairman of British Rail. But the outgoings could be a lot lower and they'd still be more than we're bringing in. Look at these figures.'

Anthony, beaming as if Princess Caroline of Monaco had left a desperate message on his answering machine to the effect that her life would not be worth living unless she had an affair with

83

him, unfolded and spread out several large sheets of paper with green lines on them and holes down the edges. Lancelot strove to grasp the import of the figures. They were not very large figures either way. Style Consultants could not go bust for much, there just wasn't enough trading involved. But it soon became clear how providential it had been that he and Anthony had each gradually come to look on their little firm as a side-line, because very soon it would not be even that.

'How did it happen?' Lancelot asked.

'Inevitable. First of all, your consultancy with Victor Ludorum is really a full-time job. So is mine with Astrotel.' Anthony spent three or more days a week as a Special Projects executive for an independent television company. 'But the main reason is historic. Nobody needs to consult us about style any more.'

'Because they've all got it?'

'Or don't care if they haven't. Other times, other priorities.'

'These figures here, are they debts?'

'Some ours and some other people's.'

'Do they balance out?'

'They ought to, but the other people's debts are mainly bad.'

'So we owe money.'

'The firm does.'

'So what do we do?'

'Wind up the firm,' laughed Anthony, as if his OBE had just come through. 'The personal cost to us should be considerable but by no means crippling. Giving Virginia a month's notice will be the main expense.'

'Munf's wha?' asked Virginia, entering with the coffee. Lancelot wondered, not very intensely, how she had heard what was being said, and then noticed that one of her ear-pieces was above the ear instead of on it, so that she could maintain contact with what he was starting to doubt could usefully be called the real world. Anthony began explaining the position to her, twinkling with self-satisfaction as he did so, as if he were H. G. Wells being interviewed by a very young and obviously smitten Rebecca West. Lancelot sat for a while lost in thought, or, more accurately, at a loss for words. Then he left them to it and walked towards Fitzrovia for his most cherished fixture of the week, the Friday lunch. It was hardly raining at all, really.

The prospect of lunch had been the main reason for thanking God it was Friday. At the end of a hard week with the empty box-files, Lancelot took spiritual sustenance from dining with his literary contemporaries. By now most of them were younger than he and all of them were more literary, it having been a long time since he had written anything. But he could still speak and in some circumstances he even enjoyed listening, so long as the periods of enforced silence were not overdone. The restaurant, an Italian establishment spread over several floors, was still called Foscari's, although both the Foscari brothers had long ago gone home. It served a cheap menu at high speed but allowed its regulars to linger over the third coffee and the fourth brandy. Lancelot's luncheon group, which Lady Hildegarde Plomley had once christened the Dregs, met upstairs in the front room. Nicholas was nowadays the leading light. The most brilliant caricaturist of the day was almost always there. Several literary editors of Sunday newspapers and weekly magazines were fairly regular attendants. Two Australian poets long resident in England turned up religiously in the forlorn hope of becoming civilised by osmosis, or at least of having their blunt features transmitted to posterity by the most brilliant caricaturist. Colin Thinwall, political correspondent of a left-wing weekly and tireless lover of aristocratic young men, made the Friday table a climactic point in his week's drinking. On the rare occasions when women attended, the talk was of literature and related topics. On all other occasions it had mainly to do with sexual scandal, although digressions into other aspects of sex, and even other aspects of scandal, were sometimes allowed. Today David Bentley was appearing for the first time, sponsored, presumably, by Nicholas. In deference to David's not yet fully brutalised ears, there were concerted attempts to discuss such normally quickly glossed over topics as the imminent economic collapse of the country.

'How much do we really *need* the railways?' asked Lancelot rhetorically, feeling a twinge in a back tooth. The minute you book a ticket for America, they start to ache, as if daring you to enter a country in which a single visit to the dentist can result in life imprisonment for debt.

'Tell us about the railways,' said Nicholas, signalling for more wine. 'You've got a theory about the railways.'

'He hasn't been on a train in years but he's got a theory,' said Thinwall, his skin gradually turning a lighter shade of green as the wine topped his system up to normal. He had woken up feeling all right that morning: always a bad sign, because it meant that he was still drunk. But after quickly being sick he had felt worse, meaning that he was getting better. Now he felt fine.

'Jesus, this snail is like a decayed Dutch cap in there,' said one of the Australian poets. 'I can't get the bastard *out*.'

'Apart from being a shameless advertisement for the class structure,' Lancelot expounded, 'the main thing the railways do is carry passengers, and coaches carry passengers almost as well. If you made the railway stations into coach stations and paved over the railway lines to make roads, you could run the coaches like trains.'

'With a cocktail bar and a superloo in each coach,' said one of the literary editors.

'They've already got that now,' said one of the other literary editors.

'Cocktail bar,' said Nicholas. '*Cocktail bar*. Yes, they've already got a cocktail bar all right. Some Chelsea Pensioner slopping gin over a formica counter. And the loo's an enamel bucket behind one of the back seats with a lot of swaying drunks all hosing into it.'

'Yes, but you could have a lot more coaches and they wouldn't need to be overcrowded.'

'They could leave St Pancras every few seconds, one behind the other,' suggested David quietly.

'Exactly,' said Lancelot.

'They could be joined together,' David added.

'Yes.'

'If you put a big engine in the first one then you wouldn't need engines in the others.'

'The possibilities are endless.'

'If you put flanged wheels on them and laid down some rails on the asphalt then the driver wouldn't even have to steer.'

'You could call it a train!' shouted Thinwall. Lancelot enjoyed his own unhorsing as much as anybody. David was definitely an acquisition. The table could use some dry wit, having always suffered from an abundance of the other kind. The noise level was already high before the subject matter switched to scandal. At other tables, various luminaries from the worlds of publishing and television discussed the minutiae of office grievances, power struggles and forthcoming franchise bids. They were well used to the row the Dregs kicked up: it was a good cover for secret talks. Lancelot could see Gillian Jackson head to head with one of her television producers. Were they having an affair? If they were, it must be in its early stages: the man was still leaning forward when he talked to her. Lancelot's tooth gave another twinge.

'Put salt on your bread and bite on that,' said one of the Australian poets.

'It hurts worse.'

'Proves you've got toothache,' said the other Australian poet.

'Everyone watch out, by the way,' said Nicholas. 'Delilah's definitely falling into bed with Dick Toole.'

'The aesthetic aspect doesn't bear thinking of,' said the most brilliant caricaturist. 'Hitler and Eva Braun. Hitler and *Mussolini.*'

'One wonders,' said Thinwall, 'if she knows what's getting into her. At least one of his wives topped herself and the other two pooled their resources to get legal advice. A pool to fool the cruel Toole.'

'Delilah sent a reporter to visit my wife yesterday,' said Lancelot absently.

'A close-up of Charlotte's knickers will be in Toole's column tomorrow,' said Nicholas.

'And a nice big candid,' added Thinwall, 'of you steering Samantha around some disco with your hand up her crack.'

'I'm no longer famous enough, thank God,' said Lancelot with barely disguised regret.

'It's a big break for Toole,' said another of the literary editors. 'He hasn't got the entrée anywhere except possibly the London Transport system. But with Delilah he's got eyes.'

'And ears,' said Nicholas. 'She's a great one for remembering what you murmur in the cot.'

'You'd know,' said Thinwall. 'You were the one who told her I was so hot for those massive hips that I was ready to go straight.'

'What happened?' asked yet another of the literary editors with controlled curiosity, as if trying to clarify a point in the relationship between Benjamin Constant and Madame de Staël.

'She came up to me in the Carambar one night and kidnapped me. I was feeling a bit unwell and I thought she was taking me to hospital. When I woke up she was sitting on my face. I thought I'd drowned in the Dead Sea.'

'He thought a whale had lain down on him and died,' Nicholas amplified.

'She's refreshingly straightforward,' said Lancelot. 'One shares that first chaste little kiss and then suddenly the air's full of flying clothes.'

'And fists,' said the most brilliant caricaturist.

'He's right,' said Thinwall. 'She isn't *that* straightforward. What she really wants is violence. She kept handing me tyre levers and things and then lying down submissively. Not my sort of thing at all. Unless, of course, the chaps actually *insist* on it.'

'You give them what they want?' said one of the literary editors.

'Honourables and above, oh yes. One will do quite a lot to be there when the quail are flailing in their death throes. I'll beat up a baronet any day of the week. I'll *bayonet* a baron.'

'He'll mug a marquis,' said Nicholas.

'He'll dump on a duke,' said somebody else. Nobody could think of what Thinwall might do to a viscount, except perhaps vilify him. Vitiate? Vulgarise?

'Anyone here *hasn't* hit the mat with Delilah?' asked Nicholas. David was the only one who put up his hand.

'Means that prick Toole's got something on us all,' said Nicholas thoughtfully.

'Your secret is safe with me,' said Thinwall, to general laughter.

'With you and Guy Burgess.'

'What *is* your secret, dear boy?' asked Thinwall. 'Why so defensive? Don't tell us you've finally inveigled that vision into the bunk?'

'I'm saying nothing,' said Nicholas, with a blank look that said everything.

'Well, well. Not a word shall escape our lips. Right, chaps?'

'No, seriously. The whole thing's got to be a complete mystery or I'm a dead duck. Anyway, even if I said I'd got there, I might be lying.' He was pleased that the hint had been given but afraid that a hostage to fortune might have been given along with it. David, he had already noticed, said very little about his private life. That was the way to play it: close to the vest. Except it was so hard to do when you enjoyed the company of the kind of men who wore their hearts on their sleeves. Vests, sleeves. The soul of this man is his clothes. There was an idea there for the novel he was writing. If he had had his notebook on him he would have written it down, but there was an unwritten rule at the table against taking notes. It was held to be a damaging influence. As Lancelot, who liked French literary references, had several times pointed out, dinner at Magny's would be an even more enthralling legend if the brothers Goncourt had not kept a diary of it. Nicholas made a mental note to read the brothers Goncourt some time before the end of the century, after he had dealt with Proust. Or with Dickens. It could all wait. Everything could wait. He let the conversation, now giving off wine fumes the way rapids in the Andes generate oxygen, swirl and pour around him while he sat nursing the memory of two nights in her arms. Tonight he would be seeing her again. Tomorrow morning they could march him out and shoot him if they had to.

After the coffee, when the bill had been paid and a new bill was being run up for extra drinks, only Lancelot, Nicholas and Thinwall were left at the table, or, for that matter, in the whole restaurant. Apart, of course, from the waitresses, who were very noble about not looking at their watches. This was the time when Thinwall liked to graduate from what he called the soft drinks and get started on a succession of little test-tubes full of some evil clear liqueur with black blobs like mouse droppings floating half submerged in its viscous surface.

'One's magazine,' he told Lancelot, 'is about to publish a tiny exposé about how your firm screws its hapless employees.'

'It's a lie. We've only got one employee and she's screwing us.'

'Not *your* firm. Ludlow's.'

'It's still a lie. How did they find out?'

'Not from you through me, so don't worry.'

'I don't think we do screw them, really. One's against all wage slavery in general, of course. Nothing can justify the way Victor carries on. But on the whole I think our people get what they're worth.'

'Not what *they* think. All the figures come straight from them.'

'Can you play backgammon tonight?' Lancelot asked Nicholas. It was no use asking Thinwall, who spent his nights in the kind of place where you paid young men to hit you when you weren't looking.

'Nights are sort of difficult at the moment. What about a game of squash tomorrow?'

'I haven't played for ten years.'

'Do wonders for you. Tone you up while Sam's away. Isn't she supposed to be back, incidentally?'

'Not quite yet.'

'Doubtless being gang-banged on Eighth Avenue at this very moment,' Thinwall suggested helpfully. 'A whole football team of giant boogies shuffling their plate-like feet nervously as she urges them on with many a shrill cry.' But Lancelot pretended extra toothache before they could improvise on that theme for more than about five minutes. Then he headed off to Victor Ludorum by taxi. He had meant to go by tube but was feeling a bit unsteady. His aim was to spend as little time as possible with Janice while he made an appointment with the dentist. He was hoping it would be for Monday morning but it turned out that next Wednesday was the earliest time possible. At that rate he would have to go straight from the dentist to the airport in yet another taxi, probably the last he would ever be able to afford. No doubt an oil sheik and all his wives were each having a full set of gold crowns installed, melted down from the dentist's ample supply of Krugerrands. Having received advice from the receptionist on what tincture to try in order temporarily to relieve the pain, he consoled himself with a call to New York after Janice had gone off to unarmed combat class. Samantha was there, with time to talk, and even sounded glad to hear from him.

'Where will you stay? Sorry.'

'Sorry.'

'No, you go next. Where will you be st . . . '

'With Yonky Vollmer in some sort of chalet arrangement that Rupe Dibblewhite half owns.'

'Good. I know just where he . . . '

'Where will you . . . '

'Sorry.'

'Sorry.'

'Sorry. I'll be at the Casa Perdida about a mile away from Rupe's along the boulevard. Do you think we'll be able to get to bed togeth . . . '

'That'll be marv . . . '

'Together soon? Sorry. Try and . . . '

'What?'

'Try and wait for a bit after it sounds as if I've finished talking in case I haven't.'

'I do, but just when I think it's all right to start, you start.'

'I love . . . '

'I love . . . '

'You very . . . '

'You very . . . '

'Much.'

'Much. Sorry. Your turn.'

'What?'

At least, thought Lancelot, after hanging up, we only had one voice each. Sometimes the voice went around the world the long way as well as the short way and gave you twice as many chances to get confused. There was a Boots on the way to the tube. He stood in the second row of people waiting at the pharmaceutical counter. He was almost the only person not wearing a turban, chador, yashmak or burnous. Getting the gum salve took a long time, during which the happiness caused by his successful telephone call ebbed away. Surely after all this he deserved a taxi home. But no, the time to start saving money was now.

The tube ticket did indeed cost a fraction of the taxi fare, but the size of the fraction was impressive – somewhere between a half and five-eighths. Down he went into the lower depths, the halls of Dis, the inane regions. It was some years since he had been on the underground and at first he thought that the system had been occupied by a United Nations peace-keeping force of Norwegian ski-troops. The platform was full of young men and women wearing iridescent anoraks and huge knapsacks that bulked far above their heads and had blanket rolls hanging neatly underneath. But when the first train arrived it was as if its last stop had been somewhere under central Tokyo. The carriage opposite him was full of Japanese. There might have been people of other nationalities in there too but it was hard to see past the Norwegians. He let the first train go, being unable to imagine that he could get in without being ground flat between knapsacks. There was a long wait for the next train. The electric signboard that was supposed to say where the next two trains were going said nothing at all. The platform was filling up again with a Gurkha regiment in mufti and the Harlem Globetrotters travelling incognito. All of them were better dressed and healthier looking than the few whites, whose clothes seemed to have been bought at the GUM annual sale in Moscow and whose complexions and general comportment were a throwback to the days of vitamin deficiency and rickets.

The large posters on the curved wall beyond the rails were only intermittently amusing when not erotically provocative. Lancelot turned round to look at the ones on the wall behind him and found them to be defaced with explicit sexual references and racialist slogans. In every poster every female figure, of whatever age, was impaled through all orifices by spitting phalluses thickly outlined with black felt-tip. In addition, verbal instructions and responses had been added. As for the political messages, they advocated pornographic violence with a stridency which would have made Julius Streicher hesitate to publish them in *Der Stürmer*. But all of this was familiar in kind, if not degree. What rocked Lancelot was the plethora of aerosol calligrams written in Arabic, or what he presumed was Arabic. The whole wall looked like unbound sheets of the Koran.

When the next train pulled in, the station was just as crowded as before and the train, if anything, even more so. This time he got on, and found himself standing face to face, at very close range, with a youngish, reassuringly well-dressed man who would have seemed quite normal if he had not been saying 'no, no' every few seconds under his breath, or almost under his breath. He didn't even look worried, which made him look different from Lancelot, who did, and increasingly so as the journey went on. Yet it was more than a station and a half before a loud clanking sound, as of an outsized pawl slotting home between the teeth of an enormous ratchet, announced a hiatus. The youngish man said 'no, no' but probably would have been saying that anyway. From halfway down the carriage the noise of singing took on a sardonic tone. Lancelot had already vaguely apprehended, through the press of bodies, that a gang of youths of the football hooligan type were on board. As the train, walled in already by the tube through which it was meant to travel, continued to go nowhere, the youths grew more vociferous. Lancelot thought it would be only a matter of time before they pulled the emergency handle. Then he heard one of them advising against this, on the grounds that it could only cause further delay. A fresh outburst of derisive congratulations indicated that one of their number had relieved himself against the closed door, perhaps partly as a gesture of defiance. Lancelot was wedged in too tightly to move his head very far but if he looked downward to his left he could see a pregnant woman sitting there looking first apprehensive and then panic-stricken. But before things could get really desperate a repetition of the clanking noise promised motion.

The train jerked forward three or four inches at a time for a distance of about twelve yards. Then it stopped again. 'No, no,' murmured the youngish man, whose eyebrows, Lancelot now noticed, had been tweezed where they met on the bridge of his nose. There was a small wail of despair from the pregnant woman, who looked as if she might be from one of those parts of North Africa where emotion is never betrayed except in moments of catastrophe. Lancelot wondered if it would be physically possible to deliver the baby into an environment already fully occupied by human bodies. The hooligans were singing what must have been the Korean translation of 'You'll Never Walk Alone'. Lancelot kept his eyes closed and tried to think of something comparatively pleasant, such as his benumbed tooth. Then the train resumed its journey at normal speed, steadily emptying itself as it got beyond the centre of the city, so that by the time he was three stations from home there was even a seat free if he wanted it. He remained standing because he felt that to sit down would be to indicate, to himself if to no one else, some degree of acquiescence in what he had just been through. Evidently everybody else was used to it. Nobody had tried to lynch the station attendant at the next stop after the big pause. Not that such an initiative would have produced a very substantial result, because no station attendant, or any other official of any kind, had been in evidence. No protests entered or apologies offered. Obviously all this was now regarded as normal.

Lancelot's station was equipped with one of those big lifts like the ones that take planes up to the deck of an aircraft carrier. By the time it had raised him to the level of the open air he had almost given up hope, so that when the door puffed and crashed open he just stood there, like an institutionalised prisoner for whom the step forward into freedom is an intolerable novelty.

~ nine ~

Lancelot came home to a home where there was no one to come home to. The children were out. One of them, he learned from a note, had already gone to the country. Mrs Hydrostatics had once again gone out for the night, or gone back to Greece, or gone insane – from her written message it was hard to tell. MESAS WINDHOVER SAI TAIK WIKIN UPH it began.

Dick Toole came home after a hard afternoon on the telephone ringing up prominent men's wives to check on the movements of their husbands and a still harder evening writing up the results. It was the kids who took it out of you: they usually gave you a lot of good stuff but only after you'd pretended to be interested in the fight to save the local school or how they had been given a green star for finger painting. He told his driver to push off until about opening time next day. Both the driver and the big dark wine Jaguar came with the job, like the expense account and the unlimited first class air travel. All of this on top of the hearteningly large salary. But Dick Toole was worth what he cost. The privileged orders who shove their wealth in your face had had it their own way too long. Dick Toole liked to see them hot and bothered. Letters of protest written on disgustingly expensive notepaper came plopping on to his editor's desk, but Dick Toole had more on his editor than on anybody else and there was no denying that his page sold newspapers. Indeed there was nothing else in the paper that did, except for the TV listings. Dick Toole wore an alpaca pile coat even in warm weather, had his eye on the kind of Scampi Belt house that they show photographs of when they advertise it for sale in the glossies, and drank excellent whisky for pretty well the whole of his working day, which started in the afternoon after a long lunch. Tonight he was home in good time to see if Delilah was keeping up to the mark. He pressed the entryphone button and heard her embittered drawl, identifiable even when transformed into a squawk.

'That you?' she asked.

'Yes. Pour me a double and get down on your knees with your mouth open.'

The door buzzed and he lurched through. So much more convenient than fiddling with a key. Having negotiated a flight of rather scrappily carpeted stairs, he paused sweating before the front door of his flat and adjusted his clothing – or, rather, did the opposite of what is usually meant by adjusting it. Then he pushed the door open and found Delilah in position as instructed. Without looking down, he drifted into place like one of those American bombers refuelling and took the half full glass from her upstretched hand.

'You're getting the idea nicely,' he said, after the first large gulp. 'No need to be quite so nippy, if you follow my drift.'

'Ongar,' grunted Delilah. 'Alamo. Ulm. Ohio.'

It was, thought Dick Toole, amazing how irascible she could sound even when thus occupied. When they were both finished he slapped her face quite hard from each direction so that she fell back on the floor crying. Only then did he remove his overcoat, of which he was very proud. His three-piece suit he had once been proud of also, but it had been some time since he had sent it away to be cleaned and pressed. As you got closer to his skin you got closer to the original story. His aertex vest and saggy Y-fronts were of a greyish blue that no industrial colouring process could reproduce. It can occur only in nature.

With these final items of clothing left scattered on the bedroom floor, Dick Toole lay back on the bed in his short nylon socks and smoked an acrid panatella. Delilah knelt on the carpet beside the bed, her wrists tied together with a stocking. Another stocking tethered her to one of the legs of the bed, with just a large enough radius of operations so that she could pour drinks and hand them to him when so directed.

'That thing between Nick Crane and Sally Draycott that I told you I thought might be on,' she said scornfully. 'It's definitely on. Thinwall says that Nick was dropping large hints today at lunch.'

'Great,' said Dick Toole. 'It's the first hiccup in that slag's façade. I'll hold off a bit and see what develops. Don't want to go off at half cock there. I'd really like to do that bitch. Toffee-nosed twat. She tried to drop me in it with the Press Council just because I rang up her mother. Her mother's got some nervous thing or other but how was I supposed to know that at four in the morning and feeling a bit tired? Those telly tarts think there's one law for them and another for the poor.'

'Charlotte Windhover's still being all brave and tolerant about Samantha Copperglaze.'

'Windhover doesn't ring too many bells by now. I'd use it but I can't see how it would hurt him. We'll save that one up in case the wife develops a new interest herself. Then we can run the whole thing as a sort of boutique of barbed wire about the idle rich and their cohorts.'

The word 'cohort' was a favourite of Dick Toole's. He thought it meant 'friend'. He also used 'mitigate' for 'militate' and invariably got 'flaunt' and 'flout' back to front. His editor, powerless to check his activities in any other respect, sent him memos about his bad English, which he flouted to his cohorts as blatant attempts to mitigate against freedom of speech.

'Samantha's supposed to be back from America but she isn't and Lancelot's frantic.'

'Good. Pressure building up. In more ways than one, incidentally.'

'Arles. Morpeth. Hanoi. Armagh.'

Elena was late home after an evening of excruciating boredom at Victor's. The place had been littered with Bourbon and Savoyard relics of such an antiquity that their hearing aids had valves instead of transistors. How Victor could do this sort of thing to her she didn't know. Or rather she did know but pretended not to, since they were never happier together than when amiably scrapping. She was already in bed when the phone rang.

'How can you *do* this to me?' she asked immediately, but it turned out to be the next President of the United States. Thinking he had woken her up, he was full of apologies, and had to be calmed down, which took time. It was a measure of his naivety that he had not realised Elena would never have taken such a querulous tone except with an intimate. One only hoped that when the fate of the world became dependent on his judgment he would be more sensitive to nuance. By the time she got rid of him the phone was overdue to ring again.

'Who on earth were you talking to so long?' asked Victor.

'Washington. I thought it was you and muttered some endearment. Then I had to stop him flying straight over in Air Force First.'

'Air Force One. I don't think he's allowed to play with that until he's President.'

'How *about* that dance of death tonight? Never will I forgive you.'

'I'm truly sorry. It all got out of hand. It seems you can't get the pretenders without the pretenderesses. They all travel around together on a bus.'

'The one you sat beside me was so near death there was no point trying. He kept telling me how he used to shoot pigs with my father and I couldn't make the dates add up. Finally I realised he meant my grandfather. They shot them with muskets.'

'I could see you were suffering but so was I.'

'I don't doubt it. You must have been choking in the talcum coming off that dreadful old hooker.'

'She was quite interesting about the Duchess of Windsor. Said she was in Palm Beach with her.'

'And at school with her mother. Do you love me?'

'Madly.'

'I leave very early for the country. Are you sure you can't come until Sunday?'

'Sunday in the late afternoon. Can I bring you back on Monday morning?'

'Could you? That would be marvellous. You can help me with the guest list for my opera ball. Very few of the people you inflicted on me tonight will be appearing on it.'

'Most of them will be dead by then anyway.'

'Now we talk about next week here. On Tuesday I'm having the Windhovers and I thought perhaps Nicholas Crane and Black and White, which I'm told is now a big affair.'

'Are you bringing them together?'

'Who, Mr Crane and Black and White? Are you jealous?'

'I meant Mr and Mrs Windhover.'

'It's common courtesy. I like Charlotte very much. And I could never be a party to Lancelot's walk-out with that Copperglaze floozy.'

'She's very pretty.'

'The girl has a simply divine figure but there's nothing in that head of hers except a lot of very small round objects loosely heaped. It shows in the face. Also I think she's mad.'

'But isn't she supposed to be highly intelligent? In the sense of dozens of A levels and Oxford double first class honours and so on?'

'They've all got that nowadays. It's the muesli and the yoghurt. But she doesn't know anything and doesn't want to know. He won't ever be able to teach her anything. It's the most grotesque mismatch I've ever heard of.'

'I think it worries him.'

'Whereas your Mr Crane and Black and White are obviously made in heaven.'

'The young in one another's arms,' said Victor, who often, when he wanted to avoid saying something himself, said what somebody else had said.

'Exactly. And the not quite so young in one another's arms on Sunday. Do you look forward to that?'

'I live for that.'

'I should think so, considering how I'm giving dinners for your editors and authors and their wives and mistresses. Do you want to come to that?'

'I see quite of lot of Lancelot and Nicholas in the ordinary way.'

Good answer, thought Elena, but not the decisive outburst of bored rejection that might have been hoped for.

'I'll get Walter and Hannah that you like so much because they just sit there and listen to you. And you can always chuck at the last moment because I've got dear boring cousin Rudolph in town standing by with nothing to do except be a spare man. Or you can come in late and scare them all away.'

'Or I can wait until they're all gone.'

'Exactly. So that's settled. You sound preoccupied.'

'One of the political magazines is running a big attack about how I'm a capitalist exploiter in a top hat.'

'You should be used to that.'

'Yes, but this time the facts and figures come from inside the building. It might look as if I have a case to answer.'

'*Are* you a capitalist exploiter?'

'As a matter of principle.'

'I'm very glad you exploit me. Are you sure you don't want to leave me for someone young and lovely who's thrilled by rare books?'

'Never,' said Victor. In Italian the word for 'never' can sound like a baby's cry or a last gasp, but is never quite neutral. 'You're already as much youth as I can take. Why don't you marry me? You know you're broke.'

He asked her that every night of their lives and she always gave the same answer. By now it was a ritual. But this time she could hear anguish in his voice, as if he wanted to be saved.

'I like my life,' she said as always. 'And we couldn't be closer than we are. I'm yours entirely.' Reminding him that he should be able to say the same.

After midnight Lancelot rang New York in the hope of catching Samantha while she was dressing for dinner, but he got nothing. It was too late to ring his wife in the country so he rang Serena instead. She was not the kind of girl who was very often home on a Friday night but perhaps she would be back from wherever she had been. She was.

'I was feeling utterly alone and lost,' said Lancelot, exploiting the convention by which quondam lovers may confess to weakness, the sub-text being that nothing has gone right since you.

'So was I,' said Serena unnecessarily. It was well known that she always felt that way. 'Anthony's just been here crying on my shoulder.'

'What was he crying about?' asked Lancelot anxiously. 'Business problems?'

'Elena. He thinks his life would be all right if only he was married to her. He wouldn't mind her being lesbian and all that.'

'What does she think?'

'I don't think he even asks her any more. She's got a dozen like him all wanting to be straightened out. But he knows she'd laugh at him so he comes to me. The last person on earth who could help.'

'You're very soothing.'

'Only because I'm completely self-obsessed. Marvellous how little help it is, knowing that that's what I am.'

'We should meet next week and talk about those writers who could draw. I think it's ideal for you.'

'Come tomorrow.'

'I could come now.'

'It's too late. Would have been nice.'

'I've got squash with Nicholas tomorrow afternoon.'

'Come for drinks after that.'

Something to look forward to. The children were still out or not coming home at all. The house was so empty Lancelot even missed the dogs.

~ ten ~

With his squash racket protruding from an acceptably unfussy canvas hold-all, Lancelot arrived by taxi in front of Nicholas's club in Pall Mall. There was nothing particularly exclusive about Nicholas's club. Anyone could be in it who had been at any time a member of Cambridge University. Once in, you were set for life. A move to expel Kim Philby had been shelved for lack of a quorum. There were bedrooms so that you could stay overnight when being thrown out by your wife or before defecting to the Soviet Union. You could eat there as long as you weren't interested in food. The squash courts were quite good. Pressing his tongue against the back of his temporarily quiescent tooth, Lancelot looked forward to this game as the first step in a new health programme by which he would take himself thoroughly in hand. He would keep his body in shape even if everything else fell apart. It could be said that a few more taxis would bring on total financial collapse but really there had been no choice. He had gone down into his local tube station and ridden a few stops, but found the experience even more nightmarish in the afternoon than it had been the previous evening. The Norwegian ski-troops had been joined by their main body of infantry. The knapsacks formed one vast interlocking mass in which one was jostled helplessly, dazzled by electric blue anoraks and powerless to guard one's squash racket from danger. So up he had come, hailed a taxi, and now he was here. Put it behind you and make every new move count.

Nicholas had purchased the kind of ball whose coloured spot indicates that it travels comparatively slowly, which effectively means that the players must run further and faster if they wish to hit it. In the early stages Lancelot was careful not to be tempted. If the ball was out of reach he let it go. But when it came near he showed signs of the positional sense and economic stroke play by which he had been able to give a good account of himself when he was Nicholas's age or even a few years older. Nicholas was impressed and said so. These accolades coaxed Lancelot into trying the occasional dramatic sprint. As a sinking cross-court shot from Nicholas drifted sluggishly off the opposite wall, Lancelot would explode into a death-or-glory-run in order to thrash it back before it hit the floor. If he succeeded, the ball would present itself to Nicholas in such a way that he could make Lancelot run just as fast in the other direction if Lancelot was so minded. Flushed with achievement, Lancelot was usually so minded. He could feel the muscles in the back of his thighs coming alive. The sweat flew off him like pond-water off a puppy. He breathed like the hooter of a police car. For three-quarters of an hour Nicholas stood in the exact centre of the court while Lancelot ran back and forth and up and down like a rat in one of those psychology experiments where rewards arbitrarily become punishments. The eventual effect on the rat is to induce immobility through neurosis. Lancelot eventually became immobile through exhaustion. He felt marvellous, but could do no more. Every little muscle in his legs, buttocks, abdomen, shoulders and arms felt as picked out and chromatically vibrant as in some anatomical illustration. He staggered in small circles, propped himself quaking against the wall of the court, and called it quits.

Having darted the usual covert glances at each other's pudenda while getting dressed at an oblique angle to each other in the shower room, the two friends climbed the spiral staircase to the bar, one of them ascending seemingly without effort and the other moving as if tethered to his starting point by a strong rubber leash. The bar was upholstered throughout in the kind of buttoned blue leather employed on cross-channel ferries, but there were no windows or portholes. Lancelot asked for a double bitter lemon with plenty of ice, as part of his new policy not to drink alcohol except when he wanted to get drunk. Also he was simply very, very thirsty.

'I hear we'll be seeing you and Sally at Elena's on Tuesday,' he said when he could speak.

'You will indeed. Daunting prospect. She's so grand even Sally might get worried about using the wrong fork. Will we be seeing you and Samantha?'

'She'll still be in Los Angeles. Anyway with Elena it's wives, not mistresses. Except for those lucky enough to be unmarried.'

'I don't know how lucky that is,' said Nicholas.

'You're that serious?'

'If I was going to be, this one would be the one.'

'There's certainly something about them at that age,' said Lancelot. 'Bring her down to Biarritz in August.'

It was an invitation to talk about Samantha instead of Sally. Nicholas accepted the invitation, partly because, although painfully eager to bring up Sally's name in any conversational context including nuclear physics, he was aware that anything he explicitly said would be repeated sooner or later.

'Samantha's staying on for a while, then?'

'That's the plan,' said Lancelot, making it sound as if he had magnanimously encouraged the postponement of her return. 'I'll be going over to bring her back. You can't blame her for being pleased about all the experience she's getting.'

'Like the experience of a great scrum of thick-necked studs with tee-shirts and no foreheads all stuffing her full of coke and queueing up to boff her.'

'That sort of thing, yes,' laughed Lancelot, as if enjoying the jest.

And so they parted until Tuesday, with Nicholas heading for Westbourne Terrace and Lancelot walking towards Belgravia for drinks with Serena. Nicholas could have given Lancelot a lift to Hyde Park Corner but Lancelot had some time to kill and anyway, walking was part of his new programme for health and economy. Also a slight stiffness was setting in, which a stroll might loosen.

He set off up St James's Street very slowly, but by the time he got to Belgravia he was moving more slowly still, not so much from lack of energy as from the fact that to move either foot too far at the one time was to induce a certain amount of discomfort at the back of the upper thigh. The last block to Serena's very smart address took about twenty minutes. Several times he came to a halt altogether. At other times he was taking steps only a few centimetres long, so that he appeared to be stationary unless you were looking at him for a long while. Several people did so but he pretended to be either lost in thought or examining the architecture of the butter-white terraces. When he pressed Serena's door button the entryphone squawk told him to come up. The lock having banged open, the crackle from the tiny loudspeaker stopped, indicating that she had hung up the receiver. Lancelot thought of buzzing her again to tell her that he might be some time climbing the stairs, but decided against it. Halfway up he came to a complete halt. Unable to go back and buzz her, and too far below to contemplate shouting, he waited until she appeared on the landing.

'I thought you'd been kidnapped,' she said, 'or just decided against it.' She looked wonderfully soft and supple, as if her shapely legs weren't hurting her at all.

'Temporary stiffening of the upper thighs,' said Lancelot. 'I think it's passed off now.'

'Poor darling. Can you make it?'

'Lead the way.' He strode manfully up behind her and on into her tiny flat, feeling with each step as if the point of a Samurai sword was being thrust deeply into the relevant buttock by a blow from a piledriver. Serena's drawing room was all beige and pastel hessian and raw calico, dominated by a yielding sofa into whose thick square cushions Lancelot lowered himself with the delicate accuracy of a fuel rod being inserted into the core of a reactor. Even then the infinitesimal jolt when his posterior came to rest was enough to impale each hemisphere of his behind on its own individual spike.

'Orff!' shouted Lancelot.

'Are you all right, darling?'

'Carl Orff. The man who wrote *Carmina Burana*. Samantha thinks it's a masterpiece, so his name's been on my mind.'

'Shouldn't she be back?' Serena had sat down with enviable fluency in a separate chair.

'Change of plan. I'm going to see her in Los Angeles next week. But I thought that before I went we should get that idea under way about the writers who could draw.'

'It's so sweet of you to ask me but the only one I could think of was Delacroix and that was because I was looking straight at Victor's picture when you asked me.'

'Delacroix was more of an artist who could write. What we're after is famous writers in all sorts of languages who did drawings on the side. Sort of in the margins. There are tons to choose from. We'll get a list made up and then all you'd have to do is go off to the London Library and look up the books.'

'Wouldn't I have to write about them as well? I'm definitely not up to that.'

'No, that's the whole idea. It's more a set of captions than a proper book. You crib the biographical facts and then string them together so that Hildegarde can go through it and put it in her own style. Start with someone obvious. Verlaine is a good example. He did those little drawings of Rimbaud that bring out the whole business of their relationship.'

'Beatrix Potter was the other one I thought of,' said Serena, nodding with feigned decisiveness.

'Yes, but she's really equally famous as a writer and illustrator, like Max Beerbohm and Michael Ayrton and Osbert Lancaster and people like that. Whereas the theme ought to be that the art side is the writer's *violon d'Ingres*.'

'Mm?'

'His hobby. At the moment, for example, you've got Zinoviev. The Russian dissident.'

'Yes. I see.'

'And that's a very strong tradition in Russia, the writer who's got a very strong pictorial imagination. In fact Lermontov would be your most gifted case of the lot.'

'He's a dissident too, isn't he?'

'In a way, yes. Perhaps more of a Decembrist. And of course Pushkin could draw very well. And you've got Proust, Cocteau, Éluard. Apollinaire's *calligrammes* count as a kind of drawing. Malraux did a sort of surrealist thing with a single wavy line, like Miró. There are a lot of possibilities.'

'Stevie Smith,' said Serena in triumph.

'Exactly. When I'm in L.A. I'll get Ian Cuthbert to help me draw up a list. He's full of that kind of information.'

'Oh darling, it's so lovely that someone's got confidence in me.' Lithely she threw herself into the sofa beside him, but not so lithely that she failed to cause a critical displacement in the precisely calculated angle of his behind.

'Arp!' cried Lancelot.

'Was he a writer? I thought he was mainly a sculptor. You see I don't know *anything*.'

Her head was on his shoulder and her mouth, as lovely now as ever, was yieldingly a quarter open not far from his, so that he could feel her breath. He managed to kiss her without moving any part of his body below the neck, but the contact thus established had the consequence, welcome in normal circumstances but disastrous now, of causing her to press herself suddenly against him.

To cry out while kissing is a practice common between lovers, but takes tact and experience. Usually it occurs in that passionate half-world where real ecstasy finds histrionic expression – the most convincing evidence which life affords for the existentialist principle that we cannot be something without pretending to be it. To have the one you adore cry out into your open mouth is a reward for skill, a prize which the accomplished donor will sometimes give unexpectedly early for purposes of encouragement. By an heroic effort Lancelot just managed to modify his yell of pain into a moan of agonised pleasure. Serena drew back, looked at him with heavy eyes, got up and walked languorously towards her bedroom, reaching behind her to undo a button. In her bedroom there was a dressing table mirror which Lancelot could just see from where he was sitting, and which showed him various enticing fragments of her body as it undressed itself and lay on the bed.

Several minutes later Serena, clad only in her velvet wrist-bands, appeared at the bedroom door. 'Don't you want me?' she asked plaintively.

'Yes,' said Lancelot, 'but I can't move.'

'Are you sure it's not an excuse? Because if one more man makes an excuse not to go to bed with me then I'm going out that window and no mistake. You can forget the razor blades and the pills. I'll be a heap of meat on the pavement.'

'My dear sweet love, you look like an erotic fantasy by Boucher and there isn't a man alive who wouldn't want to screw you helpless. But you couldn't get me out of these cushions if you packed my bum in ice. I'm the man who came to dinner.'

It wasn't quite as bad as that but almost. Serena called a taxi on her account service but getting Lancelot downstairs took so long that by the time he climbed into it the figure on the meter looked like a Weimar Republic bank-note dating from December 1922.

'I'll owe you,' said Lancelot.

'Don't be silly,' said Serena, looking wonderful in her submarine captain's roll-neck sweater and designer jeans, although not as wonderful as she would have looked lying beside him with nothing on at all. 'Karim gave me the account and he'll never get round to cancelling it. Anyway it goes with the flat. Will you be able to get out at the other end?'

'I should be all right by then. See you when I get back from America.'

He did manage to get out at the other end, but only by keeping his knees bent at 45 degrees and moving very slowly, so that he felt as if he was seeing the world from the angle of Toulouse-Lautrec or a large tortoise. Samantha by this time would be in the air between New York and Los Angeles. He felt he could survive the night alone if he had company tomorrow, so he rang his wife and suggested that he might come to the country next day.

'Has she *still* not turned up?'

'I'm very much alone.'

'Hop on a train now.'

'Well, I can't actually hop on anything at the moment. I've hurt myself playing squash with Nicholas.'

'You're a damn fool, trying to keep up with people twenty years younger.'

'Fifteen.'

'Can't you talk to them about books or something, instead of being so competitive? What did you do, break an arm?'

'It's a pain in the arse.'

'Sorry for the lecture. I imagine you've torn your muscles. Sit in a hot bath and come down on the fast train at mid-day. I'll be driving up again in the evening but at least you'll have the afternoon in the garden. It was very pretty here today. There are plenty of cushions for the garden chair.'

'I might have to lie face down.'

'I'll put you near the trellis to keep the birds off my seedlings. You *are* a fool, you know.'

'I know.'

~ eleven ~

Late next morning Lancelot went to Paddington by taxi because the only other way to go would have been in an ambulance. Just bending down to pick up the Sunday papers had taken him some time and for a long while he had been obliged to stay down there, like an old man on a bowling green who had launched a particularly finely judged wood and was executing a long follow through. But although he was, if anything, even more hampered in his movements than the previous evening, the actual pain was somewhat diminished, so that while taking his breakfast he was able to read the book review pages with unimpaired concentration. The number of implacable female critics seemed to be increasing all the time. Paula Thorax, the strictest of them all, was being scornful about coffee-table books. As an editor whose projects mainly fell into precisely that category, Lancelot felt apprehensive. He had met Paula Thorax at a rival publisher's annual party and been struck by her rugged good looks, but one hesitated to think how pitiless her gaze would have been without the dark glasses. Doubtless she had some eye injury which necessitated the wearing of tinted glasses indoors, and it was that which made her so severe.

From where the taxi set him down, Lancelot moved to the ticket hall like a slow loris. The queue could not shuffle forward too gradually for his liking. If two or three people in a row paid cash then everyone behind them had to explode forward like sprinters. People paying by credit card took much longer, and mercifully there were more of them. Cash was going out of style.

Aren't we all? thought Lancelot, taking his place at the window. At first he refused to believe the figure specified as the cost of a first class single to his destination. For reasons of hygiene or physical safety, the ticket seller was standing on the other side of a complicated glass filter through which even the air could not pass directly, so perhaps the sound got distorted too. The man – whose original language, judging from his appearance, was almost certainly not English – might have thought that Lancelot had asked for a return ticket to Bucharest or had put in a bid to purchase the locomotive. But apparently there was no mistake. Lancelot asked for a second class ticket instead, recalling dimly how Bianca Jagger or some equivalent philosopher had said that one should go first class or not at all. A good principle if you didn't mind not going. A small brushed steel turntable looking rather like a piece of Japanese stereo equipment took his credit card past Checkpoint Charlie so that the man could put it through his little printing press and thus record one more unarguable debit to Lancelot's account. Then his card came back accompanied by a ticket which was made only of cardboard, instead of the platinum or tungsten commensurate with its price.

Wheeling slowly like a rusty gun turret, Lancelot pointed himself towards the appropriate platform and picked up speed by steady increments, until finally he was travelling at the same velocity as a culture of mould forming on stale bread. The train promised to go a good deal faster. Billing itself as the 125 to indicate the number of miles it could cover in a single hour, it actually had these figures painted on the side of the shovel-nosed prime mover at each end. The second class carriages were at the further end of the train, which gave Lancelot an opportunity to wonder whether he would reach them before the train left. Getting there just as the last whistle was blowing, he was lucky enough to find a seat comparatively free of stains. Most of the seats looked as if someone had given birth in them but his merely suggested that a man had been knifed to death after a brief struggle.

The train surged into motion and went at a tremendous clip while Lancelot, who had brought the Sunday papers with him, read a brilliant book review by Nicholas which tore the heart out of some American tract about the alleged necessity to revise the English language in favour of feminism. Halfway through reading this piece, which he admired although deploring his friend's unyielding hostility to progress, Lancelot had to put the paper down while a semi-articulate but dauntlessly self-confident voice on the public address system welcomed him to the train, told him where it was going, informed him of the whereabouts of the buffet car, gave a detailed breakdown of the type of sandwiches which could be purchased there, and thanked him for listening. In the other paper there was a quite funny piece by Thinwall making game of the Social Democratic Party. Lancelot couldn't agree more. That one's politics should indeed contradict one's material interests seemed to Lancelot to be the very basis of public morality. A political party which reflected one's own social position in every particular thus defined itself automatically as an irrelevance, not to say an anachronism. As caricatured mercilessly by Thinwall, the SDP was a public relations exercise aimed specifically at people like Lancelot. No question of it, thought Lancelot, enjoying his train ride. The 125 certainly lived up to its name.

The 125 went on living up to its name until somewhere between Reading and Didcot, whereupon a sudden application of the brakes filled the carriage with a urethral odour. Abruptly the 125 became the 12.5. For several miles the 12.5 ambled along past squads of men in luminous orange jackets who seemed to be engaged in some anglicised, alfresco version of the tea ceremony. Gradually the 12.5 converted itself into the 1.25. The men outside could be studied in detail as they sat, or, in some rare cases, moved about. Then the train stopped altogether.

For the first half hour of total immobility nobody told them anything. Then the voice came back on the PA system with what sounded at first like a specially prepared script. The phrase 'owing to the engineering' occurred several times and with remarkable fluency, perhaps because it was a standard utterance, like the admonition to make sure you had your belongings with you before getting off. But then there was a lot of other stuff about the special rail-laying equipment having become derailed. How could rail-laying equipment become derailed? The voice didn't seem to know either. It stumbled over its words, interpolated crackling caesuras between sentences, and signed off with an assurance that the train would be under way again as soon as possible. Lancelot glanced yet again at his Cartier wristwatch. It was half past one and he was feeling a bit hungry.

*

After lunch, which the children gratified her by taking off their headphones in order to eat, Charlotte carried her prayer-mat into the garden and planted out a few expensive seedlings for the dogs to dig up. A taxi bearing Lancelot obstinately refused to arrive. Perhaps she should have fetched him from the station but that would have been going a bit far. Finally she went for a walk around the bend of the river to call on Elena. She would have gone the day before but certain thick-set men in blue suits had been standing about incongruously among the trees. During the previous government this would have indicated the presence of the Home Secretary. Who it had been this time Charlotte didn't like to ask. She found Elena counting tulips.

'People get off those little ships and steal them,' said Elena from under her straw hat. 'I've got some iced tea getting cold. It's about a month too early but we could test it out. Some of my guests have departed and a new lot are about to descend.'

'I'd love to,' said Charlotte, and they walked together through the trees until Elena's house appeared to them like a vision. It would have looked like a caprice by Rex Whistler if there had been any trace of tweeness about Elena's fantasy. But its simplicity was the reason she had chosen the old square house in the first place, and none of the many adornments which had since accrued made any fuss. There was a barn for younger guests. There was a summer house where the garden walls joined, so that you could walk through from a lawn into an orchard. The swimming pool in the rose garden was only just deep enough for a diving board but looked inviting under its topiary arch. The boat-house behind the willows was missing one corner of its slate roof, so that the rain had got in and made a mess of Cleopatra's Dinghy. Elena was rather proud of Cleopatra's Dinghy. It was a rowing boat that seated about eight people under a painted canopy. A wooden fairground swan fixed to the prow counted as figurehead and there was an old red plush armchair in the back for a commander. Trimmed with rope painted gold, it looked like the Venetian *Bucintoro* painted by Canaletto on the lid of a snuff box.

Elena liked the kind of visual treat that costs little in the first place and looks even better with age. One of the laurels had a fleeing marble Daphne disappearing into its storm-split trunk and when you looked down the path you could see Apollo just arriving around the corner. Unfortunately the laurel version of Dutch elm disease looked like spoiling the joke but she could always set it up somewhere else. Elena was always thinking of new things and nothing was ever quite finished. Charlotte wondered what it would be like to have so much imagination. Sometimes she doubted whether she herself had enough imagination even to wonder. But she appreciated it tremendously. She thought the world of Elena and loved talking to her heart to heart, although it had long ago become clear that the traffic was flowing in one direction. What confidence it must take, to give so little away. Charlotte would have given a lot to be enigmatic. Open books want to be mysteries.

'Pretending for the moment that the sun is really hot,' said Elena, 'try some of this.'

'It's perfect.' They sat at the white cane table on the lawn and talked. Some lone mayfly, the harbinger of thriving millions, spotted the mint leaves in the jug of iced tea and dived in, not making much of a splash.

'Later on I'm giving an opera ball to which you and Lancelot must come. My nephew is getting married and his mother is helpless to organise anything. Buggins gets the job.' Elena knew she meant Muggins instead of Buggins but the occasional malapropism was part of her defence system.

'How wonderful. Will you hire a theatre or something?'

'No, I'll put up tents and have it here. The relatives will have to stay in the villages and round about while they dress up as Otello and Boris Godunov.'

'I could put a couple up.'

'How sweet of you to offer but I wouldn't dream of giving you the bother. We'll make them all stay in hotels. The whole enterprise is insane but so is my father, and he and my sister have given me all this money to do it. Might as well spend it properly for once.'

'I think Lancelot will want to bring his girl,' said Charlotte. Elena knew this to be the key item on the agenda. She would have liked to stop the girl outright but then the girl might stop Lancelot, leaving Charlotte, who had an overdeveloped capacity for guilt, to attend alone and not have much fun.

'You should get in first,' suggested Elena, as if she had just thought of it, 'and say you're coming with somebody else. My boring cousin Rudolph is always available but why not make it an adventure?'

'I met a rather nice young man at Victor's the other night. Terrifically left wing and no doubt he'll disapprove of your relatives. But he's a wonderfully talented writer and he ought to see things. I think he wants to, really.'

'I think it's perfect. A young lover.'

'Is that how it will look?'

'Let's hope so. The professor and the brilliant young writer. Couldn't be better. People will talk of nothing else.'

'Do you think so?' Charlotte was surprised to find herself excited by the idea. It was always like that around Elena. The possibilities multiplied. The white wine grew bubbles and stung the inside of your nose.

'*And* it will do Lancelot the world of good,' said Elena, clinching the matter. 'It's the only way you can ever teach people a lesson. Giving them what they want.'

'He and I seem to have made rather a mess of things.'

'Good God no. Married all this time and still caring what each other does? That's a raging success. Some of us have a *lot* less to show for the time we've put in.'

'Then I shouldn't leave Lancelot.'

'If you want to. But it might kill him.'

Charlotte felt powerful and decisive hearing this, while knowing she was not. Elena was powerful. Look at the strength in that figure. The time sped by. She should have gone back to make Lancelot some tea but it was too pleasant here. Then the nephew of the third or fourth last prime minister arrived in a pony trap, with his singing wife Dido not far behind in a Range Rover. Dido had picked up Elena's boring cousin Rudolph from the station. Rudolph, although he didn't actually click his heels, had an impressive line in stiff handshakes and deferential inclinations of the head. His vocation was baroque art history but he had a way of bringing the subject up that had been known to make even other baroque art historians start discussing snooker instead. Finally there was the crunch, whisper and thump of a very large Rolls-Royce arriving. If it had borne a pennant it might have been the Queen Mother, but it was Victor.

'You must send that great thing back to London immediately,' said Elena, offering her cheek. 'I can't have it standing here. It blocks the view.'

Victor sent the car away. Tea gradually turned to drinks. Charlotte was urged to stay but the thought of her crippled husband nagged at her conscience. She crossed the lawn and took a short-cut through the rose garden past the pool. One of those big jets went over, momentarily shattering the idyll. She looked back and could see them all looking up, except for Elena and Victor, who were looking at each other. Charlotte had sometimes wondered about Elena and Victor. Elena was famously asexual and Victor was reputedly much less interested in that sort of thing since the dreadful shooting business, but there was something too perfect about the timing. If two news-makers both stop making news at once, that's news. Charlotte felt pleased with herself at this formulation, as if she were living dangerously all of a sudden. How disappointing to get back to the mill house and find Lancelot not there even yet. What could have happened to him?

The train had still not moved. Rioting had broken out at the beginning of the third hour, with teams of young men in Zec haircuts and Li'l Abner boots pounding back and forth spilling beer, shouting in languages which seemed to bear the most tenuous connection with English, and pausing only to form small malodorous choirs which competitively sang 'You'll Never Walk Alone'. Lancelot might have joined them if he had been capable of movement. The three other people in his group of four seats were up and down all the time on the way to and coming back from the buffet car and the toilet. The buffet car was soon stripped of everything except a few styrofoam sandwiches filled with tenderised hardboard and foot powder. The man on the PA system took advantage of the opportunity to launch himself on a career in broadcasting. He recounted similar incidents which had happened, he said, previous. He explained the perils of alighting from the train and walking along the permanent way. The slogan 'owing to the engineering' still recurred like the *petite phrase* in Proust, but in other respects his performance had taken on a fully organic, phantasmagorical bravura. He stayed on the air for longer each time and the space between announcements became progressively shorter. Eventually he broke into song, but was abruptly cut off, as if he had been overpowered by a colleague. Just after half past five the train moved. A woman who had done nothing all afternoon except shake her head burst quietly into tears.

Upon arrival there was an almighty mass sprint for taxis, buses and any other form of transport that was not a train. Lancelot was the only passenger left in the station to hear the public address system regret the inconvenience caused. He was in a toilet and laughed hollowly. By the time he arrived at the taxi stand there was not a wheeled vehicle to be seen. He contemplated going back to telephone Charlotte but was afraid of missing a taxi should one turn up. So he waited. If it was not precisely twilight then certainly the clarity had gone out of the air. A taxi arrived. He bent down to the driver's window with some difficulty and named his destination. The driver, who had a joke Hitler moustache and oiled hair parted in the middle, dared say that he could find it with a bit of help. Lancelot completed the long process of opening the back door and getting in.

'Muscular dyslexia, is it?' the driver asked cheerfully.

'Dystrophy,' said Lancelot.

'What I meant. You on that train, were you?'

'Last one off.'

'Yes, well, you would be, having the muscular. I got a short fare off that train so I nipped back hoping, and there you was. She was right stroppy too, wasn't she, the train being that late. Come down to see her mother on her death bed. Be too late, I shouldn't be surprised, what I told her. I don't know why they don't stop subsidising some of the people what've got no right to be travelling for nothing, do you know what I mean? Then you wouldn't have these breakdowns. Money for repairs, isn't it? Give you an example. Woman what her next door neighbour was in this cab March last year. No, April it was. Tell a lie, it was March. He said she goes up to London every week with her eight kids. None of them pays nothing. She pays a cheap day return or whatever you call it. Awayday, Playaway, you know, that. Kids pay nothing. Nothing! Meanwhile you and me pay the full, even if we don't go, you know what I mean? And rates on top of it. Ridiculous. Give you another example. Suppose I've got a three months' season ticket one month gone. That's eight weeks. Tell a lie, nine. Call it eight. Well, the fifth, sixth and seventh week I'm still paying something, an incremental on the third or fourth, aren't I? But what am I paying on the what do you call it?'

'Eighth,' said Lancelot.

'What I meant. The eighth week I'm not paying nothing, am I? Which other people are. Meaning their subsidence of me is the same as what mine was of that woman last March. And what I'm saying is, I should be. Because if I'm not, then they are, even if they don't go. Ridiculous.'

Lancelot, after only five minutes of this, had realised that there were going to be at least twenty more minutes of this on top of the five minutes of this he had already had. It was the first time he had ever been in a conversation to which he had been able to contribute only the word 'eighth'. He didn't see what he could do apart from suddenly opening the door and rolling out sideways like one of those crack infantrymen who drop off the back of a truck. The road threaded through several small towns and villages before dropping gently into the shallow valley which must have been worn into that shape aeons ago by a glacier even more irresistible in its ponderous attack than the tirade to which he was currently being subjected.

' . . . they ought to scrap all that lot, know what I mean? Otherwise the running costs are out of, over the, what with all, aren't they? Get rid of all that rolling stock and them engines at each end so one of them's wasted, isn't it? Just getting towed along. Rid of all that and cover the railway lines over with what's it called?'

'Asphalt,' said Lancelot mechanically.

'Yeah, that. And just run coaches every five, say every six minutes if you like, so you could catch one when you, go there when you, any time you felt like it, you know what I mean?'

'Yes,' said Lancelot, pointing out the side road that led across country. 'You could even join the coaches together so that you'd only need an engine in the first one.'

'What I *mean*,' said the driver triumphantly. 'Like you were saying. They ought to get it sorted. Don't see why they're still mucking, can't get it right. Give you another example. Just after the war, must have been 1947. Tell a lie, '48 . . . '

Lancelot was thinking of the tramlines still visible down the middle of Santa Monica Boulevard in Los Angeles. Was it Santa Monica Boulevard or the other one that branches off it? Where the road bends to the left as you head out of Hollywood towards the beach. By now the concrete would be wavering under the sunlight of late morning. Down the tracks had come the musical trolley cars to shunt and squash and cut in half the Model T Fords full of Keystone Kops in the days when Mabel Normand was the same age as Samantha. But now Mabel Normand was inside the glacier and twilight was thickening to dusk in the meadows beyond those lilac walls of fitted stones.

'. . . don't know why they don't do it, honest I don't. Cover up the railway lines with you know, easy. Three, four coaches every five, six minutes. Everybody gets what they pay for, don't they? And if you don't, you can't. No season tickets.'

'That's the ticket,' said Lancelot absently.

'Eh?'

'I mean that's the solution. You've put it in a nutshell. There's a man I work with called Frank Strain that you really ought to meet. You and he think along the same lines.'

'Along the same *lines*, that's what I *mean*. So all that money for new motorways gets saved straight away, without having to do nothing. Don't have to buy up no land. No compulsory purchase what is it?'

But by now they were turning into the gravelled loop in front of the mill house. The driver put on his glasses to read the colossal sum on the meter, and then asked for twice as much, presumably to cover his costs back to his starting-point plus depreciation on his vocal cords. Lancelot added a 10 per cent tip. Even as he did so he wondered why he did so, instead of deducting a 75 per cent listening fee. He accepted one of the driver's cards. 'LET ME QUOTE YOU,' it began 'ON MY TERMS FOR A 24 HOUR SERVICE OVER ANY DISTANCE.' How could any distance be greater than the one they had just travelled?

'What on earth happened?' asked Charlotte, helping him inside.

'Owing to the engineering, British Rail apologises to passengers and regrets the inconvenience caused. I'm famished.'

Charlotte fed him a snack to tide him over and then very shortly afterwards sat him down to dinner. Two of the three children were present, and seemed neither pleased nor displeased to have him around. The dogs were wholly indifferent, except perhaps for Feydeau, who squatted facing Lancelot's chair in order to display an erection that looked like a pink propelling pencil manufactured in Taiwan. Later they all got into the car and went back to London.

~ twelve ~

Nicholas abandoned his heap somewhere near Sally's front door and pressed her entryphone button. He was allowed upstairs for the privilege of watching her in the final stages of getting dressed for dinner at Elena's.

'This little number', said Sally, 'is the only item in the wardrobe that you don't know intimately. Now you've seen everything.'

'You can say that again,' said Nicholas, thinking how good a plain dark green skirt and little jacket effect could look if it was all put on the right person. He supposed it was made of velvet and the piping stuff at the edges of the lapels was satin, but would not have been surprised to hear that it was satin and the piping stuff at the edges of the lapels was velvet. All you could be sure of was that none of it was tacky. If tacky fabrics were cancelled on the spot, nearly everything that she had on would still be on her. He would have to take it off her himself. He made a ritual gesture towards this end, but had his hand beaten away as if it were an obstreperous pet that might be allowed back later. Would be allowed back later. Fancy being able to be sure. Bonanza.

'Where's the heavy metal conveyance?' he asked as they descended the stairs. 'I didn't spot it coming in.'

'It's around the corner in the underground car-park. I don't like leaving it in the street normally. Smart cars get scratched on principle and there's this new craze for peeing in them.'

'Let's go there in your thing and leave mine here. If I'm lucky they'll set fire to it and I'll get the insurance.'

'You like being driven around in a quick motor, don't you?'

'By you, yes.'

'You should like the car-park. All the really good cars in the district are down there.'

The car-park went down for several levels, each of them

120

clinically clean and looking like a private show-room for Arab League delegates to the UN. Nicholas had had no idea that this sort of thing was going on. There were Rolls-Royce Corniches standing next to each other with dust sheets over them. Ferraris and Aston-Martins were lined up as if for the start of a race. Cars he couldn't even recognise crouched sullenly, waiting for an excuse to unleash their powerful beauty. Sally told him what they were.

'It's like royal jelly, isn't it?' she asked rhetorically. 'Nothing down here but nutritious goodness.'

'It's probably a bit like that where we're going,' said Nicholas.

It was, too. A Spanish housekeeper who looked and sounded like a benevolent caricature of a Spanish housekeeper answered the door and showed them into a hallway which was already like a small Aladdin's cave. The hallway opened on to a reception room which was like a large Aladdin's cave. The house was in fact not especially big but mirrors leading into other mirrors made its true dimensions hard to assess. Nicholas got an impression of comfort raised to the point of luxury. Sally got the same impression but could see it was achieved by the most economical of means. It wasn't clutter, it was cunning. To prove the point, Elena was putting the finishing touches to the table. 'Nothing's finished and everything's burned,' she said as she turned towards them. 'Total, unmitigated disaster.' She offered her cheek to Nicholas, the first time that she had ever done so.

'We can see that,' said Nicholas. 'Can I introduce Sally Draycott?' Elena shook Sally's hand while bestowing on her the smile that charmed without challenging. She recognised Sally's suit immediately as being from the 1978 Chloë *prêt-à-porter* collection, not very expensive, especially when you allowed for how often it could be worn, but well chosen for someone of her height, colouring and unfussy knack with the accessories. Already at Victor's she had assessed the girl as having a good eye but here was the fact confirmed. Meanwhile Sally had spotted Elena's 1980 YSL pants suit as a *couture* original. Usually, in Sally's experience, the *couture* clothes looked good on the models and forlorn on the eventual client, but it was clear that anything designed for Elena didn't come into its own until it was hanging on her: the mannequin, by comparison, would look as juiceless as a coat-hanger. 'Is it permissible to gush about that suit?' she asked.

'It is. The poor man made it for me on condition I wore it in front of all the clever young people in London.'

'Who made it?' asked Nicholas, but they brushed him aside.

'I know it isn't done to ask,' said Sally. 'Next thing I'll be pestering you for recipes.'

'It's a delicious change to meet someone English who's also so visual.' Elena, who knew that people don't want to be charmed, they want to charm, would have pretended to be pleased with her guest anyway. But she was really pleased. How very displeasing. If the girl had so light a touch already then God only knew what she would turn into with practice. It was going to be a race. As for Sally, who had been impressed with Elena at Victor's and was now enchanted, it was only a question of how much she could take in. She had already noted with relief that her hostess wore contact lenses. At least something wasn't perfect. But how did she get so much light in her face? There must be a fluorescent tube in there.

Nicholas, who although standing beside them had no idea that any of this was going on, still felt momentarily out of it, but Elena now put him in charge of pouring drinks. All the bottles, decanters, siphons and cognate paraphernalia were grouped in a mirrored well sunk into the middle of a low table around which the hostess and her first guests now disposed themselves on a many-cushioned velvet banquette. The banquette ran around three sides of the sitting room and could have held twenty people in comfort. Three people it held in a state verging on bliss. Elena cast Nicholas as the man who did not know how to pour decent-sized drinks. Far from resenting this mockery, he found himself flattered, and mimed picking up the wrong bottle in order to improve the game. Sally already knew that nothing establishes intimacy faster than teasing but it was an education how Elena did it: Nicholas had a thin skin but he was purring like a cat. He was so accustomed to being a social catch that it did not occur to him he would have been slower to get through Elena's door if Sally had not been on his arm. Nor would Elena, though she did not much like young men, give the game away by turning cold where warmth had once been offered. Sally knew there must be undercurrents but the overcurrents were enough to be going on with. She had never felt so at ease so quickly in her life. It made her uneasy.

The doorbell rang and an expensively unkempt man of about thirty-five was shown in. Clearly he went with the furniture, because after being introduced to Sally he sat down on some of it without even looking around. Nicholas already knew him to be a dilettante painter who was one of Elena's celebrated assortment of door-opening and handbag-holding faggots. His name was Monty Forbes and in addition to his vocational expertise he was well up on opera, a subject on which Nicholas was well down. But Monty, eyes alight with obvious lust, started telling him all about it in a way that shut him out of the general conversation. Elena, who had counted on this effect when inviting Monty to arrive at precisely that time, spent the next quarter of an hour completing the conquest of Sally. She would have liked to tell herself that there was nothing to it, but it quickly became clear that the girl had much more to offer than a sense of style. Elena had long ago discovered that anybody was rated as a fascinating conversationalist who could, after saying 'Tell me about yourself' to an interlocutor, actually look interested while all the most intimate details of a mismanaged private life came pouring out. But Sally not only failed to gush about herself, she was genuinely impressive about her work, which in turn seemed to be concerned with the world at large. Elena was obliged to raise her game. A woman who liked only the kind of women who didn't like women, she recognised and responded to a fellow sufferer. It would have been almost easier having to feign interest. To be really interested was, in view of the peculiar circumstances, to feel herself threatened. But then, the girl would never do as an enemy: that had been obvious from the first. She must be made an ally. Time, that was the enemy. And this girl might know a lot for her age but about that she knew nothing. Bind her with a spell.

Nicholas had been all set to prove himself a dry well where opera was concerned, but Monty was under instructions to get him talking at some point about his latest novel. The colloquy moved on to the subject of novels in general. Monty had read a frightening amount of them in several languages. Nicholas, who hadn't known that about Monty before, found himself required to pedal hard. He also found himself quite enjoying it. Monty might be a fag but he wasn't a shrieking fag. He wasn't going to lean back and swat you with a powder puff. Occasionally these deviants were plugged into some pretty subtle vibrations, Nicholas had to admit. The front door bell rang again and Charlotte was shown in.

'Has Lancelot fallen by the wayside?' asked Elena, rising to kiss her.

'He's still outside in the car,' said Charlotte, 'and wonders if Nicholas could help him in.' Her apologetic blush blended into her Brontë sisters look with touching perfection.

'What's up?' asked Nicholas, minding his language. 'Is he drunk?'

'I should have thought you'd know better than anyone,' said Charlotte, looking rather cross. Nicholas strode bravely out into the night and bent down at the open door of Charlotte's Maxi.

'What gives?'

'My legs. They don't.'

'Don't what?'

'Give.'

'I don't get it.'

'Temporary stiffening of the upper thighs. Afraid I tried a bit too hard in that squash game. They hurt a bit afterwards and then everything went tight.'

'Christ. You're too big for me to carry you in.'

'No, I'll be able to walk in all right. But I'd appreciate some help getting out of the car so that I don't have to bend my legs too much.'

Nicholas helped to extract Lancelot's feet from under the dashboard as Lancelot lay down sideways into the driving seat. Then came a difficult and audibly uncomfortable manoeuvre by which Lancelot's body was turned through 90 degrees so that he was lying on his back with his bent knees pointing towards the top of the doorway. Then Nicholas grasped Lancelot's extended hands and attempted to pull him upright, but although his feet made contact with the footpath his head would not clear the upper door frame.

'We're going to have to push you back a bit,' said Nicholas. 'Impossible.'

'Just enough so you can bend forward. Then I'll hoik you out.'

Lancelot came out all right and straightened up very slowly, as if he had been photographed by a high speed camera. After a while Nicholas asked him whether it wasn't time he was moving inside, and received the reply that he already *was* moving inside.

'Look,' said Nicholas, after further time had passed. 'Maybe I'd better go in and arrange for your dinner to be sent out. By the time we sit down to eat you should just about be coming through the front door.'

'It's all right. Getting started is the hard part.' And indeed by now Lancelot was detectably in motion with regard to his surroundings, in the sense that they were even more stationary than he was.

Lancelot's handicap gave the evening an extra impetus of hilarity. He was pretty good at taking a joke against himself, which was lucky, because Nicholas had no intention of letting the point go. The two last guests to arrive were a shy but internationally luminous piano player and his spectacular Hungarian wife, a fountain of ebullience who did most of the talking for them both. To clue them in on the joke, Lancelot was encouraged by Nicholas to be the first to start making the trip from the banquette to the dinner table which lay glittering beyond the archway in the adjacent room. Everybody else started the journey a good deal later. This encouraged the shy but internationally luminous piano player to reminisce about just how fast the supposedly crippled Klemperer had been able to move in his wheelchair when chasing young lady violinists. General conversation had thus already begun as they sat down. Such was Elena's carefully nurtured technique: at her table there were rarely so many people that you could get stuck talking to someone on your right or left if you didn't want to. Everyone could address the whole assembly, and did so less tentatively as the wine flowed. The food, billed by Elena as an incinerated ruin, was exquisite, but nobody noticed. Lancelot was very funny and then Monty was funnier still. Then Nicholas was funnier than that. Sally, who in her short life had already found out a lot about marshalling competitive male egos into a coherent conversation, quietly marvelled at how Elena orchestrated the talk so that it never disappeared down a side street of specialised knowledge, which with Monty and the piano player present it could easily have done. They would obviously have talked about Pfitzner or Kulenkampff at the drop of a hat, but were not allowed to. The radiantly happy Spanish housekeeper and her even more ecstatic daughter kept appearing with new courses, each course ritually announced by Elena as the biggest disaster by fire since Krakatoa. Lancelot forgot first his bottom and then his tooth. Charlotte forgot she was angry with him for making a mess of the money and then running off to Los Angeles on such weak excuses. Nicholas forgot to worry about Sally, who was obviously a duck in water. Everybody except Sally and Elena forgot everything. Sally had seen Elena's kind of calm before – in a television production gallery, where a really good director, who at first sight appeared to be doing hardly anything and never spoke above a murmur, was telling people all over the building exactly what to do and when. Elena knew Sally was watching her and occasionally tipped her a wink of complicity after starting Lancelot or Nicholas or both off on some new flight of verbal extravagance. By that time they all would have been drunk just from breathing the air, but the wine helped.

Eventually they all drifted back to where they had begun, for coffee and serious drinks. Other people began to arrive. The editor of the most prominent literary magazine in London was followed into the room by the editor of the most prominent literary magazine in New York. Sally began to wonder who had been left in charge of the world: they all seemed to be here. She had read about this sort of thing but only vaguely. Now she realised why. She had read about it vaguely because it had been written about vaguely. Nobody who could write about it specifically would ever get within a mile of it. Was that a good thing? It was a fact. When people like Victor entertained you it might feel like the inner sanctum. But there was another sanctum even further in, where people like Victor were entertained. By the time you found out about it all, you were in too deep to rebel. Unless you were born there, of course. Then you could rebel, but what a misleading and untrustworthy ally you would make for other rebels.

Sally was ordinarily very good at neither staring nor taking her eyes away too quickly, but when Victor walked in she looked away and smiled involuntarily at the same time. Victor's gaze swung over her without hesitating and stopped on Elena, who rose to be kissed thinking that he had done that too well. There wasn't a normal man alive who wouldn't drink the girl in, and Victor, in that respect, was the most normal man she had ever met.

'I've decided to seduce Black and White myself,' she murmured through a smile. 'Seldom have I been more impressed. Will you join us? I'm sure Mr Crane won't mind.'

They picked their way between Nicholas and Lancelot, who were down on the carpet playing jacks with walnuts, Nicholas athletically cross-legged and Lancelot propped elaborately among cushions. Elena sat Victor down between herself and Sally, so that when she drifted away to look after another guest their conversation would at least be taking place under her auspices. That bound them to her, whereas if Victor had made his own way to Sally's side it might have been a conspiracy against her.

'Elena is throwing us together,' said Victor after she had moved away, 'in order to remind me of my age and responsibilities.'

'I've never met anyone like her in my life.'

'A woman of infinite deviousness. There isn't a man or woman here that she didn't enslave in the first hour. I once saw her do it to Yasser Arafat. From a distance, thank God. A terrible sight when that man smiles.'

Sally liked the way he talked about historically significant people as if they were a cast of characters in a play put on for the world's diversion. He seemed to know everything about what was going on everywhere. Sally's job was to think like that but it was highly informative to meet someone who had been thinking like that for a lot longer.

Towards one o'clock the Ambassador to the United States got

up to leave, presumably to go back to Washington. All the men stood. Sally hadn't seen that happen before. Elena waved dispensation to Lancelot as he struggled among the cushions. The general amusement marked the beginning of the end of the evening. Victor left not long after. Nicholas and the most brilliant caricaturist helped Lancelot back into Charlotte's Maxi: working together, they were able to pick him up and insert him like an astronaut into a capsule. The luminous piano player could not risk his fingertips in this operation but hummed Siegfried's Funeral March to appropriate effect. Rather too much laughter rang around the square for that hour of the night and Elena had to dampen it down.

'You seemed to be getting on very well with old Ludlow,' said Nicholas as Sally drove them home. 'Lucky he's got one foot in the grave.'

'Don't you believe it,' said Sally, treating the tunnel under Hyde Park Corner as an excerpt from the Monaco Grand Prix. 'Thirty-year-old men always think any man over fifty's just under a hundred. Twenty-seven-year-old women think differently. That's quite an attractive chap.'

'Did he pull you?'

'Not a bit. Elena did, though.'

'No kidding?'

'No kidding. I didn't quite get what was going on but if that's the sort of thing she's after I can see how she does it. I was wooed and won. For life.'

'I don't blame her. If I was a fabulous-looking power-crazy diesel dyke you'd be just the sort of trinket I'd want for my collection. She sort of bequeathed you to him, though, didn't she? What was *he* on about?'

'This and that. Nothing much about himself, except that he seems to be in on everything that's ever happened. He's right in the middle of the Middle East business. Bullets still coming at him from both directions, I shouldn't be surprised. I'd love to talk to him about it.'

'You just have.'

'On the air, stupid. But he never gives interviews.' They left the Porsche in the royal jelly car-park. 'You aren't too drunk, are you?' she asked as they climbed the stairs to her flat. 'I'd hate to be wasted.'

'You won't be wasted in that sense,' said Nicholas with mock bravado, although the real bravado underneath felt a trifle shaky. What had Elena put in the wine? Wine, mainly. Good wine, that was what the wine had been full of. But he didn't waste her. He was too grateful for his perfect evening, which had come at the end of a perfect day and already looked like paving the way for a perfect day after that.

'Have you got them all out?' asked Victor, telephoning from his car.

'Where are you?' asked Elena, taking off her other earring. 'Come here immediately.'

'Crossing Westminster Bridge for the second time.'

'Finally they've all disappeared. Extraordinary scenes getting rid of Lancelot. They had a funeral for him. Even Charlotte was amused. I must admit your young man Nicholas is quite funny with that filthy tongue of his. I suppose that's what she likes.'

'All his Christmases have come at once. She's an interesting young woman.'

'Meaning she listens raptly while you talk non-stop.'

'She spent the whole time looking at you. I think you've made another conquest.'

'She was just taking notes. And send that monstrous car home when you get here. I don't want anybody putting bombs in it outside my front door.'

When Lancelot and Charlotte got home there was a protracted, whispered struggle. At first Lancelot thought he would have to sleep in the car, but after complicated manoeuvrings he finally emerged. The awkwardness seems to be growing slightly less at last, thought Lancelot, shuffling carefully around the recumbent Feydeau in the hall. High time, because now that they were home and alone the running joke was wearing thin. Like all strained couples they spoke about other couples. They were agreed that Nicholas had struck it lucky. It must be good to be at the beginning of things. The trick, thought Lancelot, is to stay at the beginning of things. Lancelot would be back at the beginning of things tomorrow. You could practically call it today, because it was already tomorrow and the flight would consist largely of the time that doesn't count. Charlotte helped him take his socks off and get into his bed, sparing him all but a few sarcastic remarks about stiffness and how it might come in useful where he was going. He touched his tooth with his tongue and said goodnight.

~ thirteen ~

'Nguyen,' said Lancelot as the dentist probed and chipped at the roots of his teeth. 'Angkor. Ngaio. Ungarn. Ingres.'

'We'll just clean out some of this plaque while the filling hardens,' said the dentist jovially. Lancelot was almost horizontal and trying to focus on the discomfort of his bottom, but this by now had faded to the extent that when he was stationary it was barely noticeable. When he moved too suddenly he was instantly reminded of the benefits conferred by remaining stationary, but he was not moving now. So really he had nothing to distract him from his teeth, upon which the dentist was currently applying pressure from various angles in order to abrade flakes of scale like rust from a ship's hull. Magnified inside Lancelot's head, the noise was of trees being felled, furniture being moved and blocks of marble being split with wedges. On the upper left side of his mouth a different, steadier source of annoyance was provided by some sort of metal tourniquet which had been placed and tightened around the drilled and filled tooth. The tourniquet seemed to have a species of knurled handle effect sticking out from it, by which Lancelot's lip was forced upwards into what felt like an Elvis Presley sneer. As if to compensate, a curved plastic pipe had been hooked into place over his lower teeth. The end of it was resting irritatingly on the floor of his mouth, which felt as if it was full of enamel chips, fragments of cement and the kind of debris associated with a small archaeological dig.

'Not quite set yet,' said the dentist, smiling at his nurse. She smiled back and shook her head knowingly, as if there was always one awkward patient whose fillings set extra slowly. 'We may as well move ahead and do the bottom ones with this oriental thingummy I've just bought. Makes a pretty little squeal, doesn't it? Like a mouse at bay. Comfortable?'

'Arles. Annan. Ankara.' By crossing his eyes Lancelot could just see that the dentist was holding the latest variation on the theme of the Japanese hook, a transistorised hypersonic device for producing gratuitous pain.

'Good. When we get the clip off we can have a wash out. You've got some inflammation here so you might feel this a bit.'

Apart from feeling that his lower gums were being etched with a white hot pin while the string of his tongue was being sucked out by a bilge pump, Lancelot felt hardly anything at all. Transferred to his upper gums, the hook tried to lift him out of his chair. Finally the clip was taken off and he was allowed to wash out. The effluent looked like the strawberry and chopped nut sauce off some terrible ice-cream sundae. Then there was a bit more of the hook, topped off with a rousing five minutes from the fizzing brush coated with pink slime. During the last part Lancelot's apprehensiveness eased to the point where he was able to recall how mixed his emotions would have been if all this had not been happening. Relations over breakfast had been rather strained and his bags standing in the hall a focus of attention, with the children tripping over them and Feydeau taking the opportunity to make a territorial signal against one side of the big hold-all. It was a rather good, leather-bound canvas affair from Harvey Nichols and showed the stain wonderfully. On the other hand he was elated to be going, or would have been elated if the necessity to suppress the elation had not made him impatient. Also he wondered what was happening to his car and could hear a cold wind blowing through empty box files. Then there was the tax position, his buttocks and the tooth.

Well, at least the tooth was mended now. Having been tipped back into the vertical position, he shuffled downstairs to the receptionist's desk and was told that a bill would be sent in due course. Better than being arraigned as a defaulter by the Los Angeles police and locked up in San Quentin. Obviously it was not the first time the receptionist had seen a patient pick up luggage and head for Heathrow. She was quite sweet in a tarty way, with excellent ankles. How bright the world always looks as you leave the dentist's, even if your legs hurt. But they were definitely loosening up. He was able to strike a quite debonair pose as he hailed a taxi.

It took him to the international terminal at a cost which with his recently acquired experience he was able to believe, but only just. The final sum ran right off the conversion chart altogether and had to be computed from a second chart attached to the first one. When checking in he had trouble finding the right queue. As far as the eye could see the hall was jammed with people standing shoulder to shoulder. Every racial, cultural and ethnological variant of humanity was present and wearing national dress, as if for the first day of the Olympics. Lancelot could not see any Eskimos but presumably they were in there somewhere, incurring excess baggage charges for their kayaks and harpoons. After a while it became obvious that everybody belonged to a queue. The problem was to find which queue was yours. The only way to find out was to make your way to the correct desk and then trace your way back. It all took a long time and was hard on the legs.

After passport control things got easier. Lancelot bought some reading matter at the bookstall. Nicholas's latest novel had just come out in a bright paperback edition with an embossed polychromatic cover, like a small box of chocolates with an icon for a lid. It was all about a gang of young people so far gone on drugs that they die off one by one without the rest realising it, until finally only one is left, who writes the novel. It was called *Anything for a Laugh* and Lancelot had read it before it was published in hardback, but he bought a copy for Samantha. He also bought David's book of short stories, which he had not yet read. *Tactical Voting in the Eurovision Song Contest* was a bad title because it meant the book would usually be put on the wrong rack. But the cover was rather sexy, unless it was a photograph of the inside of a flower, in which case it wasn't. For enjoyment purposes he bought one of those collections of Victorian pornography in which the ladies manifest physiologically impossible reactions to stimuli. For some reason which he had never been able to fathom, the unlikelihood put you on rather than off. Magazines there would be on the plane, although perhaps not as many as in first class. Lancelot was going Club class, meaning that you ate the same food as economy class but with metal cutlery instead of plastic, unless you got lucky and were given the same food as first class but with plastic cutlery instead of metal.

Lancelot liked flying. A few days ago, he told himself, he would willingly have caught a slow rocket to Jupiter. Even today he was in no tearing hurry to get there. He felt he ought to be and it worried him slightly. He was worried about not being worried more but not too worried. During the mandatory one-and-a-half hour delay after boarding the aircraft and before taking off – apparently the baggage handlers were demanding to be either indemnified against prosecution for robbery or else paid overtime during appearances in court – he read David's short stories. They were all about a way of life concerning which Lancelot knew so little that he couldn't tell whether the prose was heightened realism or just realism. Everybody lived out of suitcases and believed what people used to say they believed in the Sixties, except that this lot were excruciatingly sincere and actually, instead of purportedly, penniless. But there was no doubt that the author could write. What he said, you could see.

Then the flight began. It proved as usual to take the form of an unbroken succession of meals which it seemed just as easy to eat as to hand back. The in-flight movie, Lancelot was pleased to find, was the very latest vehicle of the world's most famous young female film star. She played a journalist assigned to the life story of a presidential candidate, played by that smiling actor, what was his name, Bulk Stores. The candidate was a happily married man but he had never really known true intellectual companionship until he met the world's most famous young female film star. At the end he went back to his wife, but the end was a long way from the start and in between there was the middle. Keep the middle going, that's the secret.

Somewhere over the snowfields of Colorado, Lancelot had a shave, using a new throwaway razor from his sponge bag. If he had thrown the razor away before shaving instead of after, he would have done himself less damage. Wishing to avoid the jokey impression inevitably created by stanching the wounds with small scraps of toilet paper, he kept splashing on the free aftershave provided until the astringent effect took hold. Then he had to wait a while before giving his face a thorough hot water wash to damp down the pronounced floral odour of the aftershave, some distillate of rotting nasturtiums. At last he was ready to make a slow, 90 degree shuffling turn to the right and pull the folding door inwards. There was an impatient man just outside the door and another impatient man outside each of the other five doors just like it. Six men standing upright in small cubicles scraping hair from their faces while moving through the stratosphere at a speed approaching that of sound: it would have struck Lancelot as a conundrum if he had not already been feeling a bit sleepy.

Then they landed. By the time it was his turn at the immigration desk his internal clock was registering midnight. For the immigration officer, a black man who looked like a football player so recently retired that he was still wearing his shoulderpads under his blue shirt, it was bright afternoon.

'Windhover,' said the immigration officer. 'I caught this morning morning's minion, kingdom of daylight's dauphin . . . '

'I know,' said Lancelot.

The immigration officer looked at Lancelot without altering the angle of his head. The sole unrehearsed opportunity which life would ever offer him to recite a poem by Gerard Manley Hopkins had been interrupted.

'You haven't pressed down hard enough with your pen right here,' said the immigration officer, 'to make a clear copy on the counterfoil. Have you?'

'I guess not.'

'I guess not. You speak American pretty good. Why don't you go back there and do it all over? Just press down hard on what you've written already and it'll turn out fine.'

'Can I come back to the head of the queue?'

'Can you come back to the head of the what?'

'To the front of the line?'

'Dapple-dawn drawn, in his riding . . . '

This time Lancelot waited until the end of the stanza, and was rewarded with permission to come back to the front of the line once he had finished pressing down hard. Tracing over what he had already inscribed gave him such a perfect sense of time wasted that he felt as if he himself were being pressed down on hard in his turn. Pressed down hard and then released, the way your hand floats upward after you press the back of it hard against a wall. His head was light. Perhaps it was the heat.

Laden with bags, Lancelot walked through into America with comparative ease. Sudden moves were still self-limited by a twinge in the glútei, but he reached the cab rank at a casual stride and bent down to enter the low cab without assistance or much comment from the driver, whose name was Joel. As the cab flew low beside the armco barrier rails of the freeway, Lancelot found out, without having to ask, that there had been no rain for weeks, that many visiting British writers had found Joel to be a useful guide to Los Angeles, that the weird machine which passed them as if they were standing still was a beach buggy chromed all over and driven by a celebrated dog surgeon, and that Joel's brother ran the PX at a USAF base in England. Lancelot let it all wash over him like warm air. Joel's conversation was the verbal equivalent of the freeway: endless, easy, hypnotic. Also you didn't have to pay for it. The fare seemed to contain no hidden charges and even Lancelot, no great shakes at lightning computation, could tell that it was reasonable compared to Britain. If America became cheaper to live in than Britain, what was the point of living in Britain at all? To get Radio 3?

Lancelot's room at the Casa Perdida had a boot-shaped hole kicked through the plywood door and the carpet had not been shampooed, so that his bare feet felt as if they were secreting glue. Or perhaps it had been shampooed and the shampoo was still in it. His feet were ill at ease but the rest of him, as he picked up the telephone while the bath ran with a generous American gush, was as close as it had come for a long time to happy anticipation.

'She's in Las Vegas,' said Yonky Vollmer's brain-damaged voice. 'She said to tell you she was sorry she couldn't tell you. It happened real sudden.'

'When is she coming back?'

'Tomorrow morning. She said for you to get some sleep and she'll be with you there for lunch.'

Lancelot looked at his bath as if the only sensible thing to do was climb into it and open his veins. But he soon rationalised disappointment into relief. He was, after all, not at his best. His body would obey only the most elementary commands, and those with a sluggishness wholly unbefitting the challenge represented by Samantha, who looked on love as a variety of free-form dancing. In the morning he would be fresh and might not even feel hampered, especially if he lay now for some time in the luke-warm water. He lay in it and waited for tiredness to overwhelm him. It almost did, but the light and heat were all wrong, perceptible even through the air-conditioning and the drawn curtains. The drawn drapes. There was a theory that you should try to stay awake until the local bedtime, thus to avoid waking early in the morning. Perhaps he should try that. What about making his call on Ian now? The chances that Ian might be in were considerably increased by the known fact that he very rarely went out.

'*Lovely* that you're here. Where have they put you?'

'I forget. It's got a hole in the door.'

'Sixteen. That was Julio. A *very* exciting evening. There were squad cars in the forecourt and all kinds of lucky people spreadeagled with these wonderfully well built law-enforcement officers doing the highly intimate body search.'

'Are you available for consultation? I should be asleep but it's a bit early.'

'Of course. Can't wait. I'm the last one on the second floor just around the pool from you. Climb the wooden stairs as soon as you've settled in. I'm actually in the throes of composition.'

Lancelot finished unpacking and walked slowly out into the brilliant air, to which his body in vain said midnight. Where was the second floor? There was no second floor. Oh, of course. Second floor meant first floor. After climbing the wooden stairs one step at a time he knocked on Ian's door and was told to push it open. In the room the curtains were drawn and the lights were on. Ian was behind a desk looking with elaborate thoughtfulness at what was almost certainly a revised synopsis of *A World History of the Short.* He was sucking his pen as if he had just been told to suck his pen by Karsh of Ottawa. Then he smiled in welcome and stood up, ducking instinctively as he did so. Ian Cuthbert was six feet seven inches tall and like most outsize people had a rich formative history of collisions. Later on, his sensitivity to the nearness of the scenery had been sublimated into the inevitable, endless concern with shoes, shirts, suits and beds, but the old reflexes still showed. Seldom did you see him stand up suddenly without ducking: his central nervous system was imprinted with the continuously threatening image of a ceiling through which his head would protrude abruptly into the room above.

'Faulkner,' said Ian significantly.

'Faulkner what?'

'Faulkner. Willian Faulkner. Tiny. Absolutely minuscule. Nearest thing to a homunculus. Made Truman Capote look like Steve Reeves. It's been staring right at me. He spent half his life only a mile away from here. And you've got all those marvellous photographs Alfred Eris took of him at the Highland Hotel in 1949. He's sitting there in just his shorts and glasses tapping away at a typewriter bigger than he is. It looks like a Bechstein. We could do a whole chapter just on him. Faulkner. The bardic voice of the *bonsai* people. It staggers me I didn't think of it straight away.'

Ian was back behind his desk miming creative frenzy and remorse. Folding his gigantic right hand into a fist, he bounced the heel of its palm off his forehead to indicate the imminent possibility of rent garments. Lancelot was impressed by the number of pills on the desk. The predominant colours were red and yellow but there were others too. Ian had always been like one of those scientists who work their way back through the putative history of the universe in search of a unification principle which might reconcile the forces operating in nature, except that in Ian's case the reconciliation sought was between all the pharmaceutical products conceivably applicable to the human system. Judging from the beads of sweat on his forehead his researches were far advanced. He still made some kind of sense but it all came in fits and starts. He would be brilliant for two minutes and then sound catatonic, like a man who had just walked away from a plane crash. Lancelot persuaded him that there would be plenty of time to discuss *A World History of the Short*, but for now he would appreciate some help compiling a list of writers who could draw. He repeated the sample names he had already given Serena and was gratified, if not surprised, at the high recognition factor. Ian was off and running long before Lancelot had finished stating the general idea.

'Lermontov would be the key man, of course,' said Ian. 'In fact that would be almost cheating because he probably would have *been* an artist if there'd been time. He'd have been in the same category as Ruskin and Rossetti. And Hazlitt. Marvellous portrait of Lamb by Hazlitt. Cummings and Montale would be modern day equivalents. Both serious painters. Both pretty awful, too, but that's part of the point, isn't it? You ought to have Tennyson. Baudelaire would be a must. Did you say Montherlant?'

'No. Did he draw?'

'Bullfighters. Started when he was a child. The grown-up drawings are marvellous. Sort of thing you get on menus, only better. There's one of Belmonte fighting where the bull's all drawn in one line, like a Picasso.'

'I would never have thought of that and I read everything he wrote. You really are invaluable.'

'There's Chesterton, of course. Would Evelyn Waugh be too obvious? Kafka did some very interesting drawings, sort of halfway between Klee and Thurber. Max Brod included some of them in that first little 1937 biography. And don't forget Firbank. His notebooks are full of the most dazzling little doodles of ladies in cloche hats and madonnas with mascara. The Berg Collection's got them. New York Public Library.'

'That's just what we want. Unknown stuff by well-known people.'

'If you widened the basis from just writers you'd be opening the whole question of multiple talents right up. John Maynard Keynes did caricatures at Versailles. Caruso drew very well, of course, as well as being quite short. So did Chaliapin. And think of what you could do with Schoenberg.'

'If you think his music's tough on your ears, wait till you see what his paintings do to your eyes. Yes, that could be a good line.'

'Then you could take it full circle and include the artists who wrote. You could have Michelangelo's poems. Delacroix's journal. Reynolds. Fromentin. Whistler. Quite short, Whistler: five foot five. Van Gogh in his letters. Cellini. Beardsley did some *beautiful* translations of Catullus.'

'But that's getting . . . '

'Degas wrote sonnets that Valéry thought were amazingly . . .'

'That's getting into the area of a proper essay rather than just . . .'

'God! Why didn't I *see* it! Vasari! Thought he was a painter but really exists only as a writer! Case of not even realising which of your talents is the real one!' Ian was hopping about on his enormous feet. He grabbed a handful of pills seemingly at random and sprang hugely into the *en suite* bathroom with his head held low. Lancelot could hear him washing the pills down with water.

'Blake!' boomed Ian with a bathroom voice. 'So obvious you forget him! Lousy poet *and* a lousy artist! Edward Lear! Wilhelm Busch! Walt Kelly! Asterix! Rupert the B . . .'

Forgetting to duck as he danced out of the bathroom, Ian fetched his forehead a crack against the lintel that sent him reeling back out of sight. Lancelot found him sitting on the toilet wheezing and sobbing, but not holding the injured part. Instead his trembling, acromegalic hands were on his knees, palms upward. Either he was not badly hurt or else he experienced local damage only as a diffuse general effect.

'It's all right,' said Ian eventually, lying on his special bed. 'It's all right. Leave me alone for a day or two and I'll do a complete list. Wouldn't mind writing it myself, as a matter of fact.'

'We could consider that. It might mean abandoning *A World History of the Short*.'

'Couldn't. Must see things through. Must must must. So much time gone. So much.'

'I know how you feel.'

'Did you see Monty before you left?' asked Ian with feigned drowsiness.

'Last night at Elena's.'

'Has he found anyone?'

'Not that I know of. No, I'm sure he hasn't.'

'Isn't it awful how we don't want the people we love to be happy except with us?'

Lancelot switched off the lights and left, startled to find that it was still daylight. He ordered a room-service hamburger and watched television for as long as he could. On a local news programme a man wearing a fake-fur catcher's mitt for a wig told him that the actor who used to play Captain Video had died that morning in a Long Beach motel room which had been his residence for some time. Nobody had come to claim the body.

~ fourteen ~

'Praline,' said Lancelot, tasting his fingertips.

'Mm?' Samantha was weary at last.

'*La céleste praline*. It's what Rimbaud called it. Perfect word. Gets the thickness.'

'Wasn't he a woofter?'

'Verlaine was mad about him but he had a soft spot for ladies. Soft spot for their soft spots. Especially this soft spot here. *Chanaan féminin dans les moiteurs enclos*. A feminine Canaan enclosed in moisture. *Des filaments pareils à des larmes de lait*. Filaments like tears of milk.'

'How can you remember all that?'

'It's all I *do* remember. A few scraps of randy poetry that leave everything of mine in the shade. But there are other things in life. This, for instance.'

Through the early afternoon they had been lying there in his room, with enough light coming in through the drawn lemon drapes to excite the photosphere of her skin into incandescence. Practically singing with energy, she had appeared at his door in a tee-shirt and a pair of shorts that made her legs look more than usually endless. Slowing her down to this degree of somnolence had taken a long time, but Lancelot had never used time better. The idea of her tautness, firmness and creamy resilience had been haunting him. Now there was the fact at last. It was impossible to imagine yourself as having more conscience than you possessed, but even supposing he had twice as much, he suspected that he would still forgive himself. Men who thought they could resist this had never been offered it. By the time age turned it loose he would be gone. He looked along her stomach to where her face, slightly propped up on the pillow, was smiling down at him between her breasts.

'Bum still hurt?' she asked.

'Faintly.'

'Cost you a groaning to take off my edge.'

'There you are. You can do it too.'

'Should bloody well think so. Me and my useless double First.'

Samantha's reasons for having been in Las Vegas sounded plausible enough to anyone who believed that her reasons for being in Los Angeles were plausible in the first place. Lancelot had no intention, now at any rate, of asking any questions. But it emerged without prompting that she was bored with what she was doing. When she came back to England she would resume writing articles but she was bored with that too. Perhaps she was meant to be some famous man's wife, managing his house and going to parties with him, or having the parties right there in the house if there was someone else to cook.

All this was suggested frivolously but it put Lancelot on the alert, so that in the next few days he strove to prove that a girl like Samantha could be a moderately famous man's *companion*, with matrimony and a house left out of the picture but a lot of parties thrown in. His own connections in Los Angeles were with literary people but when he took her along to dinner she could occasionally show, if suitably prompted, what looked like real interest in the conversation. This was a relief to Lancelot, because some of his hostesses were acquaintances of Charlotte and there had been a certain amount of humming and ha-ing about blending Samantha into the *placement*. Indeed in the case of one notoriously successful husband-and-wife writing team the invitation had been resoundingly for one person only, take it or leave it. Lancelot had taken it while Samantha went to one of those roller discos where even at his most slavishly obsessed he did not dream of being seen dead — or, rather, did. Stretched out with an impacted occiput while his feet leaked small ball-bearings. Dancing below your age might merely be ludicrous, but doing the same thing on eight wheels would court disaster. Not that the simple act of dining out was devoid of hazard. The news would be back in London soon enough. He was like a man living on borrowed time, but that kind of time can do strange things to space and light. Look at her sitting there among all these lined and sagging people. Why bother to lift a face when it is no longer as fresh as hers? See how she shines.

It remained a constant wonder to Lancelot that someone with Samantha's glittering academic record should betray so little inclination to open a book now that her last examination was behind her. In Pacific Palisades they ate Mexican salads at the pine tables of some of the most literate writers in the English-speaking world. What was more, these writers, unlike most English writers, or the same writers transposed to England, which was where many of them had come from anyway, liked talking about literature in the evenings, as a necessary corrective to having spent the day helping Barbra Streisand rewrite what they had written. But Samantha's attitude was never one of deference or even of particular respect. Instead, apart from the occasional and unpredictable display of sudden curiosity, she seemed mostly long-suffering, as if wondering how long these fuddy-duddies could prop each other up. It wasn't that she laughed in the wrong places, only that she laughed as if the real laughs were somewhere else.

Several times, instead of his taking her with him, she took him with her, to clockless pulsating black vaults in which coloured sparks chased each other through slits in the sprung floor and the music kicked him repeatedly in the head. While she occupied herself in a stroboscopic frenzy like a female mythological protagonist trying to shake off a shirt of intermittent fire, Lancelot capered dutifully in her reflected glory, praying that he could get her home while he had some energy left. But when Yonky tagged along with some dreadful teenage bio-engineering millionaire of a boyfriend then the night out would go on until Lancelot had nothing left in him except tiredness and leg muscles that begged for peace.

The house parties she took him to also featured a lot of cavorting in dark rooms full of auroras and subliminal electrical storms, but there were at least some areas of comparative silence, in what would have been gardens if not for the glass walls, or living rooms if not for the lianas. Unfortunately the indirectly lit personnel had nothing to say which Lancelot could easily comprehend. If he could understand it, he couldn't understand why they were bothering to say it. Most of them were young actors and actresses or people trying to look like young actors and actresses. At the equivalent gathering in

London the cocaine would have been sequestered in an upstairs room to which only the stars would be granted unchallenged access. Here it was laid out in lines on silver trays. Samantha seemed to be taking the stuff on board like one of those pipes that sucks grain from a ship's hold. It would be an expensive proclivity – she wouldn't let him call it a habit – to take home. She had no real money of her own and seemed to be not very interested in earning any. What would she do if she were not interested in writing articles? Perhaps she would move up to being not interested in writing books. It was then that the idea struck him.

Only partly as revenge for Lancelot's flagrant absence, Charlotte telephoned David and asked him to dinner. If hers had been a vindictive nature then retribution might have been the whole reason, but in fact curiosity outweighed it. She had thought that today's young people were like her children – i.e., like her, but not old enough. David had impressed her with the specific quality of an idealism which you could not dismiss as callowness, especially when it was based, as it obviously was, on real experience. The Sixties, an era whose memory she reviled, had been full of fake rebels, but whatever David was up to was unmistakably genuine. Also he had real talent, you could tell by the way he spoke, and one of the things that made her a good teacher – she knew she was that, being surrounded by bad ones – was her instinctive respect for creativity. And he seemed to like being with her. Ringing him up would put that last proposition to the test instead of leaving it safe, so she hesitated for a whole day. But he said yes, no evening would be too soon. Well, what do you know?

David's schedule at the house was heavy that week. Race relations in the area had reached the point where Trotskyites of different colours weren't talking to each other. Gaga Ladbroke, David's companion for the last two years, was conducting teach-ins every other night in the downstairs front room. All this on top of acting in a film during the day and running the workshop at the weekends. In the workshop some of the local youth acquired skills which might or might not keep them out of gaol until such time as capitalism could be overthrown.

Press spies would have liked to suggest that they were learning to make bombs or rob banks, but David mainly contrived to keep the channels of communication open, at least as far as the radical and socialist magazines went. Also his efforts to maintain a dialogue with the local constabulary had so far managed to ward off one of those routine house-searches that leave the electricity meter lying in the bath and the bath lying in the back garden. David felt all the more involved for having rather gone off Gaga – not, he hoped, because she was tired all the time but because she was becoming repetitive. It was inevitable: staying true to your code largely entails repeating its slogans over and over to yourself as well as to anyone who will listen. David could see the political necessity for this but it grated on him as a writer. So with a clouded conscience he took a night off, plus enough money to get the tube there and back.

Charlotte thought at first of anticipating his culinary tastes. Probably he existed on revolutionary bean shoots and rice wine. But she was immediately out of her depth and anyway he had eaten those pieces of pheasant readily enough. Perhaps the thing to do was feed him up. She dismissed Mrs Hyperbolics for the evening, first of all because David might have advised her to seek political asylum and secondly because she, Charlotte, wanted to do all the cooking herself. On one level of the gas oven she set to roast a small tarragon chicken while she got on with concocting a spinach soufflé and an out-of-season fruit tart made possible by her preserves. Any children who turned up were fed hamburgers as they arrived and soon wandered away again. They were New Romantics and their hands were ever at their lips, bidding adieu.

One of the children let David in. He was instantly attacked by the dogs. Charlotte helped rescue him from his position behind the hall-way coat stand.

'It's the fear,' said David apologetically. 'They sense it. Dogs much smaller than these go completely kamikaze when I'm around. I get chihuahuas zooming up my trouser leg.'

'I'm sorry. I had no idea you hated them. I'll lock them outside.'

Charlotte sat David down at the kitchen table while she cooked. All he would drink was mineral water. She told him about a wasted afternoon of academic politics and he told her about the other kind of politics, with specific reference to Gaga and his house full of revolutionaries. David had in his jacket a copy of the magazine in which Victor's shameful mistreatment of his employers was supposedly laid bare. Charlotte found herself defending paternalism, or at any rate defending Victor, whom she knew to be fundamentally honest, even if hopelessly flamboyant. David explained that personal honesty was irrelevant if the system was dishonest, but Charlotte professed not to understand the explanation. As they sat opposite each other at the thick table, Charlotte was surprised to discover that one of her daughters, having entered and been introduced, neither seized any further food nor sought a quick exit to escape adult conversation, but actually stood there, silently attentive and almost staring. In the course of time this daughter was joined by another daughter, and finally by her son. The offspring stood in a spangled group, their eyes, for once, glistening like their sequinned eyeshadow. Their bells and chimes were almost silent, except when one or more of them shifted his or her weight from one foot or more to the other or others. Then there were questions, which David answered. The questions and answers were so technical that Charlotte could get only a fleeting idea of the subject matter, but it seemed to be something to do with popular culture. This impression was reinforced when the children brought forth multiple copies of those frightful magazines of theirs which had titles like *Fangs* and in which very few words, almost invariably misspelled, eked out reams of pictures featuring young people in cargo-cult makeup. David signed all the magazines and eventually, reluctantly, the children went away, walking backwards, as if leaving the presence of the King of Siam.

'I've brought home a hero, it appears.'

'Sorry about all that.'

'For God's sake. You've raised my status around here to the highest it's ever been. I had no idea they read short stories. I was under the impression they never voluntarily read anything.'

'I don't think it was for that. Until last year I was a bit of a musical personality. I played bass guitar in a band called Clutch Shudder. We were going quite well but it all depended on the singer and he had an accident.'

'Inside of his nose fall out?' asked Charlotte, feeling terrifically up to date.

'Wet stage.'

'Is that something else that coke does?'

'No. The stage was wet. Rain. It's an occupational hazard when you're doing open-air concerts. Lot of juice about, so it's very easy to get zapped. Rick had this ultra-complicated routine when he came on for his first song. Flinging his head around in a circle while he strutted all the way across the stage and back. Up in the air for a splits, then he dives forward and grabs the mike. Only this time he flings his head around in a circle, struts across the stage and back, up in the air for a splits, dives forward and there's a blue flash. I had my eyes shut at that point because I was playing a dramatic lick. You know, my head thrown back in ecstasy. But I could see the flash through my eyelids. I can see the exact colour now. Like the Cherenkov effect. Pure sapphire.'

'Was he killed?'

'Oh, instantly. Never felt a thing. But then he never felt a thing anyway. I took it as a signal and decided to enter the world of words full time.'

'Don't you miss your music?'

'There wasn't much of that left. We were too busy being successful. Which was never supposed to be the idea in the first place.'

'You're serious about all that, are you?'

'About all what?'

'About being against society, and so forth.'

'I don't have to be against this society. It's against itself. It's insane and I'd like to see it sane. It's sick and I'd like to see it well. It's careless and unfair and the way it's going it might end up just hopeless. You can't imagine what it's like to be young just now.'

'No. I don't suppose I can.'

It was like talking to an exceptionally bright student, with the difference that she felt as if it were she, and not he, who had enrolled for the course and would eventually be tested. His hands were beautiful but he held his fork far too low down, with his index finger on the chines. Stop that. Squash the peas if you have to but don't shovel them. Cut smaller pieces. Don't put so much in your *mouth*.

When she led him upstairs it was to show him her books, which she had been collecting since her undergraduate days at Girton.

'Wow. Are they all yours?'

'The French ones are mainly Lancelot's. There are more of them in his study. The Greek and Latin and Italian and German ones are mainly mine. And all the English ones of course.'

'It's a whole library.'

'It's a working library. I'm especially strong on English critical prose. That's what my own book's about.'

'I know. I've been reading it.'

Normally she never lent books but when David left he had an allegedly spare three-volume set of Saintsbury's *History of Criticism* under his arm, plus a copy of Desmond MacCarthy's *Portraits*, with instructions to read the chapter on Henry James. Charlotte reminded herself of someone who leaves an umbrella in someone else's house, not so much as an excuse for coming back as to establish a connection.

When Sally saw the article about Victor Ludorum she rang her producer immediately. Her producer called himself Speed Blair and wore training shoes to indicate that he was classless, a tie to establish his qualifications for the executive restaurant, trousers that were almost jeans and a jacket one step up from a windbreaker. His character reflected his attire in every particular. Not only, he assured her, had he already seen the article and got the point, he had done his best to flush that old crook Ludlow out, with predictable results.

'No way in the world, love,' Speed announced, employing that patronising tone of misplaced self-confidence which she had come to know and loathe. 'Every channel's been on to it already and can't get past his outer secretary.'

'I might have an in. Can I get it on the air if I'm right?'

'Oh *ho*,' said Speed. 'So that's how it is.'

'That's how it isn't. To get this I'll have to swear we'll treat him fairly. No dodgy cuts.'

'You can count on a full half hour. They'll jump at it upstairs.

Might even want longer. It'll be the first time he's talked since Carlos shot him.'

At Elena's soirée Sally would have made a point of not taking Victor's private number if he hadn't made such a point of not supplying it. Unfortunately that left her back at square one with all the other contenders. It would be a mistake to ring Elena. She rang the publishing house and was surprised when the switchboard put her straight through to Victor's private secretary. She was more surprised still when the private secretary asked her which number and extension number she was speaking from and told her that Victor would ring her back.

'I didn't really want to interrupt him,' said Sally, momentarily thrown. 'Just perhaps to reach him when he had a spare moment.'

'Sir Victor is in Vienna but he should get back to you very soon. I'll ring him now and if he's free he'll ring you. Vienna is an hour ahead of us at the moment but he might not be at lunch yet. If you could just hang up and stand by?'

Sally hung up and stood by. Never, never would she get entirely accustomed to the prodigies that could be accomplished with Alexander Graham Bell's invention. One of the reasons she liked machines was because they offended her scale of values. People were meant to walk there, or, failing that, send a letter. Either she was dazed or the phone rang straight away.

'Can anyone reach you that easily?' she asked, smiling. Stop smiling, dummy: it's a tele*phone*, not television.

'Your name is on a list of people who are to be put in touch with me wherever I am. It's not a very long list.'

'Which elegant Austro-Hungarian female am I helping you to keep waiting?'

'Chap called Kreisky.'

'Have you seen this stuff about you as the Simon Legree *de nos jours*?'

'I had it read to me last night.'

'Have the world and his wife been trying to get you on television to defend yourself?'

'Yes. I said no.'

'What if it was me asking the questions?'

'Yes.'

'There's a chance that they might muck it up but I . . . '

'Yes. Take yes for an answer.'

Apart from fixing time and place there wasn't much talk between them after that. Speed, for once, was slack-jawed with admiration, a desirable symptom because it shut off his knowing drawl. There were approving noises from upstairs. Anthony Easement came striding happily down the corridor to wonder if she could do a long version that he might use as a recurring theme in a projected series about the émigré intellectuals which had been going to happen for about the last five years. Also he asked her out to lunch as usual and she refused him as she always had since the end of a mercifully brief near-affair which had consisted almost exclusively of his crying on her shoulder. He had a typed list of extra questions with him. She threw him out and went incommunicado while she worked on her own questions. Victor would be already in the sky and on his way across Europe. The ancient professor of economics she had been meant to talk to had to be rung and put on ice. He asked her to lunch. To eat what, rusks? From the cuttings file and her own dossier she put together a short biographical introduction for autocue. On her note pad she put down 'Do you love me?' as one of her draft questions and then drew a line through it. Then she obscured it more thoroughly by cross-hatching it closely with her pencil. She tore off that sheet and the sheet underneath which carried the indentation. After copying out all the questions except that one she crumpled the two torn-out sheets and dropped them into the waste-paper basket. Then she reached down, took out the wad of paper, shredded it, and dropped the fistful of pieces back in.

A television studio is a perpetual count-down which involves everyone except the assistant scene-shifters in the automatic histrionics of an adrenalin high. Only two kinds of people can behave naturally in such circumstances: hardened professionals and those whose personalities, whether through unusual self-possession or the intensity of some past experience, are without a modifiable demonstrative element. Victor was one of the latter. There was neither bogus chumminess nor assumed hauteur. Perhaps he was such a born ham that he could fake naturalness, like a coward pretending to be brave. He listened to the question and then answered, although Sally could tell that while answering one question he was already preparing himself for the next. So she was not surprised, only impressed, at how he fielded the awkward stuff, which after some opening pleasantries they arrived at quite soon.

'First of all we *don't* pay editorial workers the minimum. We could pay less and still be above generally agreed standards.'

'According to the figures in this article, and I must say according to the figures we've obtained ourselves from independent sources, if you paid any less you'd have a riot on your hands.'

'I'd ask you about those independent sources if we had time. But let me resume by conceding the point. At that level of work we don't pay very much. When the same people have stayed on for a while and learned something then we pay quite a lot – rather above the rates that prevail elsewhere. But you've got to realise that when editorial workers start out they get little because usually they're giving little.'

'There are complaints here about a fifty-hour week.'

'Yes, but even if that were true, what would they actually be *doing* all that time? There's no guarantee that the average young applicant for an editorial job, even when she's got a degree or two degrees, can even spell, let alone that she knows enough to know what needs checking in a manuscript. Most of them do work that needs checking in its turn. You have to ask yourself whether it makes any sense for an apprentice to demand a skilled worker's privileges. If we're talking about membership of a guild. I only wish we were, because a medieval guild tried to make sure that bad workers couldn't flourish.'

'Are you saying your own employees don't do satisfactory work?'

'No, because they do. But they have to learn how on the job, and the real rewards don't come until they make a real contribution. I'm all for unions and even for a closed shop, but I'm not for an adversary relationship between management and labour.'

'Doesn't that make you paternalistic?'

'It would please me very much to be a patron. Especially a patron of the arts. But I lack the talent. Count Razumovsky was a patron. When he commissioned a piece from Beethoven, he could not only appreciate it, he could play it.'

'You choose to misunderstand me, or perhaps I expressed myself badly.'

'You expressed yourself impeccably. I chose to misunderstand you.'

'Let me ask the question again. Doesn't that mean you're setting yourself up as an all-wise father figure to your work-force?'

'Only in the best sense, I hope. The law doesn't allow the worst sense. And nature doesn't allow anyone to be as wise as that. Publishing is a risk business and I've made the mistakes to prove it. I was the man who published *Random Thoughts of Rossano Brazzi*. You can have a few thousand copies if you like. Not even the pulping mills would take it.'

'You've been accused of dropping novelists ruthlessly when they cease to sell.'

'All publishers do it and it always feels ruthless to the novelist. We've certainly dropped *one* novelist recently. I suspect he might be one of the principal sources for this celebrated piece of investigative journalism. He never sold very well and after six novels he had stopped selling at all, so we had to call it a day on his seventh book. It was no doubt very disappointing for him but the chance of not pleasing the public is the chance you take when you set out to please it.'

'Isn't that a thoroughly commercial attitude to art?'

'It's a thoroughly commercial attitude to commerce. As for art, it certainly has to be subsidised. But my firm already subsidises art. Most of the serious books published by us are subsidised by the unserious books – among which must be included all but the most exceptional novels, whatever the occasional embittered novelist might think. Half of the dissident writing that comes out of Eastern Europe is published by us. We publish African protest writing that hasn't even got a market in Africa. We're proud to do it, but commercially it's a dead loss.'

'But couldn't you . . . '

'No, we couldn't. Writers want to be with us because we're a prosperous firm. The firm is prosperous because it pays its way. If it didn't it would have to be subsidised in its turn by other elements in the group which make profits. Magazines, for example.'

'Which you own too.'

'Which I own too. But there again, they don't sustain themselves by magic. There is no limitless source of money into which I can dip and thus restore an ailing enterprise to profitability. I pay myself well and live high, but I've got no more pull at Fort Knox than you have. The kind of business I'm in is long on personal satisfaction but the profit margins are small. If they shrink to nothing for even a single year, no petrol for the Rolls. Two years, no Rolls. The way I live is an index of the productivity of the companies I've built up.'

'Don't you feel that it's all your personal creation?'

'All what? The world?'

'Your companies.'

'I have a lot of personal pride in what I've done but I hope humour saves me from megalomania.'

'This article says you've got a sneaking admiration for dictatorial methods.'

'As the last surviving member of a family systematically persecuted and eventually annihilated by dictators of various kinds I would take that hard if it weren't so patently ludicrous. One of the reasons why the Left is now ceasing to be a force in British politics is its habit of forgetting that modern European history is not a debating point, it actually happened to people. The ground is full of them.'

Sally followed that line up and got a surprising amount out of him about democracy and liberty, two things which, in her experience, men of his manifest intelligence didn't usually talk about in such unblushing terms. Apparently the first could be a threat to the second if the welfare mentality hardened into ideology, which in the course of time it would tend to do. She said that he sounded like a standard hard-core Tory and he, after reminding her that he had received his knighthood for services to the Labour Party, went on to point out that social democracy everywhere in Europe had been occupied with no other question since 1945. They were given an extra fifteen minutes on top of their first extension and Sally knew it was because everyone upstairs was glued to the monitor. In his quiet way Victor was word perfect and she thought that she had been pretty good too, pushing in hard behind the awkward questions, but as the public's informed representative, not as a pest. Sally Draycott, tribune of the people. *Not As a Wanker*, a novel by Sally Draycott. She was as high as a kite.

'Take this number,' said Victor, while the man was unclipping his microphone, 'and call me about what they decide to do with the tape. I'll be here in the early evening and back in Vienna tomorrow. Now I must get out of here before they inflict hospitality on us both.'

'You've still got your powder on.'

'My driver will think Elena's fancy-dress ball has been moved up. Will you be there?'

'Apparently. God knows what as.'

'Try Catherine the Great. She made torture attractive. Save a dance for an old man.'

'Which old man is that?'

Victor was right to run. Speed Blair emerged from the production gallery doing his full casually triumphant impersonation of the P-51 pilot climbing down from the cockpit after scoring six victories on one trip. 'Great stuff, kid. Fifteen rounds with Hitler. They're crazy about you upstairs. Horace says come up pronto.'

Horace, whose grey hair was so distinguished that there had been talk of giving it a separate knighthood all of its own, told her that she was wonderful. All her interviews were wonderful but this one was particularly wonderful. How wonderful that she should have the inside track, as it were, with such a man as his good friend Victor. It went to prove that she wasn't just intelligent, she was beautiful too, ha ha. So wonderful had the interview been that they would put it out straight away, tonight. Which would mean losing about half of it but that was inevitable. Because there were other things in the programme that could not be shifted. Yes, he understood that she had made promises, but Ludlow would be the first to understand that those were the risks you took. What she must do now was to look to the unswervingly wonderful future. A programme of her own, or almost her own, where there would be no question of such wonderful events being cut down or crowded out. Her own multifariously wonderful current affairs show in the evenings. They must have lunch and discuss it.

By the time Sally got back downstairs to VTR, Speed had already specified the cut and the computerised editing machine was searching for the numbers. Everything about the historical background was being taken out. 'Sorry, love,' said Speed, with every sign of sincerity, 'but it's go tonight or never go, so the best thing to do was to take out the whole chunk. It leaves the actual subject intact except for one little snip. A snipette.'

'And which is that?'

'Count Razoo-whatname. Bit of a sidetrack, that. Otherwise, perfect. Very, very sexy. The MENSA dad and daughter team. *Oh*, yes.'

When Speed gave you every sign of sincerity he left nothing out. There was even the concerned shaking of the head and the gentle encirclement of your quaking shoulders with the chaste arm. Sally restrained herself from strangling him. If she hadn't had the nerve to throttle Horace, there would be no merit in terminating his lickspittle subordinate. Who wasn't so bad, when you considered how many of the others were so very much worse.

Waiting alone in the large open-plan current affairs office until Nicholas should call at reception and pick her up, she tried ringing Victor, although he could hardly be home yet.

'What did they decide?'

'How did you get there so fast?'

'I'm still in the car looking at the back of a 27 bus.'

'They're running it tonight and taking out all that marvellous stuff about the EEC and the German trade unions. Everything that gives it depth. I'm so ashamed of myself I hardly dare speak to you. It was my fault for giving them so much to cut. I should have stopped.'

'But there won't be any trick editing inside what's left?'

'No, they won't do that. They're not dishonest. Just crass.'

'Good. Every man you ever meet tries to buy you lunch, I expect.'

'All except one.'

'You're heavily committed to young Mr Crane, I understand.'

'Yes.'

'But you owe me an apology.'

'Yes.'

'I'll be back in London as from Monday. Would you lunch with me at the house some time next week?'

'Yes.'

'And did you make a rendezvous?' asked Elena later that same night.

'She wanted to apologise.'

'I should think so. She was at you like an interrogator.'

'That's what she was supposed to be. And she did it very well. If she writes anything it should be for me. And if I go into TV production she could be very valuable.'

'And when is it to take place, this famous meeting of mutual guidance?'

'Next week perhaps. I give her lunch, listen to her plans, make some comments and she goes away. And that's all.' He reached for a lamp switch but she stopped him. There was already far too much light making its way from mirror to mirror, spilling between the heaped cushions. Not that she had much to fear from being compared with a mere child.

'Leave that off, please. Will you ring me when you get home?'

'Of course.' Taken literally, the Italian phrase means 'without anything else', so it had an automatic air of falsity. By now they both knew there was something else. The mere possibility was enough.

'Because I don't think I'll sleep tonight.'

'Don't be silly.'

For his last night in Los Angeles, Lancelot was invited to Randall Hoyle's housewarming. To this he was able to bring Samantha, who was very glad of it, because Randall Hoyle's housewarming was one of the events of that California year. You could be sure of that because it had also been one of the events of every previous year since Randall Hoyle had taken up residence in the Hollywood hills. He believed in redecorating and rewarming his house annually, as if it were the stage setting for a play featuring his wide range of prominent acquaintances, who periodically assembled so that he could get drunk and insult them.

Randall Hoyle was a screenwriter so famous that he was billed above the title in the possessive case. *Randall Hoyle's Sejanus* was thus distinguished from Ben Jonson's and *Randall Hoyle's Wallenstein* from Schiller's or Golo Mann's. Many a doomed project was taken all the way to a second draft so that Randall Hoyle could sit around his pool with the young actor under consideration and dote on his powerful thighs. Hoyle's own thighs were quite shapely in their own right but that was because his whole body was a cosmetic rebuild, like his house, which was radiating white light from every shrub when Lancelot and Samantha arrived in Yonky's spare Toyota. Samantha was getting hard to impress but she could not help gaping when she saw the first roomful of faces. She recognised them all. Anyone whose face you didn't know at one of Hoyle's parties was probably a Nobel prizewinner or something.

So Lancelot had scored a point. The previous evening he had seen boredom on Samantha's face and it had struck him like finding blood in his sputum. But it was not there now. He left her with some agent she knew – you could tell he was an agent because he looked like an actor – and went to remind the world's most famous young female film star of his existence. Once more 'Zoom' Beispiel was at her elbow. Without hesitation she made a date for dinner in London, stunning him by saying that her husband was an admirer of his work. What work? She couldn't have been sweeter. Lancelot came away absurdly hoping that Samantha had been a witness to his casual intimacy with the great, but it turned out that she was doing a bit of that herself. She was with the celebrated actor, who was smiling at something she was saying. Distracted by his perpetually bared teeth, Lancelot missed his name again. Stoke Boiler? Stiff Cheese?

'Hey,' purred Stoke through his smile, leaning against a wall that wasn't there. 'This little lady of yours was *great* in Vegas.'

'She was?' asked Lancelot. Samantha had not mentioned Stiff's presence in Las Vegas, but the fact that she betrayed no disturbance now was clear proof that everything must have been above board.

'I'm *telling* you,' smiled Stoke, 'never bet on *anything*

without asking her first. She has *radar*, this girl.'

'I know,' said Lancelot. 'I've alw . . . '

'I think I'll go in the pool now,' said Stiff. The pool was in the middle of the house. As the celebrated actor floated in it fully dressed and face up, Lancelot and Samantha were among the many people looking down at his smile.

'You'll be back very soon, now, won't you?' asked Lancelot, trying not to sound plaintive.

'Next week at the latest. Christ knows what I'll do for a living.' It was the ideal time to offer her the Gillian Jackson project.

'By now it's urgent,' said Lancelot, 'so you'd practically be on salary. And you'll do it standing on your head. You're just right for it.'

'Meaning I'm aggressive.'

'And you're aggressive. I've already got a few bedizened dowagers lined up that you could talk to before you left. Your lover just sank.'

'He can breathe underwater. It's some Indian thing. He learned it on an ashlar.'

'An ashram. You didn't answer the question.'

'He physically wouldn't be able to, honestly. He's so high he lost interest in all that years ago.'

'You're almost as high and you haven't.'

'That's because it's you.'

'You'd better get your daughter some plastic wrinkles and a grey wig,' whispered Randall Hoyle in passing. 'Remember what happened to Polanski.'

~ fifteen ~

Back in London after a sleepless flight, Lancelot went to bed for the day, but left the phone on the hook in case Samantha rang up later. Everybody except her did.

'You got shag-lag?' asked Nicholas.

'Yen. Mustab. Florfl.'

'Better get some sleep. Sounds like Sam fucked you flat. She come back with you?'

'Still there. Change of plan. Home soon.'

'I'll leave you alone. Watch out for Delilah. She's sniffing about. See you at lunch Friday.'

Lancelot went back to a sleep punctuated by the barking of dogs. Delilah was, in fact, next on the line.

'Can I speak to Mrs Windhover, please?'

'Slancelot. Zat you, De l'Isle?'

'Sorry, I thought you were the Chinese gardener or something. Are you ill? I was just calling to check up on something with Charlotte.'

'Check up on what?' said Lancelot, suddenly fully alert.

'Just a thing. But while I've got you, I'm doing a profile on Samantha Copperglaze and all the other bright young beauties. You know, the girls with the gold credit cards and the Think Tank brains. Did you see her in Hollywood?'

'Socially.'

'Where? In what circumstances?'

'Look, Delilah, she's just a trend, just a friend and I can't talk now.'

'Do you think she'll be at Elena Fiabesco's opera ball thing?'

'I don't know. You'll have to wait and see.'

'I haven't been invited.'

'Sounds as if you'll have to crash.'

Getting rid of her was like trying to clean up hot fat with a cloth soaked in cold water, but eventually he got her off the phone. Apart from the occasional dog fight there was peace until the early afternoon, which would have been Lancelot's interior morning if he had got any sleep on the plane. Then Anthony rang.

'You aren't *still* asleep?' It wasn't a real question.

'Not now, no. What is it?'

'There's been a hitch about Virginia,' Anthony said happily.

'Who's Virginia? Don't understand.'

'Our secretary. The one we're getting rid of to ease the cash-flow problem.'

'Oh yes. Right. Got it.'

'She needs six months' notice and a day's pay for every week of service.'

'I thought she was some sort of temp.'

'She's got a union,' laughed Anthony, 'who are threatening to take us to an industrial tribunal and beyond that to the International Court of Human Rights in The Hague.'

'I thought people like that didn't know how to apply for their own child endowment allowances.'

'This one does,' chortled Anthony. 'If you get one that can spell, you get one that knows Robert Mugabe personally.'

'Can we afford this?'

'Have to. We've got off lightly, it seems. If they wanted to enforce the rule strictly they could have asked for a week's pay for every day of service plus chauffeured car for life and a fully catered funeral in Trinidad.'

Not even this news could stop Lancelot from going back to sleep. Down he went below the level of elliptical nightmares into the long tunnel of Arabic script and random imagery, where the Japanese hook made its bitchy squeal, green numbers accumulated in the debit column, your car was never repaired, dogs barked far away, smiling squash-players laughed at you limping and the telephone rang as if it couldn't wait. As if it was real. It was. It was Janice, ringing from the office.

Lancelot felt that his head had been crammed into an angry policeman's loud-hailer, but after he had persuaded her to put the telephone on the desk and stand back a bit, he began to understand that she was putting Frank Strain through. Frank came through to tell him, in a few thousand clumsily chosen words, that his application to have his tax case reviewed by the commissioners had been rejected out of hand. The person doing the rejecting, apparently, was the inspector who had reclassified him in the first place. Something about this struck Lancelot as unfair but he could not concentrate, partly because Frank's sentences were very long and partly because he felt very weak. Either he had gone from the debilitating condition of not having had enough sleep to the even more debilitating condition of having had too much sleep, or else he had not had enough sleep. He promised to see Frank first thing next day, if next day was the day that came after this one.

He fell half asleep and stayed that way until one or more of the children came home and made noises that brought him half awake. Then Charlotte rang to say she was going to the opera at the Coliseum with somebody called David but that Mrs Hammerklavier would cook him something for his dinner if he wanted it. He thought of going downstairs and saying that was what he wanted but didn't see how he could do that without moving. So he had a bit of a doze. Towards midnight he woke up definitively, all set to face a brand new night.

~ sixteen ~

Lunch was at a table beside the pool. When Sally arrived, Victor's manservant Galtieri was setting out the wine glasses and the tumblers. Victor, who had probably heard the 928 crunch to a stop on the gravel of the outside courtyard, made himself manifest just as Sally was circumnavigating the pool. They shook hands like two near-strangers at the start of a business meeting, an impression reinforced by Victor's suit, which although light in weight was formally at odds with the setting. Sally was in a sort of thin pale biscuit overall which managed to look shapeless and well cut at the same time. She liked the way he did not give her an appreciative glance. Maturity, she reflected, is what they *don't* do. Why did it take me so long to notice that? Because I was immature.

'You look like a paratrooper from the Mount Olympus Defence Regiment,' said Victor. 'I suppose I should have climbed into my seersucker slacks and worn a Hawaiian shirt outside the pants. It's a bit of a package holiday out here.'

'It's perfect,' said Sally. 'Why go inside on a day like this?' This struck her as a stupid remark even before she uttered it.

'Especially when this might be the only day like this. You sit over there and let me do the squinting into the pitiless tropical sun. Actually I might well have greeted you in snorkel and flippers but at 3.30 I have to be somewhere else and if I'm dressed to go there then at least it gives me a few more minutes with you.' This must be a nice way of telling her that she wouldn't have to worry about being dragged into his lair for a post-prandial grapple. And indeed the conversation could not have been less burdened with hidden meaning. Clearly he was interested in her, but it was like an archbishop's representative, or the archbishop himself, trying to compile a report on the younger generation. Except, of course, that no cleric could have been so un-weird, so definitely not a wimp in a cassock. She found herself explaining what a provincial university was really like and how she had left journalism for television when she found that journalists who wrote tripe got paid more for less work, because tripe could be written more quickly. He didn't pretend to have read much of what she had written but said that he had heard it had been very thorough. She liked the way he did not pretend.

'I'm sorry for the interrogation,' he said eventually. 'We must get out of the habit of interviewing each other.'

'It's the television age.'

'Don't think I'm not aware of it. Fairly soon now a lot of book publishers will have to think about going into the video cassette market. It's a logical step from that to making their own programmes.'

'Have you any idea what that would cost?'

'Some idea, but not as good an idea as you. Would you consider giving me some advice?'

'If I didn't already have a contract.'

'This would in no way interfere with that. All I do is ask you the odd question. And one day, perhaps, you come and work for me. When you're sick of being famous.'

'You don't have to promise any rewards. Anything I know already I'll certainly tell you as long as it's not a house secret.'

'How do you know I'm not just looking for a cast iron excuse to seek your company?'

'Do you need a cast iron excuse?'

'It's a censorious world.'

'More fool it.'

You couldn't call it flirting, thought Sally, but it was something remarkably similar. Intimacy without innuendo? And it was catching. The late spring air helped. Or didn't help, depending on your viewpoint. What was her viewpoint? It was early summer. He had a knack for starting up a separate history which both of you inhabited, outside the real one. Even to establish where they stood would sound like a declaration of intent. After all, nothing had happened.

'You asked me whether it was a serious matter between me and Nicholas,' she said.

'Yes, I did. And you told me it was.'

'You and Elena are very close, aren't you?'

'Extremely. For many years.'

'I don't believe a man could be anything else except totally involved with a woman like that.'

'You'd be right. But total involvement becomes self-defeating if one loses touch altogether with the rest of the world.' Pick the bones out of that.

When he walked her to the car their footsteps on the gravel made them laugh. Their footsteps were self-conscious but the laughter was not. All kinds of numbers and addresses had been exchanged and put in diaries. They were in touch. If it was a pretext, she was glad it was a believable pretext. But she supposed that even if he was bent on possessing her, it was her whole personality he valued. She almost wished his interest were Platonic, it was so deliciously novel to be fully appreciated. No she didn't. She trickled the 928 into motion so as not to squirt gravel on the yellow roses. In the rear-view mirror she could see him standing there looking, hands in pockets. He was overweight all right. When she raised a hand without turning her head he just inclined his forehead and shrugged in a way that said he didn't know what the younger generation was coming to. The younger generation is coming to you, she thought. On its hands and knees, you sly old bastard.

'Hands and knees,' said Dick Toole, matching up Delilah's pose to the picture in the catalogue. It was afternoon outside but they had the blinds down and the lights on. 'Get your knees further *apart.*' She was a bit slow on the draw today.

This is an extremely erotic leisure playsuit, said the catalogue, *and we won't take responsibility for what happens when you put it on! Cast a tantalising spell over him in this ravishing creation styled in sensuous nylon and trilobal satin! The saucy bra has arousing peepholes for full nipple appeal while the daring panties offer a delicious open-crotch invitation!* Actually this catalogue wasn't as good as some of the magazines he had, but the girls were better. Scrubbers but not slags.

'OK,' said Dick Toole. 'Hold it there.'

'Lancelot and Samantha were an item in Los Angeles,' said

Delilah.

'Openly flouting her, was he?'

'He was scared she'd gone Hollywood. Anyway, she's back here now, working for him.'

'Nespotism,' said Dick Toole. 'He'll keep. Shut up for a minute.' He'd come to a particularly good page of the catalogue. *This one is the most exotic suspender-brief contribution in our range*, he read. *Ravishing frilly belt and stunning see-through rose coloured maneating crotch piece, plus the added excitement of having only a thin elasticated strip at the back to hold everything in place – phew!*

'Try putting your hands behind your back again,' said Dick Toole.

'It hurts like hell.'

'That's the whole idea, you great prat.' She was *really* slow today.

'Slow today,' said the man in the garage to Lancelot, thus explaining why he was available. 'You've a geezer what owns a pew, Joe?'

'Mm? Oh. Yes.'

'Nice motor, VAT pew, Joe.'

Lancelot agreed that the Peugeot was indeed a nice motor and wondered aloud when he could have his own particular example of the marque restored to his possession. They stood there looking at it. Nothing appeared to have happened to it, apart from what had happened to it on the day it had been vandalised.

'Been a hold-up,' said the man, with surprising clarity. Lancelot could well believe it. The man, whom Lancelot did not remember having seen the last time he was there, looked as if he conducted hold-ups for a living. All he needed was the stocking mask and the sawn-off shotgun. Elsewhere in the garage, other men sat around smoking, obviously waiting to be summoned into the prefabricated office so that the latest plan to blag a payroll could be sketched out on the back of a Unipart calendar. But in the course of a difficult conversation it transpired that the firm had gone through a change of ownership and some jobs had had to be put to the end of the list. Lancelot could rest assured, however, that in a matter of weeks he would once again be in possession of his pew, Joe.

So, as a fitful succession of warmish days began palming
itself off as summer, Lancelot took to getting himself about on a
bicycle. It belonged to his son Toby and thus had first to be
divested of various irrelevant decorations, but it had a very
useful set of five-speed gears. Lancelot had not many hills to
negotiate going to and from work, but starting off from the
traffic lights would have put unacceptable strain on his still
valetudinary buttocks, so it helped to have a gear sufficiently
low that he could get the bike into motion with almost no
pressure at all, if he did not mind his legs temporarily becoming
a whirling blur of activity. Samantha was a bit of a strain on the
buttocks too, what with one thing and another, but as a ghost
interviewer she was throwing herself into the task. On many an
occasion Lancelot found reason to visit her in her basement flat
with the small sunken paved garden where he could lounge
about feasting his eyes on her as she sat in jeans and blouse
typing at an old wrought iron pub table painted white. As he had
predicted, the famous ladies were obviously finding her the
ideal confidante: while intellect usually has only a sneaking
respect for money, money's respect for intellect is open and
unashamed. He could hardly believe some of the stuff she was
getting. Who would have thought that even the notoriously
indiscreet Sewanee Phu Sok, for example, would ever pass on
her secrets about how to keep half a dozen lovers on a string at
once? And yet there it all was in Samantha's notes. She had soon
abandoned the tape recorder as too inhibiting. All she did was
talk to them and write it all down afterwards from her fresh,
young memory. Making her read it all out helped fill the
silences. Not that he had anything to worry about on that score.
It was, of course, inevitable that she should feel caged, but there
was nothing unspoken between them.

There was nothing unspoken between them, but on one subject
they had tacitly agreed to touch only fleetingly.

'I'm having your Mr Crane and Black and White to the
country next weekend,' said Elena, 'if you think you can spare
her from your consultations.'

'There have been no consultations.'

'Not yet.'

'When there are consultations, they will be consultations.' They were speaking English, always a sign of incomplete ease.

'You've convinced me. Will you be able to come up at all?'

'Perhaps Saturday afternoon?'

'Perfect. On the Sunday we have the German ambassador for dinner. Also the Windhovers, if he can tear himself away from London.'

'I'm told that the girl is now working for me.'

'I wouldn't expect great things from that. Lancelot begged me to let her ask some questions but after half an hour I had to show her the door very firmly. She was no better than a journalist. So nervous, all that brightness of hers. I think she has bad habits.' It was another delicate subject. In the decade before last, Victor's daughter had died from bad habits.

'You could always ask Charlotte to come along,' said Victor. 'I like seeing her.'

'She has a young man which one day might be a romance, after she's asked my advice a few more hundred times. A prospective author of yours called David Whosis.'

'The incorruptible young radical. I've put off lunching with him for weeks but tomorrow it finally happens.'

'It finally happens,' thought David, crunching through the gravel of the courtyard after a circuitous and often seriously aberrant walk from the tube station. 'The very big lunch.'

Apparently it was to take place beside the pool, where a swarthy man built like a domestic boiler was laying a small table. Victor, who had probably been informed of David's arrival by closed-circuit television or an AWACS overhead, made himself manifest just as David was circumnavigating the pool. They shook hands like two near-strangers at the start of a business meeting, an impression reinforced by Victor's suit, which although light in weight was formally at odds with the setting, not to mention with the hulking bulk of the whacked-out weightlifter inside it. David had tried on the plain new blue suit which Charlotte had quietly egged him on to buy but after an uncomfortable few minutes of feeling like a traitor to his values he had reverted to his usual Red Army Faction summer walking-out dress. He regretted having shaved his face more thoroughly than usual, but there was no way back, apart from glueing some of the tufts back on.

'I see you've been sensible and dressed to suit the weather,' said Victor. 'I suppose I should have climbed into my seersucker slacks and worn a Hawaiian shirt outside the pants. It's a bit of a package holiday out here.'

'No complaints,' said David. 'Why go inside on a day like this?' This struck him as a needlessly compliant remark even before he uttered it.

'Especially when this might be the only day like this. You sit over there and let me do the squinting into the pitiless tropical sun. Actually I might well have greeted you in snorkel and flippers but at 2.30 I have to be somewhere else and if I'm dressed to go there at least it gives me a few more minutes with you.' This must be a nice way of telling him that every moment was valuable. And indeed the conversation could not have been more to the point.

'Whatever course you take as a writer, I think we should publish you. So this discussion isn't about that. The offer's there if you want it. But for my private satisfaction, how do you see your work developing?'

'Towards novels, I should think. Is that what you mean?'

'I mean do you intend sticking to the line you've been taking about the imminent collapse of civilisation in the West?'

'I'd certainly find the bourgeois frame of mind artistically very restricting. I mean on top of being politically just plain wrong.'

'That's what Karl Kraus thought about Schnitzler. He thought that Schnitzler's little world of comfort and adultery couldn't possibly be of any lasting interest. But that little world turned out to be the only one that mattered in the long run. People were literally dying to get back to it. By the millions.'

'I just think the liberal viewpoint is essentially self-serving.'

'Liberal values are the only kind there are.'

'There we'd have to differ.'

'We've been differing since about 1789. It's a perennial disagreement. But as long as we know where we stand.'

'I'm not sure,' said David, 'whether I know where *you* stand at all. You and people like you have seen this precious civilisation you talk about collapsing all around you for as long as anyone can remember. What has it ever done to protect you?'

'That's an argument for reinforcing it, not replacing it. Radical politics wants too much. Right or left, they all want too much. They want what they can't have. They think they can imagine what life should be like.'

'Isn't that what the imagination's for?'

'It's a failure of the imagination. Freud used to say that if you could manage to reduce the number of civilisation's enemies to a minority, you would have done all that was possible.'

'It sounds like pretty comfortable advice.'

'Well, he did die here in Hampstead, which I suppose is comfortable enough. But then so did Marx, more or less.'

'Or else it's a counsel of despair.'

'Despair comes with disillusionment. The great thing is not to have illusions in the first place. Being a Viennese Jew of Freud's generation was a great education in the realities of human nature. Like being an Athenian during the Peloponnesian war. Have you read Thucydides?'

'He's on my list. Along with Schnitzler and Karl Kraus.'

'My Greek isn't up to him so I've always read him in German. There's an excellent eighteenth-century translation. Do you read German?'

'That's on my list too.'

'Otherwise I'd lend you mine.'

'I'll get the Penguin. But I don't think it's going to change my mind. I'm well aware of how minds get changed, by the way. The studious life has a great appeal for me. I'm not saying that civilisation isn't *civilised*. Only that it isn't fair.'

But what, Victor argued, if the alternatives were less so, and necessarily less so? The altercation went on for the whole of the allotted time. As full of dates as an Arab pudding – 1968, 1917, 1905, 1870, 1848 – to David it felt like a supremely taxing *viva voce*, except that no English examiner, whatever his class origins, would have been so unselfconscious about discussing ideas. David couldn't decide whether this was because Victor was a South African Australian or because he was Jewish. Perhaps it was both. Anyway, it was catching. For example,

Victor thought that a provincial university background was a positive advantage for an English writer at the present time. He could, and did, back up this proposition with a wealth of historical examples about the strength of the outside viewpoint in various aspects of European culture. David found himself being compared with Berlioz in Rome, with Modigliani in Paris, with Lorca in New York. Even when you knew you were being buttered up, it was quite nice to be compared with Berlioz, Modigliani and Lorca. He was angry with himself, however, for being caught out about Picasso. Praising him as an uncorrupted radical had turned out to be a mistake, if Victor was right about how Picasso disguised his chauffeur as a taxi driver by making him wear a beret and not letting him shave. Perhaps he could borrow a good book about Picasso's life from Charlotte. It was going to be a bit awkward facing Lancelot, even though nothing had happened. Being issued with a reading list scarcely amounted to intimacy. Except that it was. Gaga had been very annoyed. Still was, in fact.

–

~ seventeen ~

Lancelot and David both arrived at lunch on time, which left them face to face until the others started straggling in. Possible embarrassment of one kind was immediately turned by Lancelot into definite embarrassment of another kind. 'I think your friendship with my wife is a positively splendid notion and I approve of it utterly.'

'Thanks.'

'Men in my position quite often harbour the guilty hope that their wives will get interested in someone else and so ease the burden on the conscience, but I actually do admire her so much and want the best for her, and of course she's just overcome with admiration for someone as talented as yourself.'

'Thanks again.'

'She has the right to an emotional life too and by this time it could be said that she has more than a right. Why should I have all the adventures? What I'm saying is, if it comes to a real affair, I'd fully understand.'

'I think I'll start with the avocado and prawns.'

Nicholas arrived carrying a bottle of champagne, which he gave to the waitress so that she might put it on ice for later. He was celebrating the publication of his new novel, all about a barrister who murders, by unspeakably hideous means, his novelist wife and their large brood of children. He buries them all in the garden and then writes a novel, all about a barrister who, etc. The novel's reception had been tumultuous, with even the irascible Paula Thorax proclaiming herself satisfied. In one of the literary fortnightlies there was a long article by Peter C. Bartelski (of Sydney, Sussex, and Sidney Sussex College, Cambridge) proving that Nicholas's sense of structure was governed by the geographical layout of London. Nicholas's novels, argued Bartelski, were multicentred, with areas of dense lexical congestion alternating unpredictably with open parkland. The most brilliant caricaturist had drawn Nicholas for one of the glossies. The drawing included a long-legged beauty languishing with adoration in the background. Obviously it was not meant to look like Sally, but you could make the connection if you were in the know. Nicholas was pretending to be angry with the most brilliant caricaturist over this, and made a point of sitting at the other end of the table from him. But the literary editors, when they arrived, busily fell to discussing the catastrophic effect on Fleet Street of Australian press ownership. The Australian poets, in their turn, wanted to know what was so marvellous about Fleet Street that it needed preserving from their admittedly rapacious countrymen. The noise level was already high when Thinwall arrived, looking forward to his first really serious drink of the afternoon. He was in a white suit, to denote the official beginning of summer. Grouped around its crotch were some spectacular pink stains, caused at breakfast by his having clutched a bottle of wine between his knees and drawn its cork with undue verve. 'Lancelot, dear man,' he cried joyfully. 'Just saw Sam in the Caram. What have you been doing to her? She looks good enough to eat me.' But Lancelot didn't want to answer, because standing just behind Thinwall was Delilah.

'Don't worry, I'm not staying,' she said to Lancelot, although the remark might equally have been addressed to the table in general, since almost every man sitting at it had suddenly taken to looking thoughtful, before engaging as stridently as possible in conversation about any topic that might happen to be going. 'I just wanted to give you this advance copy of the magazine with Charlotte's Ideal Table thing in it. You could give it to her in the country. Are you going up this weekend?'

'I'll make sure that she gets it,' said Lancelot noncommittally.

'I hear Samantha's research is coming on very well.'

'Really? Is that what you hear?'

'I just told her in the Carambar, she ought to interview Charlotte.'

'It's an idea,' said Lancelot, not specifying what kind of idea it was. Luckily everybody else was talking over this. Everybody except Nicholas, who was looking relieved, probably because it was happening to someone else.

'Why on earth did you bring *her*?' asked Lancelot, when Delilah had gone away after a long spell of standing there being not asked to sit down.

'She attaches herself to one's soft white underbelly like a remora,' said Thinwall, for whom the expression 'no whit abashed' had been invented. 'Never mind.'

'It's a miracle you haven't read all about yourself by now,' said Nicholas.

'My one consolation,' said Lancelot, not wholly without regret. 'The longer nothing happens, the more it proves I'm not news. Obscurity makes me invulnerable.'

With so many mouths waiting for it the champagne was only a gesture, but wine foundations had been well laid, and besides, even if you envied Nicholas you couldn't help enjoying his exuberance. It was clear that he would go on turning out a novel a year for ever, that his novels would be enjoyed by impressionable youth as well as being found important by Paula Thorax and Peter C. Bartelski, that pretty young females would make a meal of him and that he would breathe success like air. Good luck to you, thought Lancelot, meaning it. Anyway, Lancelot rather liked this new conception of himself as an old hand who would be wise among shadows. And he had the house to himself for the weekend. He could call Samantha over. All the children were going to the country with his wife – mainly, it appeared, because David would be there. At an opportune moment, as the Dregs were all dispersing, Lancelot took a quick look at the relevant pages of the magazine. Not only were the photographs quite good but the article, headed A DREME OF ACADEME, was free from innuendo, offensive only for being composed in that slovenly manner by which the interviewer puts quotation marks around scribbled notes and attributes the results to the interviewee. 'Here,' he said to David, 'perhaps you'd better take this.'

'Thanks.' Nobody saw them except Nicholas. And Thinwall, of course.

If David had been sitting on the other side of the train on Saturday morning he might have seen Sally and Nicholas heading in the same direction. Even though ideologically committed to second class travel, David would scarcely have avoided a pang of regret that he was not travelling with them. But they did not know he was going to stay with Charlotte; he did not know they were going to stay with Elena; and anyway the Porsche, though it made provision for two passengers in the back seat, required that those two passengers should be either without legs or else content to travel long distances in the lotus position. At least the train was physically more comfortable than that. Psychologically, however, it imposed a certain amount of wear and tear even if you had a political obligation to your fellow commoners. The woman in the seat opposite David, besides being ugly almost beyond belief, had a strange twitch, rather like – although occurring silently and at a slower tempo – that rare syndrome in which the helpless victim quacks like a duck while looking around in all directions. She continually twisted around to stare at various strangers in the carriage one at a time, as if tacitly accusing them of some misdemeanour. Meanwhile her two children, obviously well used to this behaviour, got on with consuming several examples each of those terrible multicoloured ice-creams from which the metallised wrapping paper can be separated only with difficulty, whereupon the cone explodes all too easily into the vicinity, leaving the ice-cream free to run all over the fingers, the clothes, the seat and the appalled spectators. Burying his head as best he could in the Penguin Thucydides, David survived, only to find the same family sitting near him on the bus at the other end. The bus ride took at least as long as the train ride. Meanwhile Sally's car had long ago arrived in front of Elena's house and was cooling down to the temperature of the ambient air. An occasional click emanated from its precisely machined engine block, that monument to Teutonic intolerance.

Nicholas did quite of lot of showing off on the diving board that afternoon. He could do somersaults. At a cane table bearing iced tea, Elena and Sally sat watching, Sally with a sarong over her one-piece costume and Elena also looking rather East Asian, with a cotton halter, baggy trousers and a low-pitched conical straw hat.

'So clever,' said Elena. 'Such complicated ways they have of getting into the water.'

'He's competitive,' said Sally. 'At the moment he's competing against gannets and otters.'

'Perhaps he's competing against your brilliance at the wheel.'

'Wasn't your husband a racing driver?'

'He thought he was. It was the only sport you could play that was so expensive it took all your money no matter how much you had, and he had quite a lot.'

'Did he do well?'

'He was the best of the amateurs. Not in the grand whatsit. In the sports whosis.'

'Racing sports cars. What kind?'

'I can never remember. Red ones.'

'Ferraris?'

'Those. After we separated he did a season full time. Finally he was killed in the big race that used to go all the way around Sicily.'

'The Targa Florio.'

'Exactly. Backwards off the road he went and took a whole family of peasants with him. Not a wise place to have a picnic.'

Nicholas was going backwards off the board at that very moment. Sally shaded her eyes to watch him reach up and touch his toes, then open out with an arched back and glide in, moving slightly slower than seemed credible. If only bodies were everything.

Bodies are everything, thought Elena, as Sally unwrapped herself and walked towards the pool, from which the surfacing Nicholas transmitted a startling imitation of a rutting walrus. Having looked after yourself was something to be pleased about, but not having to induced a fine carelessness. Elena left them to it and headed for the house, in which the phone was ringing. It was Charlotte, asking if she could bring David to dinner the next evening. Of course she could. In fact she should bring him over in the afternoon and help him relax before the boredom started. The conversation lasted some time and Victor arrived before it was over. From the window of the guest room on the first floor they could see the young people in the water.

'She's too pretty for words,' said Elena.

'Pretty but not lovely,' said Victor with his arm around her.

The air split as a Stratotanker, invisible from where they were standing, went over somewhere nearby. In the pool, the two young people stood looking towards the source of the noise.

'I've put them in adjoining rooms upstairs so they can make their own arrangements,' said Elena when they could hear each other again. 'Also I don't want you bumping into them on the landing.'

'Is it just us four for dinner?'

'Tonight, yes. And then tomorrow all those others. With Charlotte bringing her young man David.'

'He's against civilisation.'

'Well, he won't get much of it here. There's practically nothing to eat except a few dead birds.'

Dinner that night was hilarious. Nicholas improvised freely on the theme of Lancelot's slavish adoration for Samantha and the spiritual indignities it had cost him, along with a growing subjection to bodily pains, strains and ailments. Elena would have been grateful to hear this theme pursued even had the results been dull, but Nicholas made it almost too funny to be borne. He had to get out of his chair to imitate Lancelot dancing. The wine glasses chimed softly as he hopped about. Most of Victor's stories featured Elena as part of the scenery, which was a good thing too. By the end of the evening they were all sufficiently at home with one another to share that most intimate of all possible conclusions to a dinner party – they turned on the television, catching the last item in the late night news before the horror film started.

' . . . *breaking* the *front windows*,' said the face of the second most popular female newsreader, 'and *relieving* themselves *into* the car's *interior. Police spokesmen have described* it as more of a *craze* than a *crime. Some* drivers have *re-equipped* the *front seats* of their cars with the same *polythene covers* they arrived *wrapped* in *from* the *showroom*. But *apart* from *that*, it looks like going *on* being a *dry weekend*.'

The film was one of those not very horrifying British horror films in which two young people in a sports car arrive at a haunted house. Nicholas supplied an excellent running commentary for the first reel and then yawned. He preferred American horror films in which people cut each other up with

177

power saws. So the young people went to bed.

'No pangs?' asked Elena later on.

'Don't be silly,' said Victor, but when he got back to his room he lay awake for a long time, reading. Whereas Elena just lay awake.

'Are you going to be all right down here?' asked Charlotte, who had made sure her dressing gown was well done up. 'You can read quite comfortably in your room, you know.'

'I'll be fine,' said David. The books in the mill house were not as impressively massed and classified as in the house in London but some of them were fascinating, a type of light reading he had never before encountered. He had selected a small stack to browse amongst into the small hours. Charlotte had pushed a sort of squat, wheeled, chintz-covered square cushion effect under his extended stockinged feet. He looked up from the open pages of a small book of Disraeli's letters to smile goodnight.

'Are you sure they won't disturb you?' Charlotte added, but it was just an excuse to linger for a further moment. The children, each transfixed by a separate set of stereo headphones, were variously distributed amongst heaps of cushions on the floor, taking his presence carefully for granted.

Breakfast started so late that everybody agreed to call it lunch. 'There's just the bacon and the eggs and the mushrooms and the toast,' said Elena apologetically, 'and then I might throw some of these croissants at you, unless you want some muffins to go with this rather disgusting quince jelly.'

'Mpf,' said Nicholas, waving a finger. 'Thif morf narf.'

'He means this is more than enough,' Sally translated. Victor worked his way through the Sunday papers, in which almost every feature writer had at some time been contracted to write a book for him. He agreed to play tennis with Nicholas as long as it was understood that Nicholas must hit the ball straight to him. Actually Victor, when he did hit the ball, was not all that bad.

'You must have been a devil in your day,' said Nicholas patronisingly.

'Drobny thought so,' said Victor.

'So did Borotnik,' called Elena from the sidelines.

'Borotra,' said Victor. 'If you're going to make cheap jokes at least get the name right.'

'Nicholas wants me to marry him,' said Sally.

'What do you want to do?' asked Elena.

'Everyone asks your advice, don't they?'

'It's because they think I know what I'm doing. Actually I don't. It's just that I don't talk about myself. Which looks like self-possession.'

'So people try to tap your secret.'

'They want confirmation. Advice is the last thing they want. It might go against their interests. I let them go on and on talking until they make their minds up and then I agree with them.'

'I don't want to get married.'

'Then don't.'

'*You* did.'

'It was a hundred years ago and you can't possibly imagine how different my life was from yours. There was nothing resembling freedom for women in Italy then. There were no trials, only errors. My father was a rich old fool so I rebelled by getting married to a rich young fool. Disaster.'

'What happened?'

'Everything. At least I didn't do as badly as my poor demented sister. *She* rebelled with a rich young communist who eventually got himself killed trying to bomb a post office. As if an Italian post office needed any more confusion.'

'And you were separated.'

'Eventually. Luckily. Amid scenes you wouldn't credit. Then I came here, away from the hysteria. And I brought up my poor sister's son, who thank God is normal and unremarkable and soon getting married to a girl just like himself. So all the adventures in our family are now over.'

'I don't suppose there's much point asking you of all people.'

'Asking what?'

'If there was ever anyone you wanted that you couldn't have.'

'Lots of point. I know all about it. If the gentleman wants the lady as much as the lady wants the gentleman, it happens. The only question is how, when and for how long.'

Charlotte and David arrived walking about three feet apart. David proved to be a surprisingly good tennis opponent for Nicholas, thereby mightily relieving Victor, who had done his dash. Then Elena and Charlotte picked early strawberries while Victor went up to read and the others swam. When the German ambassador arrived everybody was still flopping around half dressed. Elena had told him to be as informal as possible so he had brought only one car-load of security men with him. They disappeared into the woods in order to stake out the possible approach routes for terrorists along the pathways lined with Queen Anne's lace and flowering hawthorn. The ambassador's wife was clad in peasant garb, which indicated a somewhat oppressive determination to join in the fun, but in the event she turned out to be quite sociable. Taking place by candlelight amongst crystal and silver, the dinner table conversation was mainly in English out of deference to Nicholas and David, although Sally, without really meaning to, hugely impressed the ambassador by knowing as much as he did about Büchner. At university she had played the third whore from the right in the worst ever student production of *Danton's Death*. David tried making a few sharp remarks about the Economic Miracle but it soon became evident that the ambassador's trade union background was beyond reproach. As well as the deep things that were said, there were quite a few funny ones, but the mood had changed. It wasn't the sort of evening you could watch television at the end of. Elena, though looking particularly sumptuous in a scoop-necked dark dress that would have left her head and shoulders floating disembodied had not the emphasis on her *décolletage* been such a reminder, especially to the smitten *Botschafter*, of the famed figure extending into the darkness below, was slightly subdued, and everybody else caught it. Most of them did not spot the source of the sobriety, but Charlotte, who was watching her hostess closely to see if she approved of David, did. Charlotte had never seen Elena look so passive. Instead of leading the conversation, she was following it. But David had enjoyed the day, that was the main thing.

'The girl adores you,' said Elena later. 'She told me.'

'Come on,' said Victor. 'She told you nothing of the kind.'

'She didn't have to tell me.'

'So that's what she told you.'

In a room above them, Nicholas was near tears. They seemed to be fighting more and more often. He hadn't expected to care so much. Or rather, he hadn't expected caring to hurt so much. More accurately, he'd rather looked forward to the hurt of caring but hadn't expected to *dislike* it so much.

'I'm not asking you not to be interested in what they say,' he said. 'Just not to forget I exist when they say it.'

'Who's ever forgotten that you exist? How would it be possible? You'd do a double somersault or something.'

'And I was the one who thought I was going to enjoy jealousy.'

'There's nothing to feel that way *about*. You're in *bed* with me. I regard that as a sure sign of my undivided attention.'

'It is, isn't it?'

'*Such* a baby.'

Back at the mill house, Charlotte and David, holding a stoneware cup of chocolate each, were talking across the pine-topped kitchen table, on which the magazine carrying the 'Dreme of Academe' lay open so that they might wonder at its prose style all over again.

'I don't want to be a bore about this,' said David, 'but would you consider letting me sleep with you fairly soon?'

'I haven't been considering much else,' said Charlotte, 'but first I have to consider whether I should stop sleeping with my husband. Otherwise I'll get terribly confused.'

'I understand.'

'You don't *have* to understand, you know. I really wish I could do it. Life would be a lot simpler. Can you wait for a little while?' She pulled back a stray strand of hair from her forehead in a way that David had come to like very much.

'Oh yes. I enjoy being with you. It's been very interesting. Elena doesn't exactly shake my beliefs but she certainly poses a challenge to radical feminism. What does she *do* exactly?'

'A lot of talented men are too busy to live. She makes an art of living. They depend on her.'

'It's a waste.'

'I'd do it if I could. Don't be such a scold.'

'Who cooked the food?'

'There's an invisible woman in the kitchen but Elena still manages to do most of it. Nobody quite knows how. You can't fault her on that. I'm sure the security men got their share of the pie. It's the first time I've ever seen her looking unsettled.'

'Unsettled? That's unsettled?'

'For her. I wonder if she's happy.'

'Would the world end if she wasn't?'

'Almost. If it can happen to her then nobody's safe.'

In London, Lancelot had the same dream as he had had the night before. It didn't happen in the same Koran-walled tunnel as where the taxis full of squealing dentists roamed, their faces lit green when they drew up beside you and peed through the window of your car. It happened in another tunnel, roughly parallel but lower down, where the Japanese hook made no noise but you could still feel it. You felt it at various points on your body, as if you were a diagram illustrating acupuncture. There was a pin-prick in the groin, then another at the elbow. Just the suggestion of one on each eyelid. Then a steady, slight but potentially skewering pressure in the neck, under the Adam's apple and above the infraclavicular fossa. He woke up to find Samantha squatting naked over him in the half light. It would have been an arousing spectacle if she had not been holding one of the long pins that Charlotte used for smocking. 'It's amazing,' said Samantha, 'how much I can do that doesn't wake you up.'

~ eighteen ~

Sadat, Sadat, Sadat,' said the wheels of the *Shinkansen* as
it raced south-west past Fujiyama on the way to Kyoto.
Victor sat back in Green Car luxury and breathed through a hot
towel draped over his face. The hot towel was the only item of
Green Car luxury that Victor found luxurious. Otherwise it was
a matter of being handed your shredded dried squid in a
cardboard box tied with ribbon instead of string. Victor flapped
the towel once to make it cold, cooled his hands with it, gave it
back to the stewardess and looked at the holy mountain. From
this distance you could not see that it was covered with pilgrims
all toiling upwards – except, of course, for the equal number of
pilgrims who were toiling downwards, having got what they
came for. Victor, who was on a pilgrimage himself, was not
contemptuous.

'Sadat, Sadat, Sadat.' All the way from Tokyo to Kyoto was
one continuous urban area that changed its name every few
miles. Victor could easily imagine what it must have been like
when it was burning. A man who suffered much from bad
dreams, he came to Kyoto almost every year at this time, not
just because the blossoms were out on Honshu but because the
moss was at its best in the temple. While other people favoured
the garden of raked sand, Victor preferred looking at the moss.
He was there on a day when nobody else was allowed in. The
head monk had arranged the privilege in perpetuity, as an
acknowledgment of the favourable terms on which Victor had
published the temple's fund-raising book in the English-
speaking countries. The same temple, and just possibly the
same monk, had once done Kipling the same favour.

Victor made no attempt to sit cross-legged. He just sat,
looking twice as big as he ought to in that context. He sat on the
edge of a small, smooth wooden verandah with his feet on the
brick rim of the garden. The moss covered the rocks in soft

waves and faded gradually upwards on the trunks of the trees. As a man without religion Victor had nowhere to seek guidance, and now the person he most trusted he could not consult. In such circumstances the best you can hope for is to set your thoughts in order. He didn't expect to find an answer, just a reprieve. The moss garden had the advantage of telling you exactly what you wanted to hear. It told you that the renewing impulse of nature could be irresistibly beautiful beyond any achievement of the human creative principle. It had the disadvantage, on the other hand, of proclaiming, subtly but in the most insistent way possible, the necessity for human discipline. How can you resist the force of new life? So go ahead and ruin everything. Accept this young blessing, make a shambles of your hard-won tranquillity, come back next year and tell us how you got on. Damned stuff isn't even grass, thought Victor, leaving. You couldn't feed a rabbit on it.

Back in Tokyo at the Imperial that evening, Victor rang Sally in London and caught her as she was getting up.

'You're alone?' he asked.

'In the morning, always. Where are you?'

'I'm not sure, but the assistant manager just ritually disembowelled himself because I complained about my television set, so it's probably not England.'

'What time is it there?'

'Night. They're just wheeling in another television set with a basket of fruit and a suicide poem from the assistant manager. Have you had your breakfast?'

'No. I've got nothing to eat and it's raining like hell. I've been out on a story for two days. Some of the things in my refrigerator appear to be growing hair.'

'The first and second television set wheelers have bowed out. Did you say you'd be in New York the week after the ball?'

'For five days. I'm seeing some people.'

'It looks as if I'll be there for most of that week. Will you save me an evening?'

'Wait a second. I've got the kind of diary that won't stay open by itself.'

'It's another British technological breakthrough. If you give me two evenings I'll take you to the opera as well.'

'As well as what?'

'What are you wearing?'

'Nothing,' said Sally, relaxing. 'You're very bold, suddenly.'

'I can talk like this when I'm in Tokyo,' said Victor.

'And when we're in New York, I suppose.'

'I hope so.'

'Not London, though.'

'No.'

Then he rang Elena and talked for a long time while she was eating her breakfast in bed. As usual, being as near to her as possible while she was having breakfast seemed the only sane aim in life, so he wondered again whether he might not be losing his mind. After making some other calls in various directions he ordered a room service dinner and, while eating it, watched one of those Samurai serials in which the veteran hero beats off attackers in groups of sixteen. The attackers were very bad actors who on receipt of a fatal sword thrust reacted as if they had been shot. When they were all dead and stacked three deep, the veteran hero renounced the young princess before strutting off. You had to admit the Japanese knew how to cook a steak. With raw fish and bamboo shoots they might be hopeless, but give them a hunk of frozen meat from the Argentine and they were like men inspired. Another Samurai serial came on. This time the old warrior kept his sword sheathed until the last scene. Then he exploded into action and wiped out the standard group of heavily grimacing attackers, several of them familiar from the previous serial. They presented themselves to be despatched in strict sequence, crying out to advertise their presence if he happened to have his back turned. Eventually they were all dead and it was time for the old warrior to renounce the young princess. It was a different young princess but a very similar crooked path up which the superannuated swordsman, clearly suffering from piles, strutted towards the moonlit cyclorama.

Next on was a news programme in which one of the items seemed to emanate from London. A policeman was pointing towards the broken front window of a car. Victor rang Elena again to tell her about it but this time her telephones were both engaged. He kept trying and finally got her.

'Are we all right?' she asked.

'Yes.'

'I can't tell you what the rain is like here. I'm doing designs for the ball but the gloom gets into them like mould. Why are you ringing me up again so nervously?'

'I love you.'

'Don't say it to prove it. I should hope you do.'

They quarrelled, half made it up, quarrelled again, and he kept on calling until equilibrium had been restored. For her it should have been reassuring, being so like one of those battles that take place after you first fall for each other, having set out for India and found America instead. It's all strange and limitless and you fight like savages. Later you get used to it and then you miss the tension. But Elena was not reassured. By now she was prepared to read guilt into his most innocent remarks, so the guilty ones sounded like sentences of death.

~ nineteen ~

When Lancelot booked the table for the important dinner with the world's most famous young female film star and her academic husband, he was careful to make the call himself. Janice, whose voice by now was in such a state of training that it carried halfway across the city, could have made the arrangements without even lifting the telephone, but nothing must be allowed to go wrong. The restaurant he had chosen was a certain Mayfair brasserie which was the recognised place for celebrities to foregather and pretend to ignore each other among pale green wall panels like the faded cardboard covers of old Hachette pocket classics. The decor and general atmosphere were beyond reproach. They carried with them, however, the penalty that the man who had brought them so lovingly into being might be physically present on any given night. He was the restaurant's proprietor and *spiritus loci*, a perennially drunken, scruffy and inconceivably foul-mouthed Celt named Flaherty, who had a bad habit of joining your table unasked, telling progressively more putrescent stories, making indecent suggestions to the women, laying his head in your mother's lap and singing sad songs of the Irish uprising. Lancelot quite liked him but did not think the world's most famous young female film star would relish his act. Therefore Flaherty must be persuaded to keep discreetly in the background or vanish altogether.

'No problem,' brogued Flaherty. 'Soap, is she really going to be here? Sand, would I like to get my. And. While she. A few dozen times.' Even Flaherty's close friends found it necessary, when repeating some of his statements, to substitute less offensive words for certain expletives and delete phrases entirely. It wasn't so much the filth of his imagination as the remorselessness of it. It wasn't like having ordure poured over you. It was like having ordure poured over you all day.

'That's exactly what you must get out of your mind,' said Lancelot. 'If she gets the wrong idea she won't be back.'

'Soaping sand. What a load of sand. Those spiritual-looking ones can't get enough of. She'll take one look at my. And she'll. Times in succession.'

'Seriously, you have to promise or it's all off.'

'Soap. Sand. All right. I won't touch a drop, soap it.'

Lancelot booked a round table for six, because in addition to the film star, her husband, Charlotte and himself, there would be the playwright Tim Stripling and his miraculous wife Naomi. Tim Stripling wrote plays at such an intellectual altitude that only a symbolic logician could follow the plots. In her first days off Broadway the film star had been in one of his plays and was now very keen to pay her respects. Lancelot's friendship with Stripling was not particularly close but the mere mention of the film star's name worked sudden wonders. The potential connection was made even neater by the consideration that her husband had apparently written a small book on Stripling's work. As for Naomi – an interdisciplinary dynamo engaged in a perpetual attempt, successful every second day, to be even more impressive than her husband – her presence would ensure that there were no awkward pauses. As the night drew near, all the signs were propitious. Even Samantha seemed acquiescent. Not that she would have had any particular objection to Lancelot's going out with his wife. Annoyingly enough, Samantha did not suffer from jealousy. Her objections to his marriage, though strident, were directed solely towards the inconvenience it occasionally cost her. The evening in question should have been one such inconvenience, because normally she would have been eager to meet someone so celebrated as the world's most famous young female film star. But for once she seemed indifferent, even listless. Lancelot wondered if this were a sign of spiritual disturbance. The business with the long pin he had put down to childish curiosity, as an alternative to putting it down to raving psychosis.

When Lancelot and Charlotte finally reached the restaurant, after driving in the Maxi backwards and forwards through Mayfair in a complicated pattern of one-way streets otherwise full of limousines loaded with the masked harems of Arabs, the Striplings, who had arrived from opposite directions each driving a white BMW, were already present and being fawned over by Flaherty. But at least he was fawning quietly.

'No soaping problem,' he whispered to Lancelot. 'I'll just soaping fade into the soaping scenery like a blob of sand for the duration. I haven't touched a soaping drop since yesterday, so soap *you*.' His breath was like paint-stripper but it would have been like that even if he had not had a drink for a week, and when he waddled off he bumped only a few of the tables. Lancelot's party had been given the star table, the one where you could see everyone else but everyone else had to swivel awkwardly if they wanted to see you. Only a few tables away, one of the three most famous cockney photographers was sitting with two of his wives, one of them the most exquisitely beautiful French film actress and the other the most exquisitely beautiful Hawaiian model. The photographer himself was not beautiful at all, and had chosen his most decrepit shirt to underline the fact. The whole display was meant to demonstrate what sheer unwashed virility can get you. It was a triumphant success, but Lancelot topped it when his guest of honour walked in. That particular restaurant was no more likely to go silent than Victor's house, but it did, and for the same reason. Lancelot rose to greet her and be introduced to her husband. The conversation, beginning then and there, went well from the start. Everybody at the table seemed to have a waiter each. From the corner of his eye, Lancelot could see Flaherty at the other end of the restaurant, sitting at someone else's table.

Lancelot could not conceive of how things might have gone better. Charlotte and Naomi had seen all the film star's films. The film star and her husband had seen all of the playwright's plays. The husband was a great admirer of Charlotte's book and even knew all about Lancelot's poetry.

'I'm sure he's very flattered to be hearing this,' said Charlotte, perhaps not entirely necessarily.

'Oh, it's not flattery,' said the husband. 'I think we'd have a very misleading view of that period unless we took the emphasis represented by such work into account. It was one of those reactions against a prevailing mood that help define the mood.' On reflection, Lancelot decided that this *wasn't* flattering, but he felt absurdly pleased to be one of the objects of admiration. What an exhilarating evening it was turning out to be. The quails' eggs were perfect. But then Lancelot took another glance in Flaherty's direction and found that he had moved a couple of tables nearer. He was still a long way off, but he was nearer.

By the time the entrée plates held nothing but chop bones and the spines of lemon soles, the conversation could be described only as brilliant. Stripling, showing off for the ladies, was in coruscating form. Lancelot was spurred on by the competition to flights of fancy that Nicholas himself might have envied. He told the story of the first night of the Covent Garden production of *Idomeneo*. Even Charlotte, who had heard this routine many times, privately admitted to herself that he had never performed it better. The husband, crying with laughter, was taking notes.

' . . . the spears were so big that the spear carriers could only just carry one each,' shouted Lancelot through the laughter, 'and there were twelve spears. Unfortunately there were only eleven spear carriers, one of them having gone home during the interval. So they had the choice of leaving one of the spears still sticking out of the stage or sending one man on to carry two. And they sent one man on to carry two. And he . . . and they . . . '

'Stop!' cried Stripling. 'For God's sake stop . . . '

'No!' cried the actress, dabbing at her tears. 'I can't stand it . . . '

'Please,' cried Naomi. 'Please don't tell us any . . . '

' . . . crucified like St Andrew,' yelled Lancelot, 'at the very moment when the Queen or whoever she was came on to complain about the . . . ' By that time he could not have spoiled the story whatever he did, which was lucky, because he had just noticed that Flaherty was much closer than before. Only half a dozen tables now separated the convivial restaurateur from what was certainly his goal.

The *crème brûlée* cracked like rime ice at the tap of a spoon to reveal a custard of such succulent texture that nobody could eat enough. The profiteroles were angelic puffballs full of cream you would have risked a gaol term to eat more of. Flaherty's chef had excelled himself. But Flaherty himself was now only two tables away, addressing one of the photographer's wives in terms which were inaudible from where Lancelot was sitting but which had obviously posed her the choice of either laughing tolerantly or calling the police.

When the coffee arrived, Flaherty arrived with it, bringing his own chair and loudly calling for champagne. Lancelot, not very adequately masking his reluctance, began the introductions.

'I *know* who she soaping is, you mad sand. And let me tell you she's soaping *marvellous*. Soap a duck. She's soaping *great*. Am I right?'

'You're right,' said Lancelot. 'It's his way,' he added to the husband, trying to make a joke of it.

'What are you soaping making excuses to *him* for, you sand? Go and soap yourself. Listen.' At this point Flaherty advanced his large, trembling, small-featured face to within an inch of the husband's and bellowed. '*Listen!* I don't soaping know who you soaping are, sand-face. You look like a weedy little sand to me but let me tell you. This soaping girl is not only soaping *beautiful*. And I mean she makes me want to take my. And. All the. Repeatedly. But not only is she soaping *beautiful*, she is a soaping *great* soaping *actress*. Soaping sand. Why don't you soaping *believe* me?'

'I do believe you,' said the husband, who during this tirade had at first surreptitiously dabbed at his face with a fingertip and then later on taken to mopping it openly with a napkin. 'I'm married to her.'

'You're soaping *married* to her? Soaping sand. Salt. Sugar. Saline solution. Why didn't you soaping *tell* me? Because let me tell you in case you didn't soaping know. This girl has got the most soaping beautiful pair of little tits I have *ever seen*.' So saying, or rather so screaming, Flaherty lunged out of his chair with his pudgy hands extended as if to palpate the nominated articles of anatomy. Since the actress was sitting as if paralysed he might well have attained his object had his aim been better, but in the event, whether from inebriation or because he had hooked his foot around the leg of his chair, he fell past her and rolled under the next table, where he briefly lay face down. Then he half rolled back again so that he lay face up, and copiously vomited.

'I had a grandfather like that,' said the actress as Lancelot helped her into her coat. 'He closed every bar in New York.'

Lancelot was grateful for the moral support, but could not help feeling that the evening had deserved a more gracious finish. The actress and her husband stepped outside into their waiting hired Mercedes limousine. As Lancelot dealt with Charlotte's coat and glumly accepted commiserations from the Striplings, he was in a position for the first time to glance into the other wing of the restaurant and see, at a small table sheltered in an alcove, Samantha, in full, carefully tousled blonde glory, talking animatedly to the celebrated actor, who was smiling at what she said. Then Samantha looked up, saw Lancelot, and waved as if pleased.

'Soaping forgot to warn you,' shouted Flaherty as he was carried past by two waiters. 'That bird of yours is here.'

'Come on,' said Charlotte. 'You've had a busy night.'

~ twenty ~

The weather for Elena's opera ball was everything that might have been expected, but luckily she had had some tents put up. From all over Europe and America her friends and relatives, nearly always not the same people, brought their engraved invitations and their more or less judiciously chosen costumes. Some people came only a few hundred yards and wore costumes put together from scraps in the old clothes box. Others had been days on the journey and weeks at the theatrical outfitters. People coming from far away were put up at the house or in the surrounding towns. Those coming up from London parked their cars in an adjoining field, from which a tented pathway led towards the house and the main marquee. Elena, who could do wonders on a shoestring, could work miracles on a proper budget, with which in this case she had been provided, her deranged father being very proud of his grandson. Nevertheless the tents and the trestles and the music and the food and the champagne had soon used up the money. What they could not exhaust, however, was her fantasy, which, stimulated by such a challenge, had soared beyond playfulness into the realm of the poetic. Everything bore her personal touch. Everyone in the district was in character. Even the security staff entered into the spirit of the thing. A locally based regiment of infantry, they had been persuaded by Elena into wearing powdered wigs, loose-sleeved shirts, breeches, stockings and buckled shoes. Some of them had gone the whole hog and put on makeup. They manned all entrance points and showed a lot of zeal checking invitations. The Shadow Foreign Secretary was one of the first detainees. He was dressed as Radames and felt pretty foolish waiting, but Elena rescued him eventually.

The Shadow Foreign Secretary was one of the twelve examples of Radames to be in attendance: on a warm night, short skirts were popular. But there were also eight copies of

Eisenstein from *Fledermaus*, ten of Scarpia and twelve of Baron Ochs. Otello, Figaro and Manrico were particularly favoured by the Italians. Siegfried was popular among the middle-aged Austrians, who were in the habit of demonstrating their sense of humour by being snide about the Germans. Like everybody else they had been on the telephone to each other for weeks trying to find out what everybody else was wearing, and like everybody else they ended up wearing the same thing. Some of them just wore black tie and a winged helmet, but the less decorous were in full Niebelung kit, complete with hunting horn and short sword. There were a lot of jovial recognition scenes when they bumped into each other among the glistening rose bushes, and a good deal of sweat dripping from under their leather pants and borrowed fur boleros.

The women, on the whole, were less inclined to make a joke of it. The younger ones mainly favoured Carmen, Octavian, Aida and Tatiana from *Eugene Onegin*. Mimi was thought too dowdy and Butterfly was not much in vogue because the clogs would have made for awkward dancing. Among women of a certain age there was a sprinkling of Turandots, but Tosca, the Merry Widow and the Marschallin from *Rosenkavalier* were easily the most popular choices. Of the twenty-three Marschallins, Victor's ex-wife had the most splendid costume, which she had borrowed from the New York Metropolitan Opera, of which her present husband sat on the board of trustees. She had it packed in a wicker skip and loaded amongst her luggage on the family helicopter, which lifted her carefully out of their Long Island estate and put her down at Kennedy, only a few minutes away. Without touching the ground, she was taken from the helicopter to the family Learjet 36. The Learjet put her down at the same USAF base in England from which the Stratotankers took off. A limousine took her to Castle That. After the appropriate amount of sleep she spent half a day getting into her costume and having her wig put on. Then she was taken to the ball by another limousine. It was something to do. She spent a lot of time, Victor had once complained, waiting for someone else to make things happen, so that she could go to them.

Having been in receipt, during the last month, of several hundred calls for advice, Elena knew that there was no point fixing on any well-known character for herself, except perhaps the Queen of the Night, which everyone was expecting her to be. But she had never been able to stand that hysterical woman, and besides, she would have sweltered. So she chose the obscure Magda de Cuivry, courtesan heroine of Puccini's least famous opera, *La Rondine*. It had been the first opera she and Victor ever saw in each other's company and they knew every note of it. To look like a vaguely operatic Second Empire courtesan made no great demands on her time and trouble, an essential consideration when she had so much else to organise: by the time the day arrived she felt as if she had been born in the Second Empire. Also it gave Victor the chance to avoid fancy dress. To impersonate her plutocratic lover he had merely to wear a top hat with his white tie and tails. Later on the hat could be quietly put aside. Half the secret of dressing successfully for a costume ball is to be able to discard your accoutrements once the joke has worn off. Strip naked and paint yourself gold by all means, but be content to look like that when you are queueing for sausages at dawn.

Sally didn't like the idea of fancy dress any more than Nicholas did, but with advice from Elena she worked out a good compromise for them both. They went as Aubrey Beardsley and Salome. Sally put her hair back with silver combs and wore her black Chloë sarong effort shot through with snail-trail silver thread. It looked suitably, if erotically, *fin de siècle* Middle Eastern, while leaving her free to dance. As a final touch she painted her lips black. Nicholas was the reverse of aquiline but with the addition of a cane and a carnation to his black tie he looked decadent enough. Dressed like that they came up from London in the Porsche, with Nicholas nursing Sally's high-heeled sandals like twin fetishes.

Starting out on the same route much earlier because they would travel more slowly, Charlotte and David came up in the Maxi. The last time David had been in the car it had been going in the other direction and full of dogs, but this time he was reasonably relaxed. Horrified by the idea of fancy dress, he had finally settled for being Jimmy Mahoney from *Mahagonny*, the only work for the musical theatre with which he was as yet intimate. Charlotte had taken him to see it at the Coliseum and he had been humming the songs ever since. But as far as the independent eye could discern, to adopt his Brechtian character he had made no change in his normal appearance at all. Charlotte had avoided the obvious ideas, despaired of the unobvious ones, and pretty well given up, but rallying at the last moment she had decided to be Leonore from *Fidelio*. Then she persuaded herself she did not feel particularly faithful to her Florestan, so she took off Lancelot's trousers, put a plaid sash on over her best Bill Gibb, and called herself Lucia di Lammermoor. That would have to do. Sally's car, with a wave from Nicholas, overtook them as they were turning into the meadow. A few rows of cars away, Samantha and Lancelot were to be seen getting out of Samantha's battered little 2CV Citroën. Charlotte immediately regretted not having parked at the mill house, but there was just enough rain to have held them prisoner there until it cleared. She felt wet enough already, what with her sash. No she didn't. She felt fine. Just odd.

For Lancelot it had been a bit of a nightmare trip. He had decided to be André Chénier and it had taken all day to get the too hastily hired satin breeches ironed properly so that they did not look as if they had been crushed into somebody's back pocket since the storming of the Bastille. All these preparations had to be done unobtrusively while Charlotte was fussing around the house. There was one peaceful interlude when she completed the ironing of the satin breeches at the cost of his lending her a pair of cavalry twill trousers, but otherwise all was tension. The final result, however, was undeniably rather fetching, especially the linen shirt worn wide open at the shoulders so that the neck might be bared to the guillotine. With a sufficiently dashing mac thrown over this ensemble he had said an awkward *au revoir* and climbed into the booked taxi which was to take him to Samantha's. The taxi driver, with a devotion to the labour movement rare in one of his calling, wanted to know what the country was coming to and would not take a closed glass partition for an answer. In front of Samantha's flat, Lancelot gave the driver the standard small bale of money and alighted just in time to be almost knocked down by a squad of hurtling blacks wearing headphones, candy-striped vests, nylon running shorts, pop socks and roller skates with yellow wheels. They were all travelling at a terrific rate and more than half of them were going backwards. One of them swerved past him so close that he could hear the music which should have been confined to the interior of the skater's head. Further along the street, the skaters broke formation to thread their way with undiminished speed through a loose pack of homicidally accoutred white youths whose heads looked as if birds of paradise had been placed on them and hit with a mallet. The main difference between the upper and lower orders in Britain, Lancelot told himself, is that the upper orders wear fancy dress once or twice a year and the lower orders wear it all the time.

Samantha didn't know anything about opera but Lancelot persuaded her to go as Manon in that character's last, Louisiana phase. The costume was fairly easily improvised by reducing an old chemise to artistic-looking tatters. He had rarely seen her looking so lovely but she seemed nearer dementia praecox than ever. Her work was still going well – was almost finished, in fact – but their friendship had become a source of grief to him. There is not a woman in the world, Proust had said, the possession of whom is as precious as that of the truth which she reveals to us by causing us to suffer. Screw you, Marcel. Samantha still refused to admit that there was anything serious between her and the celebrated actor, but anything unserious was serious enough. Anyway the actor was gone again, to a party in France where absolutely everybody, Samantha had con-tended sullenly, was going to be. Lancelot tried to remind her that there was another kind of absolutely everybody whose credentials were rather more substantial than those of the Hollywood younger set and the rock music cocaine culture, but Samantha seemed beyond listening. She had not conducted her seriously injured Citroën very far along the dual carriageway before it became evident that she was beyond driving too. Judging from the way she talked she was not drunk. If she was consuming that other stuff then it was a great mystery how she could afford it. Perhaps the actor handed it to her in a suitcase. Was that what they were up to? As long as that was all. Lancelot couldn't get a straight answer out of her so he took over the wheel and concentrated on getting a straight line out of the car, an aim not easily achieved. When at last they were parked in the meadow she complained about the wetness of the grass, into which her golden sandals indeed sank several inches. He told her to watch out for cow pats and strode off ahead, eager to disappear down the covered entryway before he should collide with Charlotte, whom he could see distressingly near and looking annoyingly pretty as she opened an umbrella over her companion, who seemed to have made no effort, a fact which rendered Lancelot acutely conscious of his wig, not to mention the scarlet velvet choker which Samantha had rather wittily given him to go around his neck.

Delilah also came as Manon, with a similar emphasis on bad living conditions in Louisiana. This gave Dick Toole a thin excuse to be a slave master and carry a whip. Neither of them had been invited, but Delilah had heard about the ball from Thinwall, who had not been invited either, but who had overheard Nicholas talking to Lancelot. This capacity to eavesdrop on the talking drums of the social tribe was the quality in Delilah which Dick Toole prized even above her amplitudinous emotional acquiescence. He, needless to say, had heard nothing. Elena's opera ball was most definitely not a press event. There are grand occasions to which the press, including a selection of gossip columnists and their attendant photographers, is invited. There are grander occasions at which the photography is done by private arrangement and the best photographs are immediately released to the social diaries of the fashion magazines. There are even grander occasions which are not heard about until they are long over. Elena's opera ball fell most emphatically into that last category. Dick Toole's chance of being there should have been General Dayan's chance of being in Mecca. But he owed it to his principles. This privileged enclave must be penetrated and exposed. And with all his rivals off in Paris chasing cave-mouthed pop singers, he would have the story to himself. So he climbed into his too-tight breeches, his rented cavalry boots with the heels worn at an angle, his cutaway coat and tricorne hat. It wasn't a bad whip, either. Delilah, looking a bit on the plump side in her slave-girl tatterdemalion, eyed the whip with interest and looked at her watch. There would be time enough and it would certainly do wonders for the authenticity of her attire.

Having retained his chauffeur for the night, Dick Toole could relax with Delilah in the back seat of the Jag and make notes while she briefed him on the expected guests.

'There should be,' said Delilah, sitting forward, 'at least three Felsenstein princesses.'

'And they're Jews from America.'

'No, the Felsensteins are Catholics from the Italian Tyrol. The *Nelson* Steins are Jews from America.'

'And what are their names, these little princesses?'

'Pupi, Lupi and Schnupi.'

'Christ. What about the Krauts?'

'They're mainly not Germans. They're Austrians.'

'Isn't Austria in Germany?'

'It used to be. First come the archduchesses . . . '

It all went very smoothly on paper, but in practice they did not get in. The peruked security men listened patiently to Dick Toole's story and then informed him that in three tours of duty in Belfast they had never heard anything like it. They turned the car back. But Dick Toole was not beaten yet. He got the chauffeur to make a dog-leg around the meadows and park on the far side of the cow pasture among the trees. By now it was dark but from where they were they could see Elena's house and the tents all lit up white, with coloured lights in the gardens and the orchards. Dick Toole and Delilah set out across the deep grass, doing their best to avoid cow pats. Then they saw a patrol of peruked security men silhouetted against the festive light. At the same time the air was shattered by the sound of a jet aircraft. 'They're using planes!' cried Dick Toole. 'Quick, let's duck in here.' There was some sort of concrete pill box just near them. They ducked into it and crouched. Dick Toole's boots sank into something that yielded with an ominous silence. There was a sudden, overpowering smell.

Everybody had arrived by now. The nephew of the third or fourth prime minister before last and his singing wife Dido, dressed as indeterminate characters from *HMS Pinafore*, had arrived by pony trap in the thronged central courtyard, where there was a small orchestra on a platform nobly dispensing, with restricted elbow room, a succession of operatic themes.

Aidas were avoiding each other. Figaros were being furtive. Kundrys collided. But some people had achieved singularity against all the odds. 'Zoom' Beispiel, whom Elena had invited at Victor's behest, had thought it was an OPEC ball and come as Sheik Yamani. The renowned and very fat American film producer Gus Disting had brought a range of hats so that he could say he was Hans Sachs, Gianni Schicchi or Falstaff, and certainly his tights, whose crotch was between the knees, suited all three characters equally. Randall Hoyle, tantalised by the prospective roll-up from the *haute juiverie*, had come as an SS officer in full regalia. If taxed on his costume he would have been hard pressed to name an opera featuring any such character, and planned to content himself with vague references to Wagner or Shostakovich's Leningrad Symphony, but as things happened he stunned people into silence. The Nelson Steins, dressed as the Girl of the Golden West and Lieutenant Pinkerton, were taking a turn through the floodlit apple orchard when they encountered Randall Hoyle coming the other way along the garden path. Mrs Nelson Stein, who was of no slight girth, stumbled sideways into a frame of wire netting meant to protect the raspberries and redcurrants from marauding birds. The apparatus did not wholly collapse, but extricating her from it took time. Randall Hoyle, to do him credit, helped.

But the most unusual costume was in a way the most obvious. Ian Cuthbert had come as Rigoletto. Somehow he had got hold of the harness Lon Chaney had worn in *The Hunchback of Notre Dame*. Wearing that under an outsize jester's costume from *The 5,000 Fingers of Dr T*, he had been able to halve his height, at the cost of hopping along bent double. The pain must have been considerable but he didn't seem to mind. He capered about snickering resentfully in the manner of a wronged dwarf. By that stage everybody had a bumper of preliminary champagne inside him but was still in character and keen to prove it. There was a lot of bad singing going on. They all had little jokes and clever quotations ready.

Dove sono?
Ah, Tosca!
Rofrano! Rofrano!
Bist du ein Tor?

Ah, Pelléas!
Krasavitsa moya!
Un bacio. Un bacio ancora.

People were applauded on arrival. There was much polite pushing and shoving because of the sheer numbers, so the champagne was already well at work before they all sat down to dinner in the main marquee. Set out on the wooden floor which had been laid over the grass there were scores of small decorated tables. Everybody had a marked place. Elena never gave a dinner of any size, no matter how large, without a fully considered *placement*. This was her biggest challenge ever but she did not scamp it. Couples who might have clung together damply had been ruthlessly split up. The most unlikely people found themselves next to each other. Nearly all of them did well out of it, although at first the revived Mrs Nelson Stein was not best pleased to find an unrepentant Randall Hoyle on her right. But Charlotte, who had him on her left, was very flattered. David, whose disapproval of the proceedings had reached such a pitch of ecstasy that he was almost in a trance, was further outraged to find himself sitting between two of the most breathtakingly lovely girls he had ever seen in his life. The one on his right was dressed as some kind of ballerina and the one on his left was obviously meant to be Helen of Troy. David had fixed political objections to the idea of anyone being allowed to have such skin, eyes and teeth, but his anger softened slightly when the ballerina on his right turned out to be an Italian communist. Speaking excellent English, she gave him a clear account of the political philosophy of Gramsci. At the University of Florence she was preparing a thesis on the difficulties presented by Gramsci's idea of culturally defined objectivity. She knew several people in the Red Brigades but disapproved of their attempts to kidnap her father, who owned one of the state industries. How could anyone own a state industry? She explained to him in detail.

David, who had been advised by an addendum to his place card that he was required to function as stage manager for his sector of the table, found himself serving up food for her from one of the large central silver dishes. When he had finished doing that he found himself doing more of the same for Helen of

Troy, who told him that she owned every record Clutch Shudder had ever released and that they were favourites at the weekly disco her brothers held at the *Schloss*. She had particularly enjoyed the last Genesis concert in Vienna. What did he think of Gerry Rafferty? David began to see how the Trojan war might have taken place for the very reason specified by tradition. Where was all the champagne coming from? The bottles seemed never to empty.

Nicholas was between Serena Blake and an American female critic he much admired but had not yet met. Serena could not have looked more sensational, with camellias at her wrists and in her *décolletage*, identifying her character and saving her from pleurisy. The critic had six different kinds of nervous tremor all pulling in different directions but she was a pitiless bitch about her fellow scriveners. Nicholas liked her corrosive jokes. What was more important, she liked his. Sally did even better than Nicholas, after a shaky start. It was no thrill to find Anthony Easement sitting opposite dressed as Don Giovanni; the wilting Wotan on her right had been an old friend of Marie of Roumania and was clearly out of it; but the moulting Mephistopheles on her left, although no chicken either, was full of sparks from the jump, so if she was going to be bored at least it would not be in silence.

'My name,' he said, 'is Thurn und Taxis.'

'How do you . . . '

'I am one of Elena's Austrian cousins. There are more than thirty of her cousins present this evening. About twenty are from Italy and the rest are from Austria. The families tend to overlap in the vicinity of Carinthia.'

'That's fasc . . . '

'Of the Austrian cousins, at least six are Thurns und Taxis. Elena has always called me the music hall Thurn und Taxis but I am never understanding this joke.'

Sally had begun to understand it and was just resigning herself to a hard time when it transpired that the old boy had been driving exotic cars since before the war and had not given up yet. He owned, among other rarities, a 57SC Bugatti. A beast to drive because the clutch was either in or out. Next time she was down that way she ought to come and take a spin. There was a *monoposto* Alfa she might like to try her hand at also, and a Delahaye with a Cotal electric gearbox. No, permissions were no problem: he had a circuit laid out in the grounds. Sally had rarely had a more enjoyable conversation, if you discounted the periodic necessity to stab the back of the randy old goat's hand with a fork.

~ twenty-one ~

Only Lancelot suffered. He would have blamed Elena for his predicament if he had thought that she had cause for malice. He knew she was well capable of it, but could not see any reason why he should be persecuted. On his right he had a Bismarck baroness who was notorious for having attended every party in the world since the Congress of Vienna while contributing nothing to any of them except a long face. If your German was good, which Lancelot's was not, she could tell you some reasonably interesting things about her love affair with Metternich, but in French all she could do was ask you who people were and then fail to understand you when you told her. The real nightmare, however, was on his left. It was Deirdre Childworth, an ageing Deb of the Year whose time of glory had been spent with the Chelsea Set, and who now functioned as a living reminder of the amount of triviality generated in the days when the words 'brittle' and 'vivacious' had been invariably used in tandem. 'Why are you so nervous?' was the first thing that she said to Lancelot. Her diamond-studded head-band sparkled angrily, like a migraine worn externally. 'You seem very impatient. Do you want to get away from me? Would you like to go and sit somewhere else?'

'How did *you* get in?' was what he should have said, but instead he said that he was not nervous, that he did not want to get away from her, and that he did not want to go and sit with someone else. Three lies in a row. What he really wanted was simple. He wanted to go and put his head in Samantha's fragrant, warm lap and murmur, so she would hear it through her thighs, that he didn't care what she did as long as she never came to look and sound like this awful, mad, wildly staring woman. Deirdre Childworth. Hell in a sanitary belt. A career open to the talons. After thanking his lucky stars that he had never had an affair with her, he suddenly remembered that he

204

had. But there was every chance that she had forgotten too.

'Do you have any idea of how evasive you are?' asked Deirdre Childworth. To say this to his face she had to lean forward round him and look back over her shoulder, because he was making increasingly more obvious efforts to be pointing the other way. 'Why don't you look at me when I'm speaking?' This last question was asked in a shout that silenced the table. Luckily it would have taken Placido Domingo in full voice to silence the whole marquee, and he wouldn't be arriving until after midnight. Far in the distance, Samantha was to be glimpsed spooning cold salmon to Gus Disting. Lancelot wanted to be there, but he wasn't. He was here.

'Bloody *look* at me when I'm talking to you!' shouted Deirdre Childworth, grabbing his chin and pulling his face towards her. In the resulting scuffle his wig was dislodged, but fortunately Deirdre was reduced to introspective tears and did nothing more effusive from then on except sob uncontrollably, so he was able to have a reasonable conversation with a Japanese teenage model in a strapless black taffeta gown sitting three places away. The Japanese model had come as herself, she explained, because Madame Butterfry would have been too rike a criché. It transpired that she was Gus Disting's friend, but she roathed Horrywood. The prace she riked best was New York, because there she could stay in bed at the Praza and watch moobies until dawn. 'Do you rike the moobies?' she asked. It turned out that she rubbed them. Her favourite moobie stars were Carorah Rombard and Rosarind Russerroo.

None of this was very rewarding but it beat talking to Deirdre, who kept picking at her food and then missing her mouth with it because her eyes were gummed up. The man between Deirdre and the Japanese moobie rubber sat looking straight ahead like an Easter Island statue, an impression reinforced by the fact that he was dressed as an Aztec. Lancelot could not think of any operas about Aztecs and the man himself was unforthcoming. He just gazed, mouthing mechanically. Lancelot guessed that he might be one of Elena's mad cousins from the Salzkammergut. Up there above the clouds there was an old Habsburg hunting lodge bung full of them, slaughtering chamois by the thousands and riding their horses up the spiral staircase to lunch. The women strode around in *Jagdkostüm* and the men, on formal occasions, wore Balenciaga ball gowns, tiaras and high heels.

Elena might not have been feeling at her best but she was certainly looking it. A spray of diamonds came scintillating out of her purple bodice like stars being born in Orion's sword. Because nobility is thus obliged, she had given herself a table full of crocks and bores, with the prospective bride's venerable grandfather droning away about the menace of the *Sozis* on her right and the senior economics adviser to the British government before last waffling on about the menace of monetarism on her left. As far as she could tell, the philosophical differences of the two old crashers were as extreme as could be possible between two normal human beings, but as neither could understand a word the other was saying, there was no conflict. While her admirers, temporarily unencumbered with wives, triangulated her from all over the marquee, Elena switched her most understanding smile from one of her basket cases to the other, playing her usual game of throwing in remarks at random and seeing how random she could make them. Sometimes you could quote nursery rhymes and still find these tottering relics nodding in agreement. At the next table on one side her nephew Gianni was in charge and at the next table on the other side the girl he would soon marry sat in the place of honour. A family with a name like theirs should have hesitated to christen a daughter Farfalla but in this case the confidence had not been misplaced. Her famously dumb mother, who at that very moment, while improbably impersonating Adriana Lecouvreur, was directing across the table at Elena a smile evidently meant to be worldly wise, had typically wanted the girl to come as Madame Butterfly, but had been talked out of it. So of all the Cherubinos, Farfalla Schmetterling-Papillon Mariposa was the most resplendent, her silk coat sewn with real pearls and her little sword made of real silver. To Elena, whose own jewels were mainly paste because she had sold the originals two countries agò, such blatant expenditure signalled the death of the imagination, but originality was obviously not the girl's forte and there was no point wishing for it. Wanting Gianni to marry someone penniless but remarkable was the same as wanting him to be someone else. He had turned out harmless, itself some kind of achievement in this age of danger, and would now be rewarded by the opportunity of joining himself to a girl whose wealth and position were accompanied by a sweet personality, flawless looks and the mandatory four languages. In the life they would share, no combination of qualities could be more ordinary than that. Separately or together, neither of them would say a startling thing for the rest of the twentieth century and well into the twenty-first. Very few of their older relatives here tonight seriously believed that life should be any other way. They expected the unexpected from Elena because she had run away to England. Anyone who could do that was capable of anything. But you couldn't *live* like that.

Looking towards the river side of the tent, Elena could see Victor coping nobly between two *hochgeborene* Austrian ladies, a *dégringolade* Dorabella and a *fadée* Fiordiligi, who had plainly been startled to find themselves sitting down with a Jew. Victor's odd willingness to volunteer for this assignment could only be explained by a need to do penance. Elena traced the line of his gaze to see where it led. Yes, of course. How sad it all was. Why did even the best of men have so little imagination that it took novelty to excite it? They had always to be at the beginning. To keep things going was too much for them.

'And how soon,' she asked the grandfather, 'did *you* betray your one great love and true mistress?' But the old boy rattled on regardless. 'And what about you?' she asked the economist. 'What furnished room is she rotting in now, the *Luxusdame* you couldn't live without?' But he was drivelling something about Keynes. Elena stabbed a strawberry the size of a sheep's heart with her fork and fed it to him in mid-sentence but not even that stopped him. As long as time does that to me, she thought. As long as it makes me unheeding. But what if it left you heeding and nothing else? Still, it would be a good while yet.

Better to be like Lancelot, forever looking into your own navel and finding nothing except fluff. She could see that the punishment she had arranged for him had perhaps worked a bit too well. To hit him with Deirdre Childworth had admittedly been extreme. She should have put Deirdre with some Americans, who cope with vocal stridency by talking more loudly themselves and regard mental disturbance as a claim to seriousness. Once, when Elena first arrived in London, Deirdre Childworth had taken her up, or, to put it more accurately, latched on to her. Elena had soon left her behind but that was all the more reason for not leaving her out entirely, especially after having avoided her for so many years. Going mad was another solution, of course. How did people manage it? In a concentration camp there would probably be nothing to it, but to do so in ordinary life you would have to see your troubles as unique, and Elena, although she had a good conceit of herself, was too intuitive to do that. Charm and cunning might buy you a reprieve, might go on winning you the adoration of everyone you didn't want, but suddenly there you were, fighting tooth and nail for what you did want, exactly like everybody else. The best you could do was never let it show. It isn't the what, it's the how. Anyway, tonight she was determined to enjoy herself. Being determined to enjoy yourself was not the same as enjoying yourself, but at least she was giving people something to remember.

From her nephew, and several of his friends for purposes of cross reference, Elena had taken advice about the best electric band. It was called the New Taste Thrills and began to play thunderously at one end of the marquee just as the younger people were tucking into their third helping of dessert. Farfalla and Gianni rose to lead the dancing, which seemed to consist of staring each other in the eye, crouching slightly, and then miming the removal of one's clothes. Very soon most of the other young people had joined them. 'Ah,' said the grandfather, *'die jungen Leut'.'* That's the only coherent thing you've said all night, thought Elena, and then almost panicked when she realised she couldn't remember which character has that line, the Marschallin or Sophie's father. Degrading to forget. But now Farfalla's grandfather was beginning the long process of getting to his feet. Was he asking her to dance or did he want her to carry him to hospital? The music pulsed like blood. Elena would have liked to swerve about a bit in the manner she had once pioneered at the Peppermint Lounge in New York, but that would have to wait, although not, she hoped, for very long. The old roué would surely give up at the end of the first dance.

Alternatively he would disintegrate. Besides, there were already so many people dancing that it didn't matter what you did. The next President of the United States gestured from a distance, indicating that he would like to dance with her as soon as possible, or that the Sixth Fleet was currently making a circling manoeuvre at flank speed. Ian Cuthbert hopped by, snickering, having no doubt spotted Monty in the distance. The Barberini boys had a kick-line going. Elena's opera ball was a fable in the making.

It was about this time that Dick Toole and Delilah, after dodging several patrols and crossing half the river in a rowing boat, arrived at the central marquee and peered in. The second half of the river they had been obliged to cross without the boat, which had disclosed the reason for its availability by quickly sinking. As Dick Toole strove to keep his Instamatic raised high, his boots had filled with water, thereby adding interior discomfort to their exterior offensiveness. So he had abandoned them. But the night was warm and one look at the tumultuous, leaping multitude was enough to tell them that they would blend in unnoticed, as long as they avoided the hostess's eye.

Elena had to survive many obligatory wrestling matches with variously ancient and incapacitated male relatives before it became seemly to dance with Victor, who told her that she was managing superbly and that the evening was a success, two facts of which she was well aware. She was angry with him but it was still a great relief. He was a feather on his feet. He would have his work cut out, though, to perform his usual trick of making her heart light, now that it was he himself who was making it heavy.

'She looks more than usually sprightly this evening, our young friend,' said Elena.

'Which young friend is that?'

'Your eyes gave you away. It's never easy to mix the generations like this but we seem to have managed it in your case.'

'Bitch. You're the loveliest woman here by a long way.'

'Don't play those games with *me*. I was getting meaningless compliments from better men than you while you were still a wharfo or whatever it is you say you were.'

'A wharfie. First I was a reffo and then I was a wharfie. While you were still in *scuola media*. You're serious.'

'No I'm not. Dance closer. Let them talk.'

Lords This, That and The Other took her over in succession. By the time she had had enough of dancing, at least for a while, the ball had passed the status of legend and had reached that of institution, as though it would go on forever. The rain had stopped. The sides of the marquees and tents were rolled up where that was possible, so that the party and its music could spread out into the gardens and the orchards and along the river bank. Cleopatra's Dinghy, carrying flares fore and aft, threw a pool of yellow light on the river. Charlotte and David were content either to dance or sit, as long as it was together. At one point there was a mild sensation when the boys in the band recognised David and asked him to join them for a set. David, uncharacteristically willing to show off, obliged. Charlotte couldn't tell the sound his guitar made from all the other guitars but she loved the way he wagged his head. A good-looking girl dressed as Helen of Troy hopped about enthusiastically just in front of him, which Charlotte found very annoying, but when he put down the guitar he came straight back to monopolise her. Charlotte liked being monopolised. She even caught herself hoping that Lancelot could see her having that done to her. Careful to be elsewhere, Lancelot compulsively monopolised Samantha and suffered when she looked around for a line of escape. He, too, was looking around, but only to steer clear of Charlotte and keep tabs on the world's most famous young female film star, whose eye he was eager to avoid catching. Elena and Sally met near the house.

'Queues for the loos,' said Sally, momentarily at a loss. Her hostess, with all the interior lights turned on, made her feel as if she were wearing school uniform.

'How refreshing to have you to myself,' said Elena. 'Walk with me in the apple orchard. Has Nicholas fainted? Most of the young men in his age group appear to have done that at least twice by now.'

'Monty keeps asking him to dance so now he's doing it. Which causes all sorts of pain to a huge man dressed as a dwarf.'

'Ian Cuthbert. A great love since many years. My poor old

apple trees are getting the life sucked out of them by those upstart climbing roses, but the blossoms are so beautiful it's almost worth it.' On the gravel path of the orchard the world's most famous young female film star and her academic husband, dressed with becoming demureness as Susanna and Figaro, went past holding hands. And over there were the Striplings, dressed as Hansel and Gretel. A clever idea, made doubly clever when you saw that she was Hansel and he was Gretel. 'So many faithful couples,' said Elena.

'Who *was* Magda de Cuivry?' asked Sally, when they had finished laughing about everybody's costumes. The artificial light turned the drops of rain water still in the foliage to shiver-pearls.

'She was a luxury lady of a certain age with a banker for a lover. Then someone younger comes into the picture. But they're together in the end because time has trapped them. A sort of grown-ups' *Traviata*, without the tuberculosis.'

'It sounds grim.'

'It ought to be but the music's lovely. Vaguely Viennese but not sickly. A *Capriccio* you can sing, or can think you can. He wrote it when his energy was gone, as if he was already dead and knew what it was like to lose everything. No longer in the first blush I see the point of those twilight operas more and more.'

'You think of yourself as someone older? It's hard to believe.'

'You'd be surprised how hard it is to think of anything else. Anyway, Magda and Ranaldo have enough sense to cling on to each other.'

'Which one strays? Him or her?'

'She does. Not like real life. I couldn't have borne to be the Marschallin. She gives up too easily. Covering up all those mirrors. And she's here tonight at least fifty times, including Victor's wife, expiring in all that ermine and brocade.'

'She's very well preserved. Did someone take him away from her?'

'No, she just talked herself out of a job by weighing down on him. A man like that can stand anything but gravity.'

'Speak of the devil.' By the long route they had arrived back at the marquee and found Victor sitting at a table empty except for bottles and debris. They sat down each side of him and helped him to analyse the costumes.

'I can see another Manon,' said Victor, 'but even on the slave plantation she seems to have been eating very well.'

'She wasn't invited,' said Elena. 'Neither was that man she's with. Him I don't know at all. Clearly some species of criminal. Her I know all too well from long ago. Delilah Ball-Hunt. Her equally poisonous mother tried to launch her by ringing me up and cadging an invitation, which I extended, reaping an immediate libel as a reward.'

'If that's Delilah Ball-Hunt,' said Sally, 'then the chap must be Dick Toole.'

'The name means nothing.' Sally told her what it meant. At this point Elena's aptly named Uncle Lothario attempted to sit down but she moved too fast. 'Lothario will take me in pursuit. We might catch them pocketing the bibelots. Meanwhile I permit you to dance together.'

They danced very formally. 'She has a way of reminding us,' said Sally, 'that we inhabit a world of her invention.'

'To a large extent she's right.'

'Don't say things like that.'

'Then don't you say them either. Wait for New York.' So they talked of other things. But as far as Nicholas was concerned they might as well have been locked in an embrace. When he saw Sally with Victor or Elena he felt left out. Either of them was such a presence. He had just got through seeing her sitting with both of them. He was pained, vengeful and extremely drunk, so he took Samantha away from Lancelot and danced with her, meaning that he stood there and nodded, as if interviewing some garrulous polymath, while she flung herself about violently. A lot of men in silly hats roared encouragement in foreign languages. She certainly had a beautiful body. Not a woman's beautiful body, like Elena's. A girl's beautiful body, like Sally's. But unlike with Sally, you knew exactly where you were with Samantha – in dead trouble. So while Lancelot was elsewhere helping Serena to prop herself up, Nicholas took Samantha out into the garden, along a path through a multicoloured miniature forest of the kind of flowers that went up instead of out, and into another garden, if it wasn't the same garden coming back the other way.

'Have you come to steal my forks and spoons?' Elena asked Delilah.

'Lancelot Windhover said the idea was to just crash in,' said Delilah. The strange-looking man in bare stockings explained that he was only doing his job.

'That has been every sneak's excuse in history,' said Elena, with a smile which clearly indicated that she was not in a forgiving vein. But she had to admit that the interlopers' costumes were not bad: both of them looked as if they had been splashing about in the Everglades for a century, and you would have sworn that the weals on the woman's back were authentic. So she let them stay, on their promise that they would write nothing. It was already halfway between midnight and dawn. With the night almost over there was no point throwing them out. If she did that they would be sure to take their revenge, whereas if allowed to stay they only might. The lewd contempt on the man's face, however, was not easy to bear. Elena could not shake off the feeling of having been plunged into a grease trap — a state of mind familiar to victims of Dick Toole's column, which she had never read, but of which she thought she had an inkling.

So Dick Toole and Delilah went out into the garden and were in nice time to catch Samantha and Nicholas petting heavily in the pergola. Dick Toole got several good angles with his Instamatic, and was down on one knee securing a particularly revealing aspect when Lancelot arrived.

~ twenty-two ~

'Waugh!' Lancelot shouted at a patch of delphiniums. 'Whoah! Warp! Whip! Whack! Wahoo!' It was amazing how much the stomach could contain, even when you couldn't remember having eaten more than a few scraps. He rested, hoping it was over, but stayed where he was, knowing that it wasn't. 'Hip, hip, hurrah! Hoohah! Hooray! Hey!'

It had been dawn now for some time. The cow-trimmed willows had stopped being silhouettes and the lights had been turned off. Sparsely populating the thin mist from the river and the sopping meadows, people in the bedraggled remains of their personae queued at trestle tables for sausages, eggs and bacon cooked in the military manner by soldiers with perukes askew. The soldier who had got lucky with Deirdre Childworth was reputed to be now hiding in the back of a three-ton truck. Elena had been saying goodbye for several hours, but only to those people she encountered by chance as, still looking as unruffled as when the pageant began, she toured her little principality. There was no formal ending to the evening. It just melted away.

'*Una serata magica!*' croaked the burned-out husk of an Eboli. '*Veramente un sogno.*' And it really had been a dream.

'*Was ein Traum!*' said the stub of a Mandryka. '*Mythologische Szenen!*' And indeed it was a myth already.

Victor's ex-wife headed back to Long Island ten pounds lighter than when she had left it. Several of the mad cousins from the Salzkammergut flew home to Salzburg without changing out of their costumes, and were told to stow their horned helmets under the seat in front. But although people went on and on departing, somehow there were always some who remained, and Lancelot was one of them. After he had finished being ill, or at any rate finished the visible part of being ill, Lancelot straightened up, saw the film star and her husband heading towards him on the gravel walk, ducked adroitly through a gateway in the hedge bordering the river path, and ran on tip-toe in the crouching position until he felt at a safe distance to stop and stand upright. When he did so, it was to see, not to mention hear, the hunched, skipping figure of Ian Cuthbert going mad among the tilted willow trees at the water's edge, while from Cleopatra's Dinghy Randall Hoyle, Monty Forbes and several epicene young Italian nobles drawled and lisped encouragement.

'The Millers couldn't make it!' shouted the capering Ian. 'Glenn, Arthur, Henry and Ann!'

'The Manns couldn't make it,' said Randall Hoyle, and added his own responses: 'Thomas, Heinrich, Klaus, Erika, Anthony and Shelley.'

'The Berlins couldn't make it!' shouted Ian desperately. 'Irving and Isaiah!'

'We've *had* that,' Randall Hoyle objected. '*Everyone* knows that one. And anyway, Isaiah's here. The Russells couldn't make it. Bertrand and Rosalind.'

'The Lawrences couldn't make it,' said Monty. 'D. H., T. E., Gertrude and Sarah.'

'The Coopers couldn't make it. Gary, Gladys, Fenimore and Diana . . . '

'She's here too, being Suor Angelica . . . '

'No, that's Mother Teresa being Julie Andrews . . . '

'*Che dice?*'

'*Ha detto che Madre Teresa è come Julie Andrews.*'

'*Buffo.*'

'The Frys couldn't make it. Roger, Christopher, Northrop . . . '

The voices sounded simultaneously loud and isolated, as if the time for them to be raised was over. They were keeping the cows awake. Not fair, now that it was another day. The sun had burned off the mist and for once the air was dry. Stopping sometimes to sit down, Lancelot went to the mill house, but the doors were locked. It goes hard, to be locked out of your own house when you are dressed for execution. He sat down for an hour or so. Then he went back along the path through the trees and came upon a vision of the night before, except that now it all lay bare under the bright morning. The people who hired out the tents and marquees had come and taken them away, so that all the tables full of coloured streamers and stacked crockery and scraps of rotting salmon were standing out under the sun, with chairs tipped over amongst the broken glass and the occasional sagging Siegfried or collapsed Cavaradossi sitting where he had finally seized up, fused at last by the extravagant stimulus of champagne from which the ultimate bubbles had long escaped. White doves from the dove-cotes in the barns found easy pickings.

Threading her way between small silent clouds of midges, an ancient woman who could only be an Austro-Hungarian archduchess if not an escapee from a Victorian asylum saw Lancelot from a long way away and came weaving slowly towards him through the wreckage.

'*Mein guter Mann*,' she said, having mistaken him for a flunkey, '*haben Sie mein' Ohrring geseh'n?*' He pretended for a little while to help her look for her earring and then bequeathed her to one of the local people who had evidently been given the job of cleaning up.

In normal circumstances Lancelot would have summoned up a pang of conscience about how the peasantry was being exploited but as a representative of the *ancien régime* who was about to be decapitated he felt that he had paid his debt to equality. Either that, or he felt awful. Yes, he felt awful. So he went into Elena's house to find a nice quiet lavatory and be sick, but when he found one he had nothing to bring up except bad air. He tried to find a room with a bed but all the upstairs bedroom doors were locked except one. Farfalla lay there asleep under a pale blue canopy, with her silk suit thrown carelessly over the foot of the enamelled iron bedstead. The sight was too pure for his red-raw eyes to take in, so he went downstairs and lay down on the floor in the library, using a cushion from one of the leather armchairs as a pillow.

He was not the first prostrate figure Elena saw that morning as she made the final round of her devastated lands. On the river bank she found Ian Cuthbert sobbing bitterly and demanding to be left alone, a request she fulfilled gladly enough. 'The Sutherlands couldn't make it,' she heard him crying. 'Joan and Graham . . . ' One of the Farinata degli Uberti Montefeltro Cavalcanti boys, she was told, had been discovered in a heap of streamers and given artificial respiration, whereupon he had coughed a sudden flurry of confetti. Cousin Rudolph's Parsifal outfit had been found abandoned in the boat-house. But by that stage they were saying anything. The celebrated actor was floating smile upwards in the swimming pool, having judged the party in Paris to be too dull and found his way here by the radar that seeks out fame. Lancelot's awful girl Samantha was sitting on the edge of the pool and listlessly pelting him with rose petals, which was all very well if you hadn't grown the rose bushes from which they had been stripped. Just because Elena was triumphant did not mean that she was in a good temper. Before dawn Victor had left for London, and with him gone the night had lost its point. Black and White had nicely come to say goodbye but that young man of hers had lurked sulkily in the background. Apparently there had been some terrible quarrel. Not good. What Elena wanted from those two was sweetness and light in large quantities. So she was inclined to be a bit abrupt when she met Whit Coburg in front of the house. Being asked to look for an earring in the midst of all this went too far. But she summoned her graciousness, promised that the earring would be searched for later on by troops if necessary, and made arrangements for the old horror to be taken back to her hotel. On the low light-grey and pitted lilac wall separating the forecourt of the house from the coachyard, the noseless stone bust of a Greek goddess looked long-suffering under its recently acquired plumed hat. Elena gathered up her skirts and climbed the steps When she saw Lancelot on the floor of the library she thought he was dead, his mouth was so white. It was a crime, how much could happen to that face of his and still leave it looking young. She could have sent him home but decided he had been punished enough. And for nothing, really. She went up to bed for a quiet hour before starting the long job of putting everything to rights. As always, she undressed in front of the mirror.

With the children and the dogs all far away in London, there was nobody in the locked mill house except Charlotte and David. Although he profoundly disapproved of almost everything that had happened during the evening, nevertheless David could not deny that it had provided rich potential material, and the last part of it had left him more pleased than anything which had ever occurred to him in his life, with the possible exception of the publication of his book. As for Charlotte, she would have said she was speechless, if only she had been able to shut up. Even though dazed by fatigue she felt as if she had been breathing laughing gas. She had already felt like that while talking to Randall Hoyle, who had been so flatteringly ready to hear her tell him about Peacock. He was just starting to read Peacock for the first time and said he would relish some advice. Charlotte had recommended Priestley's essay. 'What? Old Priestley? You're kidding.' No, it was an excellent essay. And she had gone on to prove it, quoting chapter and verse. She had felt elated as she always did when teaching an ideal pupil, although it was necessary to remember how this ideal pupil could be mortally wounding when he chose. And in fact he had gone on to insult everyone at the table except her. So he was not an ideal pupil. But she had only ever had one ideal pupil, and that was David. She had realised, while sitting there pronging a piece of the inspiringly flimsy meringue perimeter of a cream pie, that David was an unmixed delight for her. She adored everything about him. He was probably right about the necessity to nationalise the means of production, distribution and exchange: who was she to say? All she had on her side was reason. And the champagne powerfully suggested that reason was not enough. There was also feeling, and about that she had reasoned for too long. Reasoning about feeling had been her big trouble. Keeping silent had been her even bigger trouble. She should have talked. She told David about all that while they were dancing, and then told him again after she had taken him home to bed. How very handy, that home was just along the path. Across the river and into the sheets. Practically no other woman at the party who took a lover that night would be able to offer him a bed with fresh linen. A fresh hedge would be about the best they could do.

'Are you sure about this?' asked David. 'You're blotto, you know.'

'I've had about a glass and a half,' Charlotte protested. 'It's just high spirits, I promise. Help me with these buttons.'

She had absolved herself in advance from all blame, as if what was about to happen would be a transitory act of self-indulgence, like staying home sick from school when you weren't really. But instead it was a transformation. A quiet transformation, admittedly. Unlike Lancelot, David did not leave you flabbergasted. It was not a monologue, meant to astonish. It was a conversation. She felt that her body was being listened to for the first time. Everything was muted, even sedate. You couldn't imagine that a video cassette of what they did would be much of a hit on the domestic blue movie market. But on the inside she felt that she was being thoroughly gone into for the first time, like a literary subject which had previously been touched only by the kind of cerebral stunt-man who wears shoes like Cornish pasties and writes books with such titles as *Yeats and Embezzlement*, but which was now being dealt with, on a lifetime basis, by a serious scholar. Quite a nicely shaped serious scholar too, in his unspectacular way. She giggled at the wrong time but soon talked him out of his annoyance. She practically talked him out of the room.

'I thought you were supposed to be the reticent type,' he said during a lull. They lay there listening as the last cars departed from the meadow. They invented fantasies about the possible occupants.

'That'll be Sally doing a Le Mans start,' said David.

'There goes Monty and Randall Hoyle kidnapping Nicholas,' said Charlotte, 'with Ian Cuthbert giving them a push.'

'There goes Lancelot,' said David, 'and Samantha's in the back seat with the New Taste Thrills.'

'Don't be cruel about Lancelot,' said Charlotte, without looking in the least worried. David was asleep when she heard the front door rattle downstairs, but she decided not to move. If she was too happy to sleep then she was certainly too happy to get out of bed. Suddenly she realised she was dead sober, which meant that for the first time in her life she knew exactly what it felt like to be drunk. When you actually *were* drunk, of course, you couldn't know. She had underrated herself as a logician. It had been cowardly of her to back out of those lectures about Hume. Next year she would be bolder. In every respect, from now on, she would be that. Finally, able to do anything, she would stop time.

'Why are you crying?' asked David, feeling flattered because he thought he knew the answer.

On the way home, Nicholas saw no reason to tell Sally that he had made a fool of himself with Samantha, especially when the provocation that had driven him to it was not yet avenged. So instead of apologising he attacked.

'A bit more of that,' she said with a dab of the right foot, 'and you can get out and walk.' They were doing considerably more than a hundred, so the threat was hollow, he presumed.

'You always look as if you want to climb into the cot with both of them.'

'I never look anything of the kind. I'm sober and dignified at all times. More than I can say for some.'

'What's that supposed to mean?'

'You drink too much.'

'You're *supposed* to drink too much. It's a *ball*, for fuck's sake.'

'You drink too much anyway. It can't give you confidence. Nothing can give people confidence except self-control. I can't give you confidence.'

'You're right about that. I feel I'm on the verge of losing you all the time.'

'You got me, didn't you?'

'But that's just it. Before I did, and just after I did, I felt great. And then I felt too much. Now I spend most of the day in pain that only you can stop.'

'It sounds like hell.'

'There you go again.'

'What do you mean?'

'Saying you don't feel the same.'

'I don't, no.'

'You don't feel anything.'

'I do. And you're not going to lose me, except if you keep this up.' And that was the lie that made her feel guilty, instead of the lack of love which merely left her helpless. Because now she felt that he really was going to lose her, whatever happened next. And it wasn't his fault, so she would have to be decent, and not take away from him what he wanted, even though she herself no longer wanted it that much. But might again? What a shambles. The empty royal jelly car-park on a Sunday morning was a strange place to be Salome. She took Aubrey Beardsley upstairs to bed with her because it would have been heartless not to. And so lonely, too.

'It was fantastic,' said Victor on the phone early that evening.
'Talk English,' said Elena. 'I've had enough of my native language to last me.'
'Has it all been spirited away?'
'On trucks. In great black plastic sacks of garbage. Poor Ian Cuthbert is in the hospital because he had some sort of truss on and it gave him all kinds of cramps and spasms. A soldier with a metal-finding whosis has been out looking for Wini Coburg's earring that Napoleon III gave her in a weak moment. I've got Lancelot Windhover living in my library, the broken glass is all trodden into the mud for a square mile, the rotting fish smells like a whaling station, It's like that.'
'It's history.'
'That's putting it a bit high.'
'Aussie expression. When you say it's history you mean it's over. Actually in this case it *is* history. Nobody who was there will ever forget it.'
'And all they'll do is bore the ones who weren't. It's not much of an art form, mine. Nothing but hearsay.'
'At least you've *got* an art form.'
'Why so gloomy?'
'I'm not.'
'Something you've done, or something you might do?'
'Just tired. I'm getting old.'
'Feeling you can't afford to let a good opportunity slip?'
'You're my good opportunity.'
'Don't you forget it.'
'I won't.'
Elena put down the telephone and was preparing for an early night when the front doorbell rang. It was Frank Strain, dressed as Radames. He was holding his invitation as if it were a ticket that she might want to tear in half.

~ twenty-three ~

U sually when Sally was in New York she stayed at one of those old brown hotels on West 43rd Street where all the habitués of the Algonquin Round Table used to live because it was too expensive to sleep at the Algonquin. But this time, with the Americans paying half the bill and her company paying the other, she was at the Plaza, with a window on the park and air conditioning that didn't rattle even when it was full on — which it had to be, because Manhattan was already flooded with an invisible river of heat. Dinner on the first evening felt to her like breakfast of the next day, but the Americans could not have been nicer. They wanted her to be their front-person in Europe. In return for this they could offer her hard work and not much of a salary, in view of the kernt economic climate. The kernt economic climate was what came between the previous economic climate and the future economic climate. It was one of those deals where responsibility came with the freedom and well-nigh overwhelmed it. But the man who did most of the talking was so visionary that even his dandruff looked enthusiastic. His name was Saul Newman. Not Paul Newman, Saul Newman. The amazing thing about these American men was the way that if they weren't all nylon hair transplants and silicone-filled wrinkles polished with a buffing wheel then they were falling apart in front of your eyes. Saul Newman was falling apart in front of your eyes, but he was telling her that she could make her own programmes. His wife and his business associate and *his* wife and their secretary were all there too, backing Saul up. The standard way of backing Saul up, it soon became clear, was to get a word of agreement in edgeways when he drew breath and to nod emphatically at all other times, except when you were dutifully expiring with laughter at his jokes. Everything that was said was frantically energetic but nobody had any sense of irony or nuance, so that to Sally it all seemed to be happening at high speed and in slow motion, leaving her simultaneously excited and bored stiff. But that was America, and at least she could yawn with a good excuse. Making sympathetic noises, they let her go early.

From the restaurant in Greenwich Village she took a cab back to Central Park South and found herself at midnight sitting wide awake in her hotel room. While her fatigued body reflexively stirred at a phantom dawn, she watched a sophisticated late night comedian cracking eggs on the bare head of some ex-President's brother. Had the sophisticated late night comedian's hair turned lime green since she had last seen it? Was the set out of whack? It was an insoluble epistemological problem, because there was nobody else on any other channel he could reliably be compared to. They all looked like exercises in cosmeticised prosthesis. So she rang Victor.

'I'll send a car,' he said.

'Don't be silly.' She realised as she said it that she had caught the expression from him. 'I'll take a cab.'

Victor's apartment was the entire upper floor of a building on Fifth Avenue a few blocks above the Frick Collection. Indeed when Sally was shown in she thought it might be part of the Frick Collection. But she liked the original paintings less than the reproduction of Holbein's drawing of Thomas More's family. Hugely blown up so that the figures were life size, it had been heat-sealed against one of the walls and made you feel that they were standing in the room with you.

'That one was his favourite daughter,' said Victor, pointing to Margaret Roper. 'She would have been the television star if anyone had invented it. Even old Erasmus was astonished by her. My idea of family life.'

'It's all very English of you.'

'Like a flash Wimpy bar. I get patriotic when I'm away from home. Did you have a good flight?' It was a meaningless question. It's a good flight if you don't crash.

'I did, as a matter of fact. The captain was a big fan so I was on the flight deck when we made landfall. New York is very beautiful from up there.'

'It's not bad from down here, just at the moment.' He smiled with pure pleasure.

They had a fiasco but it didn't matter, at any rate not for her. For her it went without saying that just lying down together was all right, especially when she was so sleepy, or should have been. For him it needed saying, so he said it. 'Fatal at my age to think you've only got one chance,' said Victor. 'Fatal at any age, but especially at my age.' She told him that he could have as many chances as he liked. Then she made him lie still and do nothing while she took what she promised would only be a nap. After sleeping for hours while he lay awake doting on her, she woke up just as he was falling asleep. And so on. It got to be a joke. The best joke, she assured him, that she had ever been in on.

Back at the hotel she slept properly until noon, taped two interviews in the afternoon and then slept again until the middle of the evening. Victor was in Washington but he sent a car for her when he got back. It was part of the joke: a Lincoln Continental with an extra section welded into the middle and the windows tinted so that the whole world would know someone important was inside but would not be able to tell who it was. Turning left out of Madison Avenue was like driving a nuclear reactor through an English village.

But when she got there the joke was soon over. Now they were in the same place at the same time. So this is what I've been waiting for, she thought. Well, well. 'I wish you wouldn't look at me,' said Victor. 'My poor raddled corpse is such an insult to you that I feel ashamed.' But by that stage he was fishing for compliments. Eventually she made him stop showing off and slept again. A click from the telephone console beside her bed woke her at four in the morning. She found him two rooms away talking Italian. To London, of course. Jealousy struck her with the force of bereavement. She made him get dressed and take her walking. Or rather she took him walking, because clearly he had not walked in New York or anywhere else for a thousand years. She didn't particularly mind if he got shot at. She would quite like him to be strafed by a MiG. And besides, if he took her anywhere it would only be to somewhere he had been before with someone else. So she took him to that street, only a few blocks north, where the concrete sidewalk is full of little bits of metal that shine as if the earth were a reflection of the night sky.

'Why do you like women?' she asked as they walked.

'Which women?'

'I don't mean specific women. Women generally. You don't just want us, you like us. We pick it up, you know.'

'Yes, I suppose I do. I've just always found solace in them. A cruel man is nothing strange. Whereas except in Turkey and places like that, a cruel woman is a real freak.'

'There'd be plenty of cruel women if women had more power.'

'You sound envious. And anyway I don't think it's true. Irma Gries or Myra Hindley would still be exceptional. Extreme brutality is a male preserve. Some women go along with it, but most don't. Most of them couldn't.'

'When did you arrive at these strange conclusions?'

'I didn't arrive at them. I started with them.'

'How was that?'

'When I was quite small a lot of people spat at me. The woman who was taking us through to Norway said it was a local mark of respect. She seemed to me the incarnation of safety and peace even then. Now I remember her as the model of sanity. And ever since I've got from women what strength I have. Or tried to.'

'Strength you're not short of.'

'That shows how young you are. It's only by accident that I'm not helpless.'

'I should have thought that there couldn't be a man more in control of his own destiny.'

'By accident. Dumb luck. I can still imagine my father in the dining hall. In my imagination it's always called the dining hall but it was really a sort of huge hut, like a warehouse. Those places were even more hellish before the war than later on. They had to eat their bowl of slop while those who were up for punishment were being tortured in the same room. God knows what it was like to be spreadeagled and stamped on. I can't even guess. But I *can* guess what it was like to sit there and be able to do nothing, while you ate your slop so that you could live another day.'

'Stop it. Not tonight.'

'Or ever again. But that's what you're getting when you hold my poor flabby body in your strong toils of grace. Gratitude.

You'll have other men who'll love you with more stamina and more skill but you'll never meet a man who knows better than I do what he's getting. Life. You are what it means. I am the man who knows. And now, for my next publishing event, I give you lower Manhattan at the dawn of a new day.'

As they walked south on Fifth Avenue, the ridge of buildings that included her hotel gradually stopped looking like boxes of pearl grey smoke. The sun came up and they went back to bed. Later on she took him to the fifth floor of Bloomingdale's for a breakfast of frozen yoghurt. 'I feel like an adult in a children's playground,' said Victor, balancing on his high stool.

'It won't kill you. Stop being patronising and admit this tastes terrific.'

'It does.'

'Why did she want Gianni to marry that well-connected zero of a girl?'

'She's not a zero. She knows all about the history of art, for example. Which you don't. But the answer to the question is because there wasn't any girl like you who wanted the job instead.'

'Why marry him off anyway?'

'Because that's what ordinary people do.'

'What's ordinary about *them*?'

'But that's exactly what they are. They're just rich ordinary people instead of poor ones. Very nice, very ordered lives, more bourgeois than the bourgeois. What would they do better? You can't imagine how rare it is to want the sort of life you want. I mean *really* want it, not just play at it.'

'You two are always telling me what I can't imagine.'

'It's the only thing we've got that you haven't. Experience.'

'Don't say "we".'

'If you said "you two" I thought it was all right to say "we".'

'So did I, but it wasn't.'

'Let's talk about something else.'

When Sally got back to her hotel she found among her messages a note saying that Nicholas had rung that morning. She had a heavy afternoon ahead but she called him after having appropriately luxuriated in a bubble bath. It turned out, however, that his annoyance at having found her out at such an hour was offset by an apologetic note on his own behalf. It was easy enough for her to say that she had been out walking, because she had been, really. But he was having trouble clearing his side of the air. Finally he managed to choke out that Dick Toole's column had carried an account of the ball which included their names.

'That's not so bad,' said Sally, as she lay there on the made bed, extending one leg vertically and examining her pointed toes. 'I suppose it had to happen. Why don't you read it to me?'

'It's pretty bitchy about you.'

'I'd be insulted if it were anything else.'

'There's a lot about the ball. "Publicity-shy Elena ran tight security to keep out interpolators. Was elegant Elly worried that the great unwashed would pinch her spoons? Or was she afraid that the locals might start harping back at so many Germans and Italians in comic opera uniforms, when not so long ago, in the hell of WWII, they were fighting them in their Afrika Korps tanks?" You can see that he's well down to his usual standard.'

'I like "interpolators". Read the bit about us.'

'It says, "Telly-girl Sally Draycott, playmate cohort of novelist Nicholas Crane and *alias* known as the Golden Girl of the Goggle-box, appears to have decided that she belongs with the *nobless oblige*." I think he means with the élite.'

'I know. It doesn't sound too terrible. Is that the lot?'

'Well, no, actually.'

'Why don't you just read it out and I'll tell you when to stop?'

'Here's the next bit. "Our Sally may have moved up in the world, but she was reportedly furious when supremo novelist Nifty Nick flaunted the rules. He was off grappling in the gazebo, if I may borrow a terminology from one of his own novels, with his fellow scribe Samantha Copperglaze, the girl who lives like something out of one of his own *oeuvres*. Fading Sixties 'poet' Lancelot Windhover, Samantha's regular literary adviser, made a rapid *exeunt* from the scene." His Latin's on a par with his English.'

'Is there anything in what he says?'

'There's a picture.'

'What picture?'

'Me and Sam. I'm afraid we did have a bit of a snog and Delilah must have snapped it. I can remember thinking I saw a flash at the time but I must have thought it was just part of being drunk. Which I was, very. And wanting to punish you for having such a good time with the oldies.'

'Some punishment. Like sticking your head in the garbage and yelling "Look what you made me do". What's in this picture, exactly?'

'I've sort of got my hand up her dress.'

'Find anything up there that you liked?'

'Nothing surprising.'

'Is she an old friend, then?'

'Just after Lancelot discovered her, yes. Very briefly. When she was still at Oxford. I kept it dark because I didn't want to hurt him.'

'You didn't want to hurt *him*.'

'No.'

'It seems you missed a few out when you read me your *curriculum vitae*.'

'It was meaningless.'

'The ones you told me about were supposed to be that.'

'I suppose I was a bit scared of ever having known her that well. She isn't quite all there, you know. We said goodbye after she tried to serve me the bottom of a broken milk bottle in a plate of breakfast food. I hardly laughed at all.'

'It's all right.'

'Lancelot's forgiven me. I think he was pleased to get a mention.'

'So have I. I said it was all right. It doesn't matter.'

'Why doesn't it matter? I thought it would matter like hell. That's why I'm telling you. So that nobody else will tell you first. You might have had old Delilah ringing you up to ask for your comments.'

Suffering from a bad conscience, he was unable to take offence with a whole heart, so she got away with her indifference. Which would have left her with a bad conscience of her own if she had felt less elated, but she had made a pact with herself that time would not start again until she got back to London. Victor wanted to take her to *Der Rosenkavalier* because she had complained about the way everybody talked about it in front of her as if she was supposed to know the plot. But he had obviously seen it all too often in company with other people. She didn't feel like treading on other people's ground just now. So she made him take her to the movies at the art house opposite Lincoln Center. She had seen *Otto e mezzo* only once and he, so he alleged, had seen it eight and a half times. God knows who with. But at least not in this city, or so he said. Making him sit through it again was supposed to be her test of his claim that the film was inexhaustible, but he obviously enjoyed it. Too obviously: she had to stop him mouthing the dialogue. It looked to her like the greatest work of art in the world but in her present mood she would have felt the same way about *Firemaidens from Outer Space*. Afterwards they walked to a restaurant she knew on Columbus Avenue where you can sit at a table on the sidewalk while the waiters whizz around on roller skates. It wasn't Victor's usual sort of thing at all. After receiving his assurance that there was small likelihood of his being assassinated, she settled back to enjoy the way he looked apprehensive when two servings of chopped steak went whirling past his head. It was so seldom that you ever saw him – what was the word? – discombobulated.

'Do you think he's right about men?' she asked, genuinely wanting to know. Because if she didn't get the answer now she never would.

'In what respect?'

'In the movie he gives himself a whole seraglio. Is that what you all want?'

'Do you mean "you all" in the Deep Southern sense of just me, or do you mean all of us in general?'

'Answer the question.'

'No. He's saying he can't help his imagination being like that, but that you can't live your life that way either. It's just struck me that if you play the ASA NISI MASA game on the name of the game itself, you get ANIMA. Soul. Mozart and his sister used to play a word game just like it.'

'Don't be irrelevant. Can you help *your* imagination being like that?'

'Like what?'

'Devious sod. I'm asking whether you imagine your various

women getting on like a house on fire while you're busy creating.'

'I don't create. And what I envy the creative genius is his creativity, not his privileges. Did you know that Casanova in his old age fell in love with a young female mathematician?'

'Answer the bloody question.'

'This is about us, isn't it?'

'Of course. I'm trying to get some idea of what I can expect.'

'All right. The answer's yes. I don't want to lose what I've got simply because I've found something else that I want just as much. I can imagine how the two things could be reconciled. But that's only what I imagine.'

'So I'm on borrowed time.'

'You underestimate your power. It would make someone else extremely unhappy, and no doubt me along with her, but all you would have to do is insist. Did you ever come to this place with anyone else?'

'Yes, but it didn't matter. Nothing I ever did before I met you could possibly matter. There's only one of us who's got a past.'

'What about Mr Crane?'

'That's all your fault.'

'How?'

'For not meeting me earlier.'

'If I'd met you any earlier you would have still been at school. And then there would have been no doubt about it. I would have been a dirty old man for all to see.' He sat back contentedly as he said that, just as a waiter raced past behind him on urgently sizzling wheels. A portion of banana cream pie came within an inch of shattering his reserve.

'What are you laughing at?' asked Victor.

'You, looking annoyed.'

'I must admit that in my usual haunts there's less chance of ending up with the dessert sitting on top of my head. But perhaps I've been missing something.'

'Take me home and I'll show you what you've been missing.'

There is a stage all lovers go through in which they tell each other everything that has ever happened to them, or pretend to. It happened with these two in several long instalments over the next few nights. Sally felt that her side of the exchange was a pamphlet compared with an encyclopedia, but that was what she had always wanted. As she lay beside him and listened, she could actually feel what he was saying coming into her and making her wealthy, as if she were some science fiction heroine strapped down under a tin cap and being supplied with a superior brain by electrical impulses. But her few days were taken up with interviews, talkative business lunches and more opportunities to hear Saul Newman wax eloquent, so when the time came for her to leave the laboratory and fly back to London the transference was by no means complete. She wondered if it ever would be, and what he had taken from her in return, apart from all that stuff about solace. 'We didn't see much of you,' said the nice young man as she checked out. Though patently a fairy he looked quite wistful. All the world loves a lover.

~ twenty-four ~

L ife for Lancelot was coming apart with such thoroughness
that he wondered why his bicycle was still working. Every
day, with never a puncture or a broken spoke, it took him to the
office so that he could hear more bad news. Ian Cuthbert was
recuperating in a clinic, where, after they had straightened out
his spine, it had been found advisable to detoxify him. Lancelot
had sent Serena along to extract from the convalescent some
amplification to the list of writers who could draw and artists
who could write. Whether out of misogynist rancour or a
deranged mind, Ian had sent her off in search of a document
called *Mrs Ruisdael's Diary*. She had wasted days on the search
and was to waste many days more in useless tears after Lancelot
told her that she had been led up the garden path. Brian
Hutchings continued to be tardy about supplying his manu-
script. Lancelot had put Janice on the job of badgering him but
Brian simply refused to talk to her, a standpoint he was able to
back up with force, because he had acquired a Janice of his own,
called Katja. The thought of those two communicating by
telephone aroused visions of the Four Horsemen of the
Apocalypse riding around your living room. Meanwhile Lance-
lot's tax case continued to acquire complications, like a cloud
shading from violet to steel blue. And Elena, for some reason,
seemed to be holding him responsible for her opera ball being
mentioned in the newspapers. But at least Samantha had come
through with the goods, in the literary sense at any rate. Things
might have been tolerable if she had been equally forthcoming
in other departments.

But she was being hard to find, and, when found, hard to
please. Several times he had parked his bicycle outside her
basement flat at the appointed time in the early evening, only to
discover that she was not at home, and with no note left on the
door. More often, she was physically present but mentally

absent, muttering vague generalisations about his lack of commitment to her. Employing a stratagem against theft which he had learned in New York, he would chain his bicycle to her area railings, loosen the wing nuts on the front wheel, carry the wheel down the steps and lean it against her wall before lying down with her to enjoy the only reliable privilege the English summer affords – the possibility of fornicating on the bed instead of in it. Even with her mind elsewhere she still had the body to make all the pedalling worth while, but things were not what they had been and he wondered how he might restore them to their former glory. He had planned to get out of going on the family holiday to Biarritz. Now that Charlotte was refusing to sleep with him he had every excuse for staying in London. Let David build the driftwood shelters. But Samantha announced that she would be going again, to the big house just down the coast where he had first met her. Once again she would be with her father, who disapproved of Lancelot, and her step-mother, who absolutely hated him, for trifling reasons arising from a too abruptly terminated affair twenty years before. But he would be able to meet Samantha in secret, or at any rate idolise her from a distance. He felt his need for her increasing as she slipped away. It was a pretty staggering thing for his need to do, when you considered the pitch of intensity it had long ago attained and never looked like losing.

Lancelot was still allowed into his house, but was required to lie down alone at all times. Charlotte had explained to him about David. Lancelot judged the embargo to be very reasonable but almost immediately began to feel hard done by. After all, it was not as if he were having an easy time with Samantha. He could have used some placid solidity to fall back on. Hints in this direction, however, were met with a certain impatience. He could come on the holiday if he wished, but he would have to sleep downstairs on the same floor as the children, even though David would not be there. Well, at least he would be able to keep up appearances.

The Windhovers' prospective house guests in Biarritz had not as yet come to any such crisis, but the easy days were gone. Sally had surprised herself by being able to go on sleeping with Nicholas: anyone who had dared tell her she would ever be capable of such a thing she would once have treated with contempt for the imputation as well as outrage at the intimacy. But the ructions which she was assured were going on between Victor and Elena left Victor little time to spare, so her time with him in New York still seemed like an interlude, and anyway even if she had wished to give Nicholas his cards she was not sure she knew how. He was so entertaining when he wasn't being the opposite, and he was only ever the opposite because of the intensity of his feelings. The worrying intensity of his feelings. Worrying because she didn't share them. This is how whores must feel. Although if they did, they wouldn't do it, would they? Let it all wait until after Biarritz. Victor would be in Salzburg or somewhere. The whole of London was breaking up for the hols, pip pip. Every living soul except ninety per cent of the population was getting ready to move out. Until then she went on enjoying Nicholas, while pretending to herself that she was not a hypocrite. It got harder to do that when she caught herself living for the telephone.

'You've got good nerves,' Victor said to her during one of his breakfast phone calls.

'I don't *want* to have good nerves,' she pointed out with some acerbity. He had the grace not to laugh.

He had nothing to laugh about, really. Elena had not taxed him directly on the subject but she didn't need to. Her intuition would have told her, even if his attentiveness had not given him away. Remembering her birthday had been a particularly glaring mistake. So against her standing orders, which forbade mentioning such a thing should it ever eventuate, he mentioned it.

'It's all your fault,' he said, in a foredoomed attempt to make light of it. 'You made me like the world.'

'If you see her in secret I might just about put up with this,' said Elena, with a serenity that boded ill. 'But if you acknowledge her even once, I'm gone for good. My pride wouldn't stand it. I'll just go back to Italy and preside over the final disintegration.'

All of which having been said and a lot more on the same lines, grief played its usual trick of repristinating passion. But the way the tears taste tells you what that's worth. She blamed life, not him, but he would rather have taken the blame himself.

When they weren't together they were on the telephone far into the night. Elena withdrew from social life and the word went out that she was indisposed. But she and Victor had made arrangements to be in Salzburg together and felt that they might as well go.

So the exodus began. David and Gaga went furthest, to an Indian lake where they took up residence on a raft which had a little colour-washed plaster and lath replica of the Brighton Pavilion balanced on it to keep off the sun. At Gaga's request they had gone there in search of their first simplicity, but they could not find it, because when you have to look it's too late. In a by now desperate flight from capitalist values, the beautiful Gaga submitted herself gladly to her surroundings. She willed the primordial listlessness of the place to enter into her. Unfortunately some form of amoebic dysentery entered into her as well, and their holiday became a nightmare best left undocumented. The newspaper which had sponsored the trip received from David an article which could have gone equally well in a medical section as in a travel supplement. The editors could not make their minds up, so they spiked it.

Dick Toole and Delilah went to a Caribbean island where one of the British princesses was taking a holiday during pregnancy. They had to come ashore at night in a rubber boat and found themselves outdone in terms of aggression by the French, German and Italian photographers, who had built hides in the undergrowth, disguised themselves as palm trees and were regularly delivered, wrapped up as parcels, on the verandah of the royal villa. But Dick Toole and Delilah picked up a lot of useful information by using Delilah's contacts and getting a few hangers-on to talk off the record in confidence. And the climate was so benign that even Dick Toole stripped down all the way to his grey vest, while together he and Delilah found several interesting new uses for her hired Scuba gear.

Charlotte, Lancelot and the children left for Biarritz in the weekly Caravelle. When the children had been much younger the annual trip had had some point, with even Lancelot glad to be away from some importunate *innamorata*. Now that the children were grown up there was less reason for going, in his opinion. The children still liked it because the town had all the same discos and Space Invaders machines as London but there was an even greater opportunity to spend their father's money. Apart from that the only real advantage was not to waste the house which by some old arrangement they took every year. It was poised on one of the few stretches of cliff above the Côte des Basques which showed as yet no signs of collapsing into the sea. Further south there was another beach on which Samantha annually appeared like a Homeric nymph, and then further south than that was Spain, represented, on a clear day, by mountains as delicately blue as the veins in a girl's breast. When the weather changed it gave you bad dreams, but when the sun shone it was a dream pure and simple.

Sally and Nicholas came down in the Porsche, stopping off when they felt like it and so taking two days for the trip. It should have been bliss and some of it even was. Nicholas loved it when Sally put her foot right down and the poplars lining the road turned into a picket fence. He loved hearing her talk French even if the waiters loved it too, not to mention the proprietors and half the other men in town, who would suddenly drop in to stage a spontaneous gesticulation competition. But something was going wrong in the nights. Until he had met her, he would have sworn that the body was the incarnation of the self. Looking at her as she lay stretched out, it was hard to believe that if she could give you all that then there was anything left to hold back. But she would not say the words.

In Biarritz she still wouldn't say them. Walking beside her on the beach gave him a hint of what it must have felt like to be Alexander the Great Sod or one of those characters. Frogs sucked in their stomachs and walked into each other. There were a lot of terrible Australian media types reputedly in search of a perfect wave that would remind them of the beach back home at Bang-Bang or Kogra-Wogra: the kind of Australians who carried a lot of food around with them just so they could talk with their mouths full. They moaned low as they stared up with crinkled slit eyes from under the brims of rat-eaten straw hats, saying things like 'Stone the crows'. It should have been ideal. He was friends again with Lancelot, whose children were less terrifying to look at without their bells and spangles, and whose wife looked happier than he had ever known her.

Nicholas had the queen of the beach on his arm. In the cliff-top restaurant at sunset, with the sky the colour of faded pink geranium petals, her peach-skin tan was framed against the pale green tamarisks and the silver water like a meal for the eyes. But in the ground floor separate flat which they had been assigned, she would never say the proper things during the night. It was torture. At least Lancelot could be certain that Charlotte was all his, even to the extent of his being able to fix her up with a handbag holder like David. What was Lancelot's secret?

Only Charlotte knew exactly where she was. Usually she was under the driftwood shelter, reading up for a series of lectures on Burns. What a joyful spirit he had. What a *man* he must have been. She could see the idea of him now. That rhythm of his was something she now recognised as the pulse of her own bloodstream. It caused a stir under the cutty sark. Sometimes she almost felt like asking Lancelot into her bed again, but it would have spoiled things. All she had to do was wait. What a change, to know a man whose promises were worth something.

Lancelot suffered. He did not mind so much being barred from Charlotte's bed, as long as nobody knew. But the obvious happiness of Sally and Nicholas was more than he could stand. On the day after Samantha was supposed to arrive he rang her house and got her father, so he said 'Sorry, wrong number' in falsetto French and hung up, rather abashed that in his haste he had translated these words literally instead of using an idiomatic phrase. The next morning he rang again and got her, but all she could say was that it was difficult. So that afternoon, and all the afternoons that followed, he took the long walk south, hoping to catch a glimpse of her. Eventually he did, and she was with the actor. Everyone in the vicinity was staring towards that smile. Some of them were taking photographs. It was a topless beach and the sight of her digging her hard bare breasts into that man was transmitted to Lancelot as the stab of a spear under his own heart. He looked wistfully across the rippling shallow water which at mid-tide divided the two beaches and decided not to cross. He felt himself to be an ashen-faced Aschenbach watching Tadzio outlined against the sunset, or the hero of *La Dolce Vita* straining, against the sun's glare and his accumulated hangover, to keep the young girl – his picture of innocence – in focus. Except that this one was not innocent. But what did he care about that? She saw him, waved him towards her, and when he did not move she came swayingly stepping, dragging her toes, towards him through the ankle-deep water, as once Nausikaa must have walked towards Odysseus where he lay face down in the foam, so that when he looked up through salted lashes he saw her as a curved shadow in the sunburst.

'Don't be a wet fart. Come and talk to us.'

'I can't.'

'Ring me in London then.'

Each day after that he would make the same journey, but lay in the shelter of the rocks like a frogman spying out an invasion beach. He watched them in secret. There didn't seem to be much going on. The actor spent a lot of his time floating on his back. Lancelot prayed that they would not walk north and they never did, or at least not until Sally and Nicholas were gone.

Sally went first. While Nicholas and Lancelot were down showing off to each other in the morning surf she said her goodbyes to Charlotte.

'I *thought* there was something wrong,' said Charlotte. 'Is it anything you can talk about?'

'Not really,' said Sally. 'I can't thank you enough, you know. It's been perfect from every aspect, except what's going on in my own thick head.'

'Someone you miss?'

'Something like that.'

'I know.'

'I hope I don't saddle you with a glum Nicholas.'

'We'll look after him.'

Sally loaded her bag into the back seat of the car. When the men came up to lunch she took Nicholas for a walk in the market and explained, or rather failed to explain. He wanted to come too but she wouldn't let him. When she was gone he explained how pressure of work had been haunting her. Two days later, after a record number of fruitless telephone calls, he got the weekly plane to London. But if he had gone straight away by train, or hired a car, he wouldn't have been back much sooner.

238

Lancelot should have left too but if he was going to be haunted he might as well stay near the ghost. She never came walking towards him along the Côte des Basques as she had done the year before and the blessed year before that, but on the second last night of their stay he saw her in the town centre. Having drunk everything in the house during and after dinner, he had staggered along the cliff path into town, there to find further sustenance. The lights and music in the old fishing port reminded him that it was the night of the Grand Bal. In the town centre there were thousands of people all crowded together and cheering the procession. Floats covered with crêpe flowers, coloured lights and pretty girls came swaying through. One of these was a particularly clever pastiche biplane made of paper flowers, with girl wing-walkers in white one-piece swimming costumes and goggled flying helmets. The central wing-walker, the one with the most beautiful figure, was Samantha. There was a big cheer for her and an even bigger one when the crowd saw that the smiling actor was the pilot. With his leather helmet and silk scarf he looked the part. He was always going to look the part. Lancelot wanted to go home.

So did Elena, oddly enough. After only a few days in Salzburg she announced that the ball had provided enough operatic experience for a lifetime and she could stand no more. So in the cliff-side house he took each year Victor was left to play solitary host while guests arrived and departed, sat down for grand meals, sallied out in blasé parties to attend the Festspielhaus, or toned their often ancient muscles by swimming against the artificial current of the indoor swimming pool. It would have been a good season, too. The Wittgenstein princesses never looked lovelier than they did that year, all sitting in a row for the first night of *La Clemenza di Tito* in the Felsenreitschule. Wini Coburg died during the performance and nobody realised until after the final curtain, when it was noticed by the house manager that she was still sitting there after everybody else had gone off to a late dinner at the Hirsch. So she had lost her earring for the last time.

There was a lot going on but the festival felt empty without Elena, even though she had plainly been less than herself. Even Gus Disting could see that. He arrived in the company of the

Japanese model, who was very keen to see *Araberra* and *The Magic Fruit*. Victor installed them in the summer house at the top of the garden.

'Vot's wrong with Elena, looking so sad?' Gus Disting asked Victor privately. 'A vooman in the prime of loveliness, it's not right.' Victor couldn't say, and not just because he was flabbergasted as usual by Gus Disting's caricature of an accent.

He couldn't say because what was happening was a secret even from themselves. They did not discuss it. Elena, who valued self-control above everything, would rather have died than utter a reproach. But when they were alone together she fell silent. For the first time in many years she was taking things to make her sleep. They didn't make her sleep but robbed her of the quality she prized most – the capacity to mask her feelings. Victor sat on the edge of her bed looking useless, a position which did not become him. So she packed her bags and went home. All the way home.

From Milan the Settebello took her to Florence and at Florence she was met by a nondescript car driven by Sandro, almost the last of the old staff. Nobody owned a grand car any more, because of the kidnappings. Stopping several times for the provisions on his list, Sandro, whom she was saddened to find so very vague, took her out beyond Poggio a Caiano to a brown hill patched with olive groves and cypresses. The villas in that area are set within stuccoed walls, like the outworks of little fortresses. A single villa was all that was left of their once large estates. There had been a time when you could have looked out from the loggia and seen, with your gaze directed by avenues of cypresses, nothing but land belonging to the family. Now the avenues of cypresses led your gaze to the dye works, the light-bulb factory and the warehouse for blue plastic crates. But around the last house there were still some orchards and terraced vineyards, and there was no denying that her father still looked the part, with due allowance for all the doddering and shuffling. He received her in the library. They embraced, although from her side it might as well have been a formal hand-shake.

'Everyone says it was a great success.'

'It was, I have to admit. Your money was well spent, don't

worry.'

'They say you and the *cicisbeo* dance cheek to cheek now.'

It was not a very profitable conversation. Why had she come? The heat was stunning.

Her sister was out in the fields and it was too hot to go looking, so she went upstairs to lie down in her old room. Probably that was why she had come. On the way there she looked into her father's study, where he kept what he called his real books. Complete leather-bound and gold-embossed editions of Gentile's philosophy and Mussolini's speeches: dross got up as treasure. The little marble bust of Mussolini was still there, with its silver eyes that lit up in oblique light. What a miracle that the Communists had never got in here and ransacked the place. Instead they were proving themselves model citizens by the way they administered all the surrounding towns. But no revolution had been necessary to kill all of this off. It had just died gradually of exhaustion. She was relieved to find herself so unashamed. There was nothing left to be ashamed of. Her father had remained loyal to his cause until the end. In Italian there is an expression for it: until the last day. People they knew had died on the quarry staircase at Mauthausen while her father continued with his scholastic researches into pure Latinity. He was still at it; loyal until the last day and beyond; proud, upright, kind, gentle and as mad as a hatter.

She slept fitfully but at least she slept. When her sister came in from the terrace they sat together over cold drinks in the tile-floored cool of the lobby where they had once raced tortoises in lanes made of books.

'You should have been there,' said Elena. 'The boy carried it off well.'

'I know,' said her sister. 'But there was so much to do here. The photographs were splendid.'

'Do you never get away at all?'

'I can't leave him for long or he'll be stumbling around shouting in his old uniform. And I can't be with people any more.'

'Will you come to the wedding?'

'I don't see how I can.'

'Perhaps that's what I should do,' said Elena reflectively.
'What?'
'Retreat from the world.'
'You? You must be very unhappy to say that.'
'Do I look it?'
'To someone who knows you.'
'It will pass.' But until it did it was killing her, so she poured it all out. So *that* was why she was there.

When the next President of the United States rang from Chicago the following morning she already felt, if not precisely better, at least alive enough to make a date with him for lunch in Paris early the week after next, and when Victor rang from Salzburg soon afterwards she made a point of letting him know. Then she went out into the vineyards with her sister and didn't talk to anyone else for days. It was a bit like talking to your reflection but at least your reflection didn't *want* anything. At first it seemed as if there were scorpions everywhere but later she noticed them less and with a length of strong wire bent into a hook she got the water flowing again from the lead pipe that lay hidden in the laughing mouth of the little green bronze Triton in the grotto – the Triton that might or might not have been by Giambologna. Water flowed from the peaches too, and the nectarines and the black grapes.

~ twenty-five ~

Sally got back to her flat in the morning and rang Salzburg before she had even bathed. It was a risk, but she got Victor.

'Stay where you are,' said Victor. 'I'll come straight away.'

'What about her?'

'She's in Italy. Tell me the address of that place.'

'You'll never get up the stairs.'

'I want to see how you live. I'll be there by nightfall.'

He was, too. She went down to meet him.

'You were right about the stairs,' he said as she showed him in. 'Good Lord. You mean this is all there is?'

'This is it.'

'Why should I waste my imagination on myself?' said Victor, in quotation marks.

'Who said that?'

'Diaghilev. In Petersburg. He showed Karsavina the room where he slept and there was nothing in it except a little bed. She asked him why he, of all people, should want to live so simply.'

'She must have been lovely.'

'She was, but he was the wrong sort of man. Why are you back so soon?'

'I ran away. Why have you still got your clothes on?'

'Come home with me,' said Victor.

'Later.'

'Now would be better.'

'Why? Not grand enough for you? Not enough towels? Need more room to show off?'

'Suppose my heart gave out?'

'Don't be silly.'

'I'm not being silly. It happens all the time. I'm exactly the right age and I've just climbed exactly the right staircase. You wouldn't relish having my death on your hands. People would never forget it.'

'You're serious.'

'You wouldn't be the only one hurt, either.'

'You win, damn it.'

Sally tried to compromise by persuading him into her car, but after having retraced his steps down the infernal staircase he asserted his right not to try shoe-horning himself into what he claimed to regard as an illegal weapon. So they rode in the back of his car, which meant that she was in his power instead of he in hers. But at the house she refused to contemplate sharing his bed, denouncing it as the centrepiece of a bordello. He took her upstairs to a small bedroom with a simple bed in it. It would have been for the daughter.

'She was already gone when I built this house. I stopped well short of making it a shrine, as you can see. No teddy bears. I already had enough to be ashamed of without that. It's just a useful room. It can always be yours, if you want it.'

'A niche.'

'What?'

'Nothing. All right. This is the spot.'

They lay down together then and there. Victor wanted to darken the room but she wouldn't let him. They were there again the next night and for a good part of the day between, but finally she caught on.

'It's over, isn't it? You just had me like the last glass of water in the world.'

'I think it has to be. Unless you can see us keeping it going in secret. And I don't think I've got what it takes.'

'You said all I had to do was insist.'

'Yes. But you won't.'

'She made bloody sure of that, didn't she? That's why she pulled me at the start. So that on the day when you gave me the elbow I wouldn't fight it. She saw it all in advance.'

'I wouldn't put it past her.'

'The bitch.'

He went off to make a pot of coffee and had a speech ready when he came back.

'It's for the best, you know. You would have hated it later on and so would I. It's all very well for me to revel in my autumn show of strength, but it can't last long. And when I wasn't up to it any more I'd have to watch you pretending to be pleased, and then pretending not to be pleased elsewhere.'

'It wouldn't be like that.'

'It would. I'm just the start for you. Whereas for her I'm the last big adventure, if I behave myself. Those other blokes in the wings will never get on stage unless I let them. So it's to my advantage.'

'And you had all this sorted out but you thought you'd just use these few days when nobody was checking up on us to get a good long lucky last snuffle at the trough.'

'Francis of Assisi would have done the same.'

'You've ruined me, you know. I can't go back to Nicholas. I'll just have to go and find someone else. And when I find him I'll parade him in front of you, you old rat.'

'I've already seen him. He'll be alive when I'm dead. Lying in your arms when I'm breathing oxygen in a plastic bag. I saw him the night I met you. Some young twerp wearing my skull for a mask. But I got in first.'

'Well, you're not getting in again.'

Nicholas arrived on her doorstep next morning. She wouldn't let him come upstairs. He drove her in his wreck to the Carambar for an early lunch. It was practically deserted. There, over a bacon and lettuce salad that neither of them much more than touched, she told him that they had to stop sleeping together if they were to stay friends. The message is easier to deliver when you leave out the real reason, although it is questionable if that makes it any easier to receive. Nicholas got very angry, so there was nothing else to do but get very angry as well.

'You're just not old enough,' she said. 'It's no crime.'

'I'm exactly the right age.'

'And that's not old enough. I did my best,' said Sally. 'I got it pretty thoroughly established that I was never going to talk to those people.'

'What people? My friends? Who are we talking about?'

'Journalist people. Gossip people. I hated them right from the start. Even the best of them were as thick as two short planks and the worst of them were so ghastly it was farcical. Illiterate, grubby, mean and sly. One of them sent me a note telling me that if I didn't talk to him it would be worse because he'd just make it all up. One of them rang up my sick mother at four in the morning and when I protested to the editor they ran a photo of me coming out of my front door and they put my address under it so that every sex maniac and dope addict could write to me or hang about outside. I tried to get the editor Press Councilled for that and lost because I was a public figure. I had some smooth old Press Council wanker asking me why I ever went on the television if I wanted to avoid publicity. *The* television. All this went on and on until finally they all got the message that it wasn't a ploy: I simply didn't want to cooperate. And I had a lot of pressure from upstairs, I might add. String along and they'll make it easier on all of us. Just jolly them along. But I didn't and eventually everything died down and I was able to just get on with my work and not be involved in any fatuous talk except for the *TV Times* occasionally. And then what happens?'

'I just made one little harmless drunken pass at an old girlfriend.'

'But *they* knew you were with *me.*'

'I never said a word to anyone.'

'You didn't *have* to say a word, did you? Just not deny it when one of your pals was making the suggestion. Lancelot, I shouldn't be surprised. Poor knickers-in-a-twist Lancelot. And I don't suppose *he* said a word. But then somebody else who knows you both – I bet it was Thinwall – somebody put two and two together and *he* said the word.'

'She, probably.'

'Who?'

'Delilah.'

'That lethal tart. How can I run around with a man who knows someone like her? I'll bet you've even gone to bed with *her.*'

'Don't be silly.' He hadn't, really. You couldn't call that going to bed. Going to the wall, perhaps.

So they split the bill and she got a taxi home. On her way up the stairs she heard the telephone ringing. She had made it a rule never to run for the telephone but she broke it this time in case it was Victor. It was only Nicholas.

'What you're saying is that you were never in love with me, right?'

'I suppose so, yes.'

'That's why you could never say the words.'

'Yes.'

'But you still went to bed with me.'

'Yes.'

'Well, if you weren't in love with me but you could, how come that now you can't?'

'I can't say. If you love me you won't ask.'

'What kind of answer is *that*? I'm coming over.'

This time she told the porter to let him come upstairs, or there would probably have been the most dreadful scenes right there on the street, and if there was anything she hated about the middle class it was the way they fought in public. ('I'm not your *slave*, John!') Besides, she felt guilty about having fobbed him off with an excuse. She would have had to see him again anyway. But bed was definitely out. By the time he reached her she had piled all the books on it.

'What kind of answer *is* that?' he continued. 'You aren't in love with me but if I'm in love with you I'll do what you want? That's the kind of reasoning that got women their richly deserved bad name.'

This was clearly a prepared speech so she didn't answer it.

'So why could you before?' he pressed.

'Because then I wasn't in love with anyone.'

'Who is it, then?'

'I can't say. Not possibly.'

'It's Elena, isn't it? You're a closet dyke. You have been all along.'

'She's very lovable, yes. But it's got nothing to do with sex, really.'

'I'll bet.'

'Not everything has, you know. It's not that you lack anything. You've got everything. You're sexy and bright and you make me laugh. But not enough has *happened* to you. You keep telling me that I'm the biggest thing that has. And I've enjoyed being part of your education but if I'm to learn anything myself I

247

have to be with someone who's educated already. I already spend every day in a job where real experience doesn't count. Nobody remembers the past except in manila folders. I want to be in love with the twentieth century, with somebody it all happened to, or some of it anyway. Someone who's been through it and wants to tell me just by the way he touches me.'

'Sounds like you want to fuck Winston Churchill's corpse.'

'Why do you like women?'

'I don't like women. I like you.'

'Yes, but why do you like women instead of men?'

'Because I'm that way, thank Christ.'

There was nothing she could say. Nicholas wanted to make love one last time but she said no, gratefully aware that he would not turn nasty. It was a thought often in her head, on the way back from the car-park: if she was mugged she planned to cross her arms over her face and let them kick the rest. What an absurd thought to have now. Saying 'I'll ring you' as if they had a future, Nicholas went.

Which left her facing the late afternoon and the endless night, plus a few more days before work started again. But she didn't want work to start again: not that work, anyway. She could stand no more of Horace's distinguished blarney, of Speed Blair's finely tuned mediocrity and of Anthony Easement striding dynamically down the corridor towards her with the announcement that he had an idea – the idea always being that *she* should have an idea, which he could package. It was time to move on. As Saul Newman's European roving reporter she would be calling her own shots and cutting her own tapes. She would probably also be drawing her own water and baking her own bread. But she would get a green card out of it. The 928 would have to go. You wouldn't catch her dead in a 924: might as well have a Cortina. But if the programmes were sold to British television she might even make up some of the financial loss. Who was it who had called 'residuals' the most beautiful word in the English language? Probably Saul. There was nothing seductive about Saul except his passion for the task. The dandruff on his shoulders was without charm. There were specks of it in his eyebrows, looking like the husks of dead nits. Either an abortive hair transplant had contracted phylloxera at the roots or else his scalp was really like that. The paunch was not very appealing either. As though clairvoyant, she could see the pass he would eventually make. It would be all the more embarrassing for their having done so much work together. He would say he had never done anything like this before. He would cry. He would leave his wife and children anyway, even if she did not requite him. Which she would never do, because he did not attract her. He did her the great favour of honestly admiring her work, and she repaid him by finding him unattractive. Thanks a bundle.

That side of things was a mess in advance, unless she was being conceited. But she was not responsible for other people's dreams. At the moment she was at the mercy of her own. She trusted her current explosion of decisiveness no more than the wife of a long-term manic depressive places abiding faith in his feeling suddenly elated. She mixed a packet of nuts and raisins into some plain yoghurt and called that dinner. One of the jokey little stories at the end of *News at Ten* showed a couple of senior policemen examining the broken front window of the Lord Mayor's Rolls Royce Phantom VI. It should have made her laugh or at least shake her head, but it didn't. Why was that? Because it was how the world was. Good luck was getting home safely from the underground car-park to your front door. No, good luck was to be robbed without being raped. Ordinary luck was to be robbed and raped. Bad luck was to be robbed, raped and have an eye kicked out. Oh, good *luck*, darling! Hold on, though. That couldn't be right. There was still a lot more of that in New York than here, but in New York she hadn't noticed.

It was late. Wearing nothing but her sandals she looked at herself in her long mirror. She knew how lucky she was and that she would never look better. But she felt as if she were assembled out of non-vegetable fats, monosodium glutamate and artificial colouring matter. She got rid of the sandals, sat on the bed and rubbed cream on her face. Usually it soothed her, but tonight it felt as if her forehead were getting tighter still. She rubbed cream into her breasts, a process which in normal circumstances she vaguely enjoyed at the very least. They felt like something that had just been slapped on to a wheel in a pottery class for beginners. For some reason she didn't want to sleep naked tonight, even though the summer was as yet only marginally threatened by encroaching autumn. They must still be burning the straw out in the fields. But she needed protection. From a lower drawer she got out her schooldays nightdress that she usually wore only on the worst nights when the heating gave out. She lay down on top of the bed but didn't turn out the light. She turned to the wall, afraid of what was coming. She dreaded it like being sick from the stomach. It was something she absolutely never did. Never since daddy had left home. Never never never. She lay still, fighting it off. Then, very suddenly, it went from nothing happening to everything happening. The tears were everywhere, all over the place like spilled oil. She couldn't stop the noise. She did everything except call for mother. Knowing that you will survive, that a broken heart counts for nothing in a world of broken bodies, doesn't mean that you can bear it.

'No pangs?' asked Elena on the telephone late at night.

'No,' said Victor.

'Charlotte keeps asking if she should bring home her young man and lock Lancelot in the broom cupboard. I tell her if that's what she wants, go ahead. She says thanks for the advice.'

'He's got it coming, I suppose.'

'For whoring after youth.'

'It's odd, isn't it?' asked Victor rhetorically. 'People whose lives are comedies behaving as if their lives were tragedies.'

'Whereas with some of us it's the other way about.'

'That's putting it a bit high.'

'Speak for yourself.' She was very definite about that. Just because she had won didn't mean that she felt triumphant. Even if she looked it.

~ twenty-six ~

M ister Strain wondered,' bellowed Janice, 'if you could see him as soon as possible.' There was no question by now that the bottom-strengthening exercises had also done great things for her voice.

'Has my tax position been clarified?' Lancelot asked Frank straight away, hoping to cut things comparatively short. Gradually it emerged that the tax position had indeed been clarified. But before it emerged that the tax position had been clarified, Frank had first to explain in detail how complicated it had all become. During the course of the next half hour it several times occurred to Lancelot that things were getting finally and irrevocably out of hand. The day after getting back from Biarritz he had called in at the garage where his car was being repaired and found that the whole area had been bulldozed. Enquiries at the police station revealed that the business had moved to new premises in Cricklewood. Upon telephoning the new premises, he was told that his car was top priority. Samantha, now that her work was not just complete but on the verge of publication, was almost impossible to find. Yet everybody else in the world seemed to be part of some ecstatic unit of two. Nicholas, having explained that his affair with Sally required all his attention, had disappeared from the face of the earth. He had even disappeared from the Friday lunch at Foscari's, although Thinwall claimed to be still seeing a lot of him. Elena and Victor spent so much time smiling at one another that people had begun to wonder. Serena and Anthony had once again become lovers, which meant that Anthony could cry on her shoulder about the continuing impossibility of pensioning off Virginia, while Serena could cry on his about her inability to dig up unknown drawings by known writers. Randall Hoyle and Elena's cousin Rudolph were such an item that they had been photographed naked in each other's arms for

Courage in Profiles. It was even rumoured that Monty Forbes had at last succumbed to Ian Cuthbert's tearful importunities. That would do much to explain Ian's total unavailability. People were huddling together against the portentous chill of the gathering autumn. But Lancelot was out in the cold, or at any rate confined to his room.

On returning from Biarritz, Charlotte and the children had rejoined the dogs to hold a family conference from which Lancelot had been excluded until the end, when he was admitted in order that he might hear the verdict. He was allowed to stay on in the house if he wanted to, but strictly as a guest. David would henceforth be regarded as the man of the family. For part of the week David would be with the diaphanous Gaga, aiding her in her community activities until such time as she had thrown off the effects of a variety of oriental diseases. At all other times David would be master in Lancelot's house. Everyone at the conference except the dogs, who liked David almost as little as he liked them, evidently regarded this as a desirable arrangement. Even Lancelot could see nothing against it from the viewpoint of simple justice. What unsettled him was the certainty that if he *had* seen anything against it his opinion would have made no difference. He was an unarmed prophet.

But his tax position had been clarified. He had lost. He was now on PAYE. He should never have been on Schedule D. Which would mean, of course, that at least a proportion of his deducted expenses would have to be refunded. Lancelot didn't know why Frank Strain was saying 'of course'. The tax people no doubt said 'of course' as a matter of course, but why was Frank Strain saying 'of course'?

'Is that the lot?' asked Lancelot.

'Well, no. In fact that wasn't why, except of course it's better if, and now that we have, well at least we don't. But that wasn't why I asked you up here specifically. Of course, since you *were* here, it would have made very little sense not to have discussed the . . . '

Even more gradually than during the world record for gradualness which had already been established, the real reason for the meeting emerged. Loosely bound rush copies of the uncorrected proofs of the Gillian Jackson lifestyle book had gone out to one or two magazines and in a roundabout way one of them had got into the hands of one of the interviewees, who had loudly claimed that the views attributed to her in quotation marks were ones she had never uttered. Some discreet checking had revealed that several more of the interviewees were in a similar case. In short, the young lady appointed by Lancelot to do the ghosting had faked the whole thing. The proof copies had been rounded up, brought back and placed under lock and key, but even after such limited exposure there was still a strong chance of a successful libel action, because the chief complainant, Choochoo Strapontin, was not only very rich and very touchy, she was also vengefully litigious. She had taken particular exception, apparently, to finding herself quoted *in extenso* on the subject of the desirability of having one's backside lifted. Not only had she never said anything about this, her *derrière* was still in its original position. Independent authorities insisted that no other part of her was, but if that meant anything it meant that her bottom had, in effect, been lowered. No matter how many assurances were given and mollifications murmured personally by Victor, the great names in the book would be disinclined to laugh the matter off. Putting the business to sleep would take time, effort and expenditure.

All this took Frank Strain most of the morning to say, so Lancelot had plenty of time to take it in. But he could not take it in. He phoned Samantha all afternoon but she was never there. On his way home he parked his bicycle outside her basement flat and rang the doorbell, but she still wasn't there. When he got home he phoned her again from his study. She was there, receiving a visit from her father. She told him to come over at eight o'clock, when her father would have gone away. Until it was time to head in her direction, Lancelot rode around in the vicinity of the Little Boltons, rehearsing what he was going to say. It was lucky he had brought his front lamp: the nights were drawing in. Then he rode straight over to her place, chained his bicycle to her railings, undid the wing nuts on the front wheel, and with the wheel under his arm trod decisively down her little iron staircase and rang the doorbell.

When she opened the door to him she was wearing nothing

but knickerbocker glory pop socks, which he thought was a good sign. He leaned his wheel against her small dining table and reached to embrace her, but there was something wrong with the way she was giggling, like a child whose elaborately planned joke on a parent was about to be sprung. There was an almighty crash from the bathroom. Samantha swept her hand towards it like a magician's assistant signalling for applause. Lancelot opened the bathroom door and found Nicholas just getting to his feet with one foot still caught in a pair of trousers more than half drawn up the other leg.

'Shelves,' said Nicholas.

At least two glass shelves with their full complement of bottles, jars, atomisers and aerosols had hit the floor. Nicholas was ankle deep in the aromatic junk that struck Lancelot with its quintessentially feminine spectrum of odours even in this lowest of all moments. Lancelot cried a good deal while Nicholas, having fully achieved his trousers, shouted reproaches at the helplessly laughing Samantha.

'I'm sorry,' Nicholas told Lancelot during a pause in the uproar. 'She told me you two were finished and I'd just been scrapped myself.'

'It's all right,' said Lancelot, as if that was what it was, instead of being as all wrong as it could get. Nicholas resumed giving Samantha what for until she unilaterally got into bed, pulled the covers up to her chin, and lay there looking demurely abstracted, as if facing the prospect next day of being enrolled into the Girl Guides. It all went on for quite a while with nothing gained, and Lancelot subsequently had even better reason to regret that he had not left immediately, because after he had retrieved his wheel and climbed with hanging head up the little iron staircase it was to find that his bicycle was missing. The padlock and chain, strangely enough, were still there, properly done up. So they must have had a key. Well, at least somebody knew what he was doing. As Lancelot stood there with his wheel under his arm like a less grateful St Catherine, it was raining lightly, but after a while it stopped doing that, and started raining heavily.

~ twenty-seven ~

By decision of the family council, Lancelot was obliged to knock on Charlotte's bedroom door if he wanted to enter for some reason. He knocked, and David gave him permission to enter. David was sitting up in bed reading *The English Comic Writers*. 'Sorry,' said Lancelot.

'She's down in the kitchen, I think,' said David absently. He wasn't being rude; he was merely under the spell of Hazlitt's prose; but Lancelot took it hard, packed his holdall and moved out to Serena's. Her affair with Anthony now once again over, as far as either of them could tell, Serena was ready to welcome a Platonic relationship, which for the moment was all that Lancelot was capable of. So Lancelot moved into her living room.

'I hear Lancelot has gone to Serena,' said Elena after dinner at the British Embassy in Paris. Stunning *en grande tenue*, she swept the room once slowly with the lighthouse effulgence of her upper works, just to keep them all on their toes.

'These lovers fled away into the storm,' said Victor.

'He was the one that did the fleeing. She never moved. Do you envy him his decisiveness?'

'As long as he gets some work done.'

'You look worried,' said David, breaking an egg into the batter for the wood-pigeons.

'Not worried: just preoccupied,' said Charlotte. 'If he's here I don't have to care about him.'

Thinwall, after a long lunch in the magazine's boardroom, joined Nicholas at the Carambar for drinks before dinner.

'Lancelot's done a bunk,' said Nicholas.

'With Sam?'

'No. Serena.'

'Bridesmaid Revisited.' It wasn't one of Thinwall's best, but it went around town like influenza.

Padlocked by her wrists and ankles to the iron bedposts, Delilah was wearing the top half of a wet-suit plus hood, mask and snorkel.

'Is that ponce Windhover still living in the broom cupboard?' asked Dick Toole.

'Mpf,' said Delilah. 'Eem gom doom Zhorinum.' Behind the small panel of glass, her eyes were wide at what Dick Toole obviously planned to do with the tweezers.

Before the week was up, Lancelot had returned home with his holdall between his legs. With the best will in the world, Serena had been unable to cope with the logistics of giving him a spare set of keys. He had been locked out three times in as many days, and on two of those occasions it had rained. Also she cried all night, every night, over her off-again liaison with Anthony, which was based, Lancelot now learned, on her eternal gratitude for Anthony's having helped her with the fashion articles which had made her name. The help, it transpired, had consisted merely of taking her book of notes, adding a lot more notes, joining the notes together with words, and typing up the results. But slight as the assistance had been, it had come at the right time. Lancelot could have absorbed all this with ease as supererogatory evidence of the world's tendency to entropy. Also it spoke well for Anthony, who had never mentioned any of these facts to Lancelot, obviously out of chivalrous regard for Serena. It should have been a heartening discovery. But the noise kept him awake, and thus prey to his thoughts.

So he moved back into his room to regroup. The inglorious homecoming was made more bearable by a family council plan to spend the weekend at the mill house. Charlotte, David and the children, whose main aim in life seemed to be to go everywhere David went so that without interruption they might gaze at him in worship, all went off in the Maxi, leaving Lancelot with the dogs. David, it was by now well established, wasn't too keen on the dogs. Lancelot had never been too keen on them either, but had made the mistake of not saying so when it mattered. Instead he had given them their witty names and generally played the part of squire in his populated household. Mrs Hypotaxis went off to Athens for a few days, no doubt to perform her tour of duty as a caryatid holding up the Porch of the Maidens. She left Lancelot a set of instructions about the garbage disposal unit:

MISA WINDHOVER SED DOAN YUS GABIJ DUSPOASL EFIW CAN US CAN INSTED GABIJ DISPOASL IS BROACUN MAN WIL COL IS NUMBA 798 8818 EFIW COL TUNAT AFTA 10 AND AT HOAM 723 7861 EFIW COL TOMORROW

How could she get a word like 'tomorrow' right when she got a word like 'use' wrong? It was the kind of riddle often presented to the reader by the prose of Dick Toole, as Lancelot was amply reminded the next morning. He opened the popular newspaper to Dick Toole's page and found two photographs of himself, one for each startled eye. In one photograph he was twenty years younger and receiving a British Press Award for Best Feature Writer from a notable who had since been sent to jail for fraud. In the other photograph he was dressed as André Chénier and was bent awkwardly over a patch of delphiniums. There were plenty of other recognisable faces too. Sally Draycott looking simultaneously very attractive and very angry; a standard million-dollar Norman Parkinson portrait of Elena dating from a *Vogue* spread in the mid Seventies, Victor smiling after being knighted; Serena smiling as if she had just knighted him; the often reproduced Snowdon study of Nicholas looking like a fallen cherub; a photo-booth mug-shot of David; a wanker's fantasy full-length pin-up of Samantha which Lancelot remembered as having decorated a *Nectar* feature on the bright young things of her Oxford generation; a photograph of the actor with all 54 teeth on glittering display; and a picture of Charlotte looking tragic in her kitchen. The entire cast was there. The whole two-page spread dealt with the one item. It was headlined DAISY-CHAIN THAT EXPLODED and an equivalent standard of metaphorical exactitude was kept up throughout, coupled with Dick Toole's usual fastidious handling of grammar and syntax.

'In the high-stepping world where the Beautiful People meet the *literatis*,' it began, 'the daisy-chain has exploded. Remember who brought you the exclusive story of golden girl intellectual Samantha Copperglaze letting her traces down at Elena (countless different types of countess) Fiabesco's so-called Operas Ball, much to the umbrage taken from Golden Girl of the Gogglebox, Sally Draycott? See our tell-tale snaps if you need reminding. But I am now able to reveal – and I reiterate again, it's exclusive – that there were latent, hidden ramifications unaware even at the time even to this column.'

But latent *means* hidden, thought Lancelot, the verbal centres of whose brain were still functioning, even though the rest of his cerebral cortex, like the whole of his body, was frozen as if by the instantaneous arrival of a new ice age.

'For Not Only,' the article went on, 'was Samantha's escort and literary adviser Lancelot Windhover visually put out (see our picture, premiered here for the first time), But Also Lancelot's long-suffering wife, top academe Charlotte (nay, Darley-Huckswin), was in the process of becoming very-close-friends-indeed with that rising young "writer" of the horror school, ex-punk rocker David Bentley. A long-term, live-in boom companion of loony leftie Gaga Ladbroke, Charlotte felt protective towards poly-boy David, who graduated from a New Wave guitarist to become an *intelligentsia*, but nobody thought he would ever leave his humble cohorts in the lurch. Alas, but the high life proved too allusive, for now he is a regular visitor to the Windhover £250,000 home, a phenomena to which the Windhover children are only too proud to say, as they told me exclusively: "We think Dave's brill."'

The family council missed that little point, thought Lancelot. A clear directive to say nothing on the telephone should have been high on the agenda, just after the allocating of very small rooms to husbands.

'But the daisy chain,' Dick Toole continued, 'was only just gathering speed. It was still a long way from, in the Latin phrase, a *fait accompli*. For only the most intimate of nifty Nick's flash friends knew that his all-too-public gesture of affection at Samantha was the occasion of his jealousy for Sally's ill-concealed determination to get herself adopted by those most ill-assorted of all well-heeled couples, Lancelot's boss the ostentatious "Sir" Victor Ludlow (they call him Vulgar Vic) and the psychopathically publicity-shy Elegant Elly, or so she would have us think.

'Almost as secretive herself, not even this column knows to exactly what lengths Sally went, but this much is certain: things between the two jet-setters were never the same again. Some friends say that Elly pined because Vulgar Vic and Suck-up Sally were suddenly inseparable after a fiasco television interview. And there can be no doubt that they were a visual age-gap in New York. Hitting the fashionable restaurants like Big Daddy Warbucks and Little Annie Oakley, mutual friends saw them in close conference over the *fettucino*.

'Other friends say that it was Elly and Sally who were comparing recipes while Victor fretted for his usual attentions from the plush hostess. But whatever happened, Nicholas blew his famous cool. His revenge was to coax Samantha off Lancelot. Meanwhile, still as gorgeous as when her name was all over the glossics like a rash, Lancelot consoled himself with old flame Serena Blake, a direct descendant of playwright William and now one of his ghost writers, a lucrative cynosure by any criterions.

'By any standards, suicidal Serena is not as much chop as her notorious forbear would have been when he was writing those plays. Sources close to this column say that her glossy articles of the Seventies needed help, and that Lancelot's business partner, *alias* known as yet another old friend of my-life-is-my-own Sally, ageing Etonian Anthony Easement, may have had more than a hand in her success. But as ghosts at Victor Ludorum go she rates comparatively high prestige. For Samantha, given a top job by Lancelot, is currently in low odour.'

Oh no, thought Lancelot. Not so soon. How did they get it? Every loophole was supposed to have been plugged. He had told everybody one at a time that the whole thing was a matter of mental health and that lives hung in the balance. Not that you can ever keep things bottled up for long. He scanned the rest rapidly.

' . . . fashionable women eager to flout their expertise found Samantha a ready listener. But she was even readier to make things up out of thin . . . threats of libel suits came flooding in like artillery . . . she may have Hollywood in her sights . . . effects for Lancelot could charitably be described as not a million miles from discomfiting.'

Hooray, thought Lancelot: he's got a word right at last. 'Discomfiting' is actually the appropriate word. Total defeat. Utter destruction. Cannae. Actium. Call to me all my sad captains.

The telephone rang. If it wasn't a quadrophonic tape-recording of a Force 12 gale then it was Janice. 'Sorry to be ringing on a Saturday morning,' the voice howled, 'but have you seen the papers?'

'Hold the telephone a bit further away, darling. Yes, I have.'

'Afraid that last bit was my fault,' said Janice happily. 'So I thought I should ring to say sorry. Some woman rang me up and told me they already had the story but they wanted to check the details.'

'Yes. It's a standard technique. The thing to do is say nothing.'

'I realise that now,' said Janice impatiently, 'but she said she was an old friend of yours.'

'She is, in a way. Don't worry about it. Sweet of you to ring.'

'See you on Monday.'

'I'm not sure I'll be in, so don't bother about getting the cottage cheese.'

He put down the receiver and headed upstairs to shave, bathe and dress. His head was bowed, so it was not until he got to the top of the stairs that he noticed what looked like an iridescent saffron brioche festering on the carpet. Undoubtedly it was the work of Feydeau. Right, thought Lancelot. That does it.

The doorbell rang. He stood where he was without turning, magnetised by a dumb animal's cloacal achievement. But the doorbell rang again, so down he went.

'You've a geezer what owns a pew, Joe?'

'Good heavens.' Lancelot had never seen the man before, but what had startled him was a sight almost as unfamiliar and by now completely unexpected. There before his front steps stood his car. Physical mobility had been restored to him at the very moment of final and irreversible mental paralysis.

It was too late. The car was there, looking splendid in its beads of rain, but there was nowhere he wanted to go in it. He wrote a cheque which he knew would bounce all over the bank like a squash ball, but by then he would be beyond caring. He rang Nicholas to say goodbye, but there was no answer. So he wrote a letter instead. He spent the whole afternoon writing a letter each to everyone. For dinner he heated a tin of chili con carne, not wanting to cook anything in the oven, which for his purposes needed to be free of the smell of fat. The bulk of the evening he spent working on his will. In an early version he made a list of edifying books which should be extracted from his library and given to Samantha. In later versions this idea did not crop up. The final version left Charlotte everything, such as it was. It seemed easier, and besides, he had a sneaking suspicion that it was the law of the land. The love letters from Samantha he burned. There were only two of them and their paucity of expression made him ashamed. It took an age to get the dogs out into the garden, so it was well past midnight before he was ready.

He turned on the gas tap of the oven without touching the ignition button. After the gas had run for a while he turned his head sideways and inserted it. The fit was uncomfortable so he took out the internal shelf and moved it down a notch. But he had not thought the thing through. Standing up was no good because when unconsciousness supervened he would fall out. What he needed to do was sit down. He drew up a chair and sat down but when he leaned forward the shelf was too high. He took it out altogether but when his sensitive cheek made direct contact with the bottom of the oven it detected the presence of a film of fat. Mrs Hydroponics must have finished off her cleaning with a rag dipped in cold water instead of hot. Physical disgust was not the last emotion he wanted to feel. Also it belatedly occurred to him that this new gas from the North Sea was supposed to kill you much more slowly than the old sort, or perhaps didn't even kill you at all.

He left the gas on, went upstairs, and assembled all of Charlotte's sleeping pills into the one spot. It was a formidable array: eloquent testimony to the dance he had led her. He owed it to her to swallow them all, washing each one down with a mouthful of water, so that there would be no premature rejection by an overloaded stomach. Then he lay down and waited. By the time the smell of gas reached him he was already slipping away. He had always admired Chénier's bravery. It must have been hard, letting go of so much. In the Conciergerie the condemned would talk together all night before the tumbril came. Letting go of so little was proving to be considerably easier, except that there was nobody to talk to. It was like talking to yourself. *Déjà ce corps pesant se détache de moi.* But if this heavy body is detached from me, thought Lancelot, then I should be floating up, not going down into this tunnel. This very recognisable tunnel with posters made from pages of the Koran. Going down into it in this car. This car with the taxi meter of green lights. Youths on roller skates with hair like dead tropical birds broke the window, hauled him out, and held him down for the dentist with the Japanese hook. But the back of his legs and his bottom must have been cut by the jagged glass. It hurt. Then it hurt the same way around his chest and throat, which could not be right. Hurt so much that he had to contemplate abandoning the whole idea, especially when the needles came in through his eyelids.

But he could still see, except for a dead spot in the centre of each eye, like Degas. Into whose arms fell the ailing Ingres. Look back in, Ingres. Lancelot hated puns and took it personally that one of them should dare show its face at such a solemn moment. Puns made his blood run cold. It was very cold, inside the glacier. Which was full of people, like a circle in Hell. Lancelot had expected Hell to be full of moustached men in paisley shirts, flared trousers and Cuban-heeled shoes made out of overlapping pieces of leather, but actually it was quite sweet. What a pity to be alone there. Imagine the sweetness of going down there to live together. That was Baudelaire. Ian Cuthbert, thought Lancelot, must have a memory like mine, only worse. Better and therefore worse. Like the library of Alexandria, full of the smoke of burning books. Reading stops you writing, if you can't forget. A sense of proportion, that's what you must lack. You need a drunken boat. Steady doesn't do it. He had been too honest with himself. Malraux had had the right approach: tell lies that will become truths later. Malraux told his wife that. Was it she who wrote it down? A book about lying writers would be a good idea. Tell a lie: a very good idea. He was having his best ideas too late. It was all in the timing. That was another idea for a book: careers. That was a *really* good idea for a book. Must get back and start a box-file on that one.

He tried to turn around and a ball of light went off against his palate. Then he tasted praline with his eyes and smelt silk with his ear. The lights went off again. Went off like a bomb, not off like a light. Out like a light, that was the expression for when lights went off. He was on a hillside, dug in, and a lot of smiling Chinese holding silly guns with perforated barrels were coming up through the wire. They had knapsacks on like Scandinavians. They weren't supposed to have those on, so they took them off. It was Korea, not Copenhagen. But Lancelot had never been in Korea. He had done his National Service with an intelligence unit at Bletchley, compiling a NATO chain of command chart in three languages and six colours. The last time people in uniform had come running at him had been in Paris in 1968, but then you could duck around a corner or flash your passport. Here you couldn't. Imagination to power! But it had no power. That was the whole point. Real imagination wasn't interested in power. The Chinese were pointing towards him. They were telling each other where he was. How could they know that when he didn't? He must be having somebody else's memory. Anthony had been in Korea. Must ask him if Korea was so loud. The noise was tremendous. Janice was with them. They were all singing 'You'll Never Walk Alone'. More flares kept going up and hanging there. Then they all went out at once. Out, not off. Out! Off! Out! Off! The whole light was going out and off at the same time as the noise. Tracer chased itself like sparks through a black ceiling. The Chinese looked as if they were dancing in a disco. Samantha was there too. How beautiful she was when she slid her hip sideways. It matched the curve of Botticelli's Venus. When she lay down on her side it reminded him of Velázquez's Venus. When she lay on her breasts with her legs open the back of her thighs followed the same line as Boucher's Venus. Venus O'Murphy. When her hand stroked him it looked as long and tapering as the hand of Leonardo's lady caressing the ermine in Cracow.

But none of these images lent life to her outline. She lent life to them. She brought everything alive. She was doing it now. He was going to come from looking at her. It was lovely. It kept on coming out. It felt as if it would last for a long time, like a really good day's reading in the Bodleian. Like a page of pregnant alexandrines. Charlotte had enjoyed that. He could see Charlotte at a table on the other side of the library, but there was someone else in the chair beside her. Some young man. They were both reading from one book. Then they each put a finger on the page to mark the place as they turned to each other and kissed. It made Lancelot feel lonely. It plunged him into solitude. One can acquire anything in solitude, except character. Who said that? Who *said* that? Come outside and say that. That. They had that in common, he and his wife. The meaning of words. They didn't mean everything, of course. That was the whole point. Except now they did. So there was no point. Tremendously significant and tremendously vague. I'm sorry, darling. I didn't mean it. What I *mean*. Mm? Mm.

~ twenty-eight ~

Foch! Grock!' squawked Lancelot. They had finished with the stomach pump some time before but he was still turning himself inside out, a process which for some reason kept reminding him of the Cotswolds. 'Klee! Clouet! Klimt! Braque! Cranach!'

Chance had saved him. It's all that saves most of us. Between midnight and dawn, long after Lancelot had taken the pills and was well embarked on the journey to the Elysian Fields, a pack of polychromatic skinheads, far from their home territory, happened to recognise his car as one of the same type as another car they had paid attention to in the early spring. Here was the chance of a ride home. Failing which, the interests of aesthetic symmetry required that the same vengeance should be taken as before. Once again a hot-wire start was ruled out by an unbudgeable Krooklok. So they smashed in most of the windows, paid their urinary tribute from all angles, and moved on. Towards dawn, almost too late, a policewoman and a policeman came strolling along, furtively hand in hand. Entering Lancelot's gravelled forecourt in order to embrace, they saw his wrecked car. They smelled it, too, but not as clearly as they smelled gas. They rang the front doorbell repeatedly but there was no answer except the howl of dogs from the back garden. Windows which had not lit up at the noise of a car being violated were now lighting up all around. While the policewoman radioed headquarters, the policeman broke in and opened all the windows he could find. While doing this, he found Lancelot. The policewoman radioed for an ambulance. In commendably brief time it arrived and took Lancelot away. Only then did the policeman enter the kitchen to turn off the gas. Unfortunately the first control he touched was the ignition button. There was not much gas left by then but it was enough to make a considerable thump. The explosion did the constable no great harm beyond the embarrassment caused by the loss of several articles of clothing. But it gave a shock to the front wall of the kitchen which was enough to impart a decisive shear load to the portico above the front steps. The portico shifted forward until the columns on which it rested began to pivot. With dream-like precision the whole neo-classical assemblage, weighing about a ton and a quarter, swung outwards and fell on Lancelot's car.

Everyone came to see Lancelot in hospital. Lancelot had had no idea he was so popular. All thanked him for his touching letter and told him that if he had sent it earlier he would have soon been talked out of doing anything so drastic. Serena was full of mute reproaches and despairing shakings of the head, which was a bit much coming from her. Elena paid him one brief visit during which every consultant and senior surgeon in the hospital found some reason to be present. She gave him a book to read. To ask him how he could have done such a thing, Janice came all the way in from the street, instead of just saying it from the bus stop, or from home. Thinwall arrived joking. 'I know what you need,' he cried. 'A nice steaming glass of hot pork fat.' The idea had been supplied by one of the Australian poets but nobody thought that even Thinwall would actually go through with it. Thinwall reported the alleged results at the next Friday lunch. He didn't have to exaggerate by much.

'Extraordinary thing for Lancelot to *do*,' said one of the literary editors. 'I should have thought that he of all people had life pretty well worked out.'

'Cushy job, perfect wife, lovely young raver of a girlfriend,' said another literary editor. 'Where do you get despair out of all that?'

Dick Toole had arrived independently at the same opinion. 'Flouting his artistic temperament, the ponce.' Delilah would have agreed if she had been able to speak, but the clamps were too tight.

'I can't talk for long,' said Sally. 'I'm clearing out my desk. Where are you?'

'The can at the Caram,' said Nicholas. 'Is it your last day?'

'Yesterday. Officially I've already left.'

'Lancelot said you came to see him.'

'He gave me a book.'

'So he told me. Some posh frog.'

'*Les Liaisons dangereuses*.'

'What's it like?'

'Depressing. Elena swears by it. She says we're all in it.'

'And are we?'

'In a way. It's full of people coldly assessing the caprices of desire and speaking frankly to each other at all costs. Clinical honesty.'

'Is that us?'

'No,' said Sally. 'We're better than that. Or at any rate a bit younger.'

'Can I see you for a drink?'

'I have to meet Saul.'

'What about tomorrow?'

'What about Samantha?'

'She's gone back to L.A.'

'Is she why Lancelot did it?'

'She's reason enough, God knows. But I expect it was a bit of everything. Did you hear about Thinwall's joke?' He told her.

'You make it sound funny,' she said. 'I wonder if it really was.'

'I make everything sound funny. Which you miss. Admit it.'

'Yes. I do indeed.'

'I excited you to a frenzy with my masculine crudity. Admit it.'

'A sedate frenzy. A poised frenzy.'

'You loved my lewd tongue. You creamed your Calvin Kleins.'

'Don't be disgusting.'

'But you liked being disgusted. You liked it when I danced around the room wearing your knickers for a balaclava. Go on. Own up.'

'It's a fact.'

'Then see me again. I can't bear my life.'

'Don't be silly.'

Victor couldn't see why Lancelot had done it. It had taken him completely by surprise.

'Of *course* it shocks you,' said Elena, languid among pillows. 'You're such an egomaniac that you can't believe anyone else is really there.'

'But he'd been doing so well. That business with the Gillian Jackson book was a bit unfortunate but I might have put him in a false position there. Do you know what he told me? He told me that he thought he'd been irritating me.'

'What did you say to that?'

'I told him I thought he was the most charming man I know. Which is pretty well true, isn't it?'

'And what did he say then?'

'He said I should have told him that before.'

'Well, people need flattery.'

'I don't.'

'Only because you're a genius.'

Victor might have been straining the facts when he said that Lancelot had been doing well, but there was no denying that things picked up after the crisis, and that Lancelot was the catalyst. The world's most famous female film star – who, it turned out, had relished her evening at Flaherty's – not only signed a contract in the course of time but in the course of further time got on with writing the book. Brian Hutchings, perhaps remorseful, actually supplied the last of his copy for the book on the iconography of literary London. Though no great commercial success, the book was much discussed in literary circles: at least half a dozen poets never spoke to Brian again, and would have combined to assault him if they had been speaking to each other. And the book on writers who could draw was a success on every level. Ian Cuthbert never did get started on *A World History of the Short*, and the lists of writers who could draw which he had supplied to Serena were destroyed when she accidentally set fire to her flat. But copies resided safely in one of Lancelot's box-files. The copies, having been copied again by Janice, were given to David Bentley, who, after much study but in short order, produced a set of captions which helped make the book a pleasure to possess. Even Paula Thorax had to admit that as picture books went it was something of a minor classic. Thus David was launched on a useful second line of work to help finance him while he composed his novels, the first of which was one of Victor Ludorum's big hits of the following season. The story of how a young radical couple grow apart politically during a trip to India but achieve unity on a spiritual level, it held irresistible appeal for David's contemporaries, although Charlotte, usually sympathetic to his work, did not much care for it.

But she would have been the first to put that down to jealousy. In all other respects the arrangement worked out well, after Lancelot's initial over-reaction. Obviously, to confine him to his room had been too harsh. Mrs Hepatitis was keen to go home after the destruction of her kitchen. In fact she had gone without discussing the matter, leaving a note saying I GOINC HOM TU GRIS. Following Elena's advice, Charlotte had not replaced her. David was awkward on the subject of servants anyway, and more than willing to share the cooking. That left the basement flat free for Lancelot to move into.

Once installed, he flourished. Loss had left him without distractions. Samantha, after the smiling actor had drowned at one of Randall Hoyle's parties, came back from Los Angeles and was offered a post by the Think Tank as a long-term planning officer working on the disposal of nuclear waste. Lancelot rarely saw her, and only as a friend. Besides, he was too busy. The book about literary liars sounded so juicy a project that Brian Hutchings was almost tempted to volunteer for it, but Ian Cuthbert, transformed by his possession of Monty – restored, in fact, to the full productive genius of his early years – demanded to take it on, and, after the usual hiccups, made detectable progress. The book on careers Lancelot gave to the Australian poets, who were so naive that they considered the large advance as an obligation to work diligently. The result was a first-rate piece of cultural sociology, so entertaining that it became a best-seller.

Most remarkable of all, Lancelot himself became a writer again. Not of poems: that impulse was gone, if it had ever really been there. But he had an idea for a book that would avoid the usual trap of being about writers and publishers. Some writers, apologetic about knowing nobody except writers and publishers, disguised them as painters and gallery owners, or actors and impresarios. Other writers went further and set their books about writers and publishers down coal-mines or in supermarkets, so that you had sensitive, neurotic young face-workers and check-out clerks, or cultivated, worldly-wise pit-head supervisors and area managers. Lancelot would appear to grasp the nettle by simply and unashamedly writing a book about writers and publishers. But really all his principal characters, women included, would be different versions, variously idealised, of himself, with the hero nothing but a *deus ex machina*, or chapter of accidents. Which is really how life feels, he had decided: when you look at others you see yourself reflected, and when you look at yourself you are nowhere to be found. So he changed his name to several names, dressed each of them differently in bits and pieces of made-up bodies and imagined histories, withdrew from the centre so that his creatures could all meet in the same glass room, and then wrote down what they did. A mirror hall for voices, it might not have been a proper novel, but it certainly wasn't anything else. This, of course, is it.

NOTES by Peter C. Bartelski

one

What he saw Feydeau doing on the stairhead landing   By naming the dogs Feydeau (Fido?), Scribe and Sardou, Lancelot-as-author makes a preliminary statement about the theatrical propensities of Lancelot-as-character. Taking precedence over the two melodramatists, Feydeau the *farceur* is invoked both at the beginning and at the end of the main action, thus to reassure Lancelot that the travesty in which he is caught up has at least the saving grace of aesthetic symmetry. A female dog could have been called Labiche: an opportunity missed.

Nor would it have done even to, say, Colette   As might be expected, Chéri's 'physiognomy' is analysed in the eponymous novels *Chéri* and *The Last of Chéri*, but other, less obvious works by Colette are on Lancelot's mind and thus operative in the text, most notably *Julie de Carneilhan*, whose introspective heroine is transparently one of the models for Elena Fiabesco. Lancelot's frame of reference is so undeviatingly Frenchified that we must wonder how he contrived to read but one language at Oxford. As well as choosing Chéri for a personal prototype in this first encounter with one of the book's many mirrors, Lancelot might also have thought of Maupassant's *Bel Ami*, another quasi-literatus who married for advantage.

an Adrian Stokes archive   Until his late stiffening into Freudianism the most supple of all British aestheticians, Stokes was the more remarkable for arranging his acute perceptions on the apparently unyielding framework of binomial schemes, with such antinomies as smooth/rough and inside/out. The mention of his name at this early point is strategic, since a binomial sentence pattern of either/or is to be recurrent throughout the text, paralleled by a Kierkegaardian either/or at the metaphysical level. Sally Draycott's black/white imagery, quintessentially Stokesian, might have been taken directly from his masterly book *Venice*, particularly when it is considered that Sally is a Coco Chanel figure to Elena's Misia Sert, and that Chanel and Misia were together in Venice for Diaghilev's funeral.

enamels and cameos   Obviously Théophile Gautier, author of *Émaux et camées*, is the poet principally meant, although the text otherwise suggests that Lancelot's poetic sensibility is haunted by the more familiar tropes of Rimbaud and Baudelaire. But Gautier, even more than Baudelaire, was an art critic as much as a poet, or at any rate thought himself to be such; and Lancelot prides himself on the same combination of interests.

the masonry was showing some ominous cracks   Thereby heralding the collapse of the social fabric. Visually the image subsumes the ruins-in-a-landscape of the French pastoral tradition from Poussin and Claude down to Watteau and Fragonard. Verbally it conjures a seismic portent.

grisaille fans on which no Mallarmé would ever write a poem or Conder paint a pink Arcadia   Mallarmé regularly transcribed poems on fans for his admirer and patroness Misia Sert, who in turn is clearly one of the models for Elena, just as the artistic symbiosis of Misia and Diaghilev is paralleled in the relationship between Elena and Victor, and embryonically in the mutual attraction between Charlotte Windhover and David Bentley. Prominent among the many models for Elena's opera ball is the ball that Misia and Diaghilev staged (the appropriate verb) in the Versailles Hall of Mirrors in 1923. Charles Conder blasted his gift with drink, to the regret of Beardsley, whose dislike of him was coupled with admiration. Lancelot's troubled mind dwells often on artists of truncated promise. Beardsley illustrated Malory and thus 'captured' Lancelot's image.

two

in Andrei Bely's great novel 'Petersburg'   Although the present critic's propensity for finding significance in the geography of novels is made game of at one point in the text, it is nevertheless worth pointing out that this mention of *Petersburg* can scarcely be fortuitous. Bely combines pin-point specificity of topographical detail with deliberate vagueness concerning the whereabouts of the main centres of the action – the protagonist's house, for example, seems to wander around the city like a raft. The present text has some of the same characteristics. Where does Lancelot live, or Elena? If Sally and Nicholas drive home to Knightsbridge through the Hyde Park underpass after dinner at Elena's, then Elena can scarcely live anywhere west of Mayfair. But how could she have a house in Mayfair if she has no money? It is doubtful if such questions are meant to have answers. More profitable is to note that in Bely's symbolist scheme the colour red recurs obsessively. Here the colour green does the same. Red and green constitute a disarmingly trite structuralist matrix.

what Gide had said to Roger Martin du Gard as if he had been there to overhear it   Ian Cuthbert might indeed have been there to overhear it, if as a precocious youth he had visited Paris in 1949, before Gide's last illness. Gide reread Proust in his last year, as Tolstoy reread Dostoevsky. Considering Ian's proclivities, it would be of particular interest to him that Gide's and Martin du Gard's is the only known case of a love affair between winners of the Nobel Prize for Literature.

Balthus had given him a small drawing   Very unlikely, Balthus's drawings being concentrated in the hands of so few owners. But Balthus prepared a set of illustrations for *Wuthering Heights*, and the Brontë sisters, most obviously in the presence of Charlotte Windhover, are incorporated in the text's *leitmotiv* of female threeness.

the most nearly successful attempt to revive the reputation of Denton Welch   Strangely missing from both Lancelot's and Ian's lists of writers who could draw, Denton Welch favoured Thackeray's devotion to small beer, i.e. to the 'tiny' (his word) things of life, the minutiae of homes, meals and possessions. An uncomfortable name to be invoked, in a text so impressionistically cavalier as regards concrete detail.

stories about Cocteau and Radiguet   Cocteau's play about Misia Sert and Coco Chanel, *Les Monstres sacrés*, will be recalled when Elena and Sally form their antagonistic friendship. Radiguet's *Le Bal du comte d'Orgel* is one of the image-networks contributing to Elena's country setting, while Radiguet himself, author of two masterpieces and dead six years younger even than Beardsley, understandably nags at the self-esteem of Lancelot-as-author.

framed wall paintings by Paolo Veronese   Another portent of collapse. The walls of Venice held too much water to allow use of the fresco technique, so most large Venetian paintings are done on canvas. We are reminded of the structural weakness of Lancelot's portico and, by extension, of his life.

three

even if he had dressed ... like the Count Robert de Montesquiou   The reference might be pretentious but is not necessarily Proustian. The physical appearance of Proust's Charlus was based not on Comte Robert de Montesquiou but on the obscure baron Doazan. Proust met de Montesquiou at the salon of Madeleine Lemaire (clearly one of the prototypes for both Elena and Charlotte in their educative roles), where he also met the Comtesse Greffuhle and Mme de Chevigné, part models for the Duchesse and the Princesse de Guermantes respectively – although, as Proust was always careful to point out, no character in the book has fewer than ten different real-life 'inspirations'. Madeleine Lemaire, an amateur artist of professional attainments, illustrated Proust's early and unsuccessful book *Les Plaisirs et les jours*, a publication which would be much on Lancelot's mind, since it so exemplifies just how little early promise can mean without later achievement. The most famous portrait of de Montesquiou is by Boldini, with whom Lancelot shares an admiration for long-legged women.

the average domestic pot dating from the Sung dynasty An imprecise image as to colour – which could be anything from 'hare's foot' black to *ch'ing-pai* white – but clear enough as regards thickness, although probably Lancelot-as-author is referring less to the glaze itself than to the underlying body, which tended to a particular fineness during the Sung period, mainly owing to the widespread use of clays with a high felspar content.

the job of ritually eviscerating Schubert A favourite offering of the Plaza Palm Court string quartet is 'Death and the Maiden', which has obvious relevance to Lancelot, who courts one through love of the other. Also Schubert died not only young but full of achievement, to the point that we might wonder not just what he would have done if he had lived as long as Beethoven, but what he would have done if he had lived as long as Mozart.

four

as in a Verdi aria, the same melodic figure The preponderance which Verdi will later have in the text's background music is often forecast in the early stages, thereby providing mimetic examples of the very principle here referred to. The operatic structure of the plot proceeds historically through arias, duets and *pezzi chiusi* to the through-composed extended ensembles of the opera ball, before fragmenting into a neo-classical, and finally atonal, aftermath.

'Like Flaubert' Sally's kinship with the great novelist is not through Emma Bovary but through Salammbô, spiritual cousin of Salome. To Sally, the opera ball is like the celebration in Hamilcar's garden, at which Salammbô seduces all men by knowing the language of each. (Sally's Porsche, in its power of conquest, is a Hamil-car.) Nicholas is her Mâtho, to whom she offers the city ('Carthage est à nous; jetons-nous-y!') if he has the courage to take it. (Marina in *Boris Godunov* offers the same contract to the false Czarevitch.) Lancelot paid oblique tribute to Flaubert when he named one of his dogs Feydeau. Flaubert wrote to Feydeau's father in July 1859, complaining about how people failed to understand that in order to bring Carthage back to life one had first to become sad. The success of the novel was reflected in the frequency with which the Court and the salons drew on it as second-hand inspiration for their costume balls. At the Court Ball for 9 February 1863, Mme Rimsky-Korsakov was Salammbô with a *décolleté (sic) transparent et généreux*. Flaubert, now a social lion, began attending the *dîners Magny* and in the imperial salons conceived a passion, which some say she returned, for the fabulously beautiful Jeanne de Tourbey. So complete was Flaubert's identification with Carthage in the public mind that Berlioz consulted him over details of the *mise en scène* for *Les Troyens*. The reference is thus, at a second level, operatic.

five

what Victor was fond of referring to as his Goering period   Victor has found a typically boastful way of being unfair to himself. In fact Goering's eclecticism consisted mainly of greeting real and fake with the same enthusiasm: he was a particular sucker for van Meegeren's dud Vermeers. But the deeper reference is to Klaus Mann's *Mephisto*. Victor's enervating appeal for Lancelot is an obvious echo of the Goering/Höfgen relationship, and his house has much in common with the art-palace Mann's *Komödiant* (the 'red' Mann preceded Greene in his use of the term!) built for himself in the *Tiergarten* district of Berlin.

Portrait busts by Troubetzkoy and Golubkhina   Troubetzkoy spent most of his career outside the Soviet Union but his pieces are not easily purchased, while Golubkhina's time abroad was mainly confined to periods of study in Paris. Victor most probably, or least improbably, inherited these works from his father, which raises the question of why he could not have inherited the Morandis too. There are many Fairweathers in English collections: a particularly fine one hangs in Somerville College, Oxford. If Victor received Nolans of the Ned Kelly period as gifts, it must have been a profound friendship the artist's prices were already high by then. The earlier, surrealist phase would have been more credible. But the émigré intellectuals and connoisseurs in Australia after World War II were characteristically given first choice of important works by rising young indigenous artists simply as a reward for having granted them the free run of personal libraries brought from Europe.

a huge yet weightless Delacroix watercolour study   Delacroix is Lancelot's obsession rather than Victor's, so Lancelot is the one whose mind is ravished. In 'The Death of Sardanapalus' the sultan watches his harem being slaughtered – a wish-fulfilment comparable to the Fellinesque seraglio dwelt upon later in the text. The Moroccan window is in the same range of eidetic inspiration as *Salammbô*. Delacroix, although he patronised him *vis-à-vis* Mozart, had a close spiritual kinship with Chopin, who in his turn is shortly to be invoked. There is almost no theme in Lancelot's text which Delacroix did not treat, including the shipwreck of Don Juan and the raising of Lazarus. Delacroix, who detested Ingres's 'Raphaelism', is at the colourist end of the range of Lancelot's visual affections, with the linear Ingres at the other. In this regard, if nowhere else, Lancelot can pique himself on his completeness.

He had once called her Madame X dressed by Madame Gres   Lancelot means to evoke John Singer Sargent's 1884 portrait of Mme Pierre Gautreau, *née* Virginie Avegno, the American-born Parisian *grande dame* famous for her chiselled profile, lavender-white complexion and plethora of influential lovers. Mainly because of

Sargent's keen emphasis on her alabaster *poitrine*, the portrait was a scandal even before it was hung, and was called *Madame XXX* in the catalogue in an unsuccessful attempt to veil the identity of the sitter – or, in this case, stander. Sargent kept the picture himself until 1916, regarding it, very plausibly, as the best thing he had ever painted. Although Madame X's gown, in its sensually draped simplicity, was very advanced for the time, it could not, needless to say, have been designed by Madame Gres, who, under her early name of Alix, first came to prominence only in the 1930s. Madame Gres, like Balenciaga, was an intensely sculptural designer whose clothes looked best on tall women. Madame X was noticeably short in the leg, which Elena is not. So Lancelot's witticism builds up an ideal portrait.

the most beautiful magazine ever published   Our author is being cagey about naming *Mir Iskusstva* (*The World of Art*), the magazine published by Diaghilev, whose name recurs throughout the text in connection with Victor Ludlow, but whose success in actually creating a world of art would grate on Lancelot sufficiently to make him want the phrase suppressed. The two Benois gouaches of the countess in the pool, both called 'The Countess of the Cupola', date from 1906 and can be seen, excellently reproduced, in N. Lapshina's *Mir Iskusstva* (Moscow, 1977), as can most of the Somov portrait heads, which mainly date from 1907–1915. Somov's 'Love Letter' of 1911–1912 is almost certainly one of the models for Elena at the ball. Somov left the Soviet Union in 1923 and lived in Paris from 1924. Soviet critics, typified by the relevant sections in such would-be encyclopedic works as *Ruskaya Kudozhestvenaya Kultura* (see particularly *1908–1917*, vol. 4, Moscow, 1980), continue to allege that the *Mir Iskusstva* group – being primarily concerned with decadent bourgeois liberalism – was already a spent force when the proletarian Revolution overtook it. None of the specific plates mentioned could have appeared in the magazine itself, which ceased publication in 1904. Lancelot has conceived an ideal publishing enterprise.

Or did the cherub belong to Titian?   Yes, but not playing a lute. In the 'Venus with Organist and Small Dog', painted at Augsburg in 1548 for Charles V and now in the Prado, the cherub whispers warnings to Venus while the young man plays the organ. The rows of trees in the background remarkably hark forward to Benois's garden exteriors in both versions of the 'Countess of the Cupola'. In Fragonard's 'Les Hazards heureux de l'escarpolette' (London, Wallace Collection), the onlooking cupid is made of stone, but seems animated. Lancelot is most likely to be thinking of the Ingres 'Odalisque with a Slave' (Fogg Art Museum, Harvard), in which the slave is female but holds a lute. Lady Hildegarde's three daughters obviously constitute a preliminary appearance by the Three Graces, an impression reinforced by the fact that they are not individually named.

a Gontcharova ballet backdrop   Gontcharova designed the scenes and costumes for *Coq d'or* in Diaghilev's 1913 Paris season. Fokine's last ballet for Diaghilev, it starred Karsavina (clearly one of the models for Sally) in her favourite role as the Queen of Shemakhan. Benois sat with Misia Sert at the premiere. But Victor's wall-covering most probably came from Diaghilev's London season at the Lyceum in late 1926, in which Gontcharova's decor for *Firebird* was a particular hit – a crowded panorama of pink, red and gold cupolas which would make Victor's bedroom seem like a courtyard in the Kremlin.

three matched Boldinis of a fine lady getting out of her clothes   There is no such sequence of pictures by Boldini, although individual paintings on the theme are common enough among his works. His emphasis on the elongation of the neck, like Sargent's on the elongation of the arm, is usually attributed to flattery, although it is a nice point whether the artists influenced the women or the women the artists – the original of Boldini's magnificent 'Consuelo, Duchess of Marlborough' of 1906 was actually pretty much like that. Nor is it easy to see why what is acceptable in Parmigianino should be derided in Boldini, whose home town of Vicenza has sensibly given him his own museum. So aware of women's clothes that it is possible to identify the dress designer in almost every picture, he is assured of survival on the documentary level at least. The reference to Boldini is plainly a contributory image to the iconography of Elena, who, even more than Sally, is continually represented in terms of unusual height.

One of the Medici had had three Uccello battle scenes in a similar position   Only one battle scene, divided into three panels; and more than one of the Medici. Cosimo probably commissioned Uccello to paint the 'Rout of San Romano' at some time in the middle 1450s, but the earliest documentation dates from 1492, when the three pictures are described as decorating Lorenzo's bedroom. The pictures are now divided between the Uffizi, the Louvre and the National Gallery, London. The broken lances lying on the orthogonals of these bold exercises in perspective would be a signal to Lancelot of his impotence.

a Raphael pope's cassock   Either Julius II or Leo X, the only two popes during Raphael's short career, and both of whom, of course, he immortalised. Raphael is one of the master spirits at the root of the text's iconography. The Rovere Pope Julius is an obvious armature for Victor's self-conception: a rough man of action yet an inspired patron of Bramante, Raphael and Michelangelo. The Medici Pope Leo (son of Lorenzo the Magnificent) is a precursor of (and pre-curses) Lancelot: more cultivated than Julius, he yet was unable to retain the allegiance of any of the titanic artists except Raphael. Julius's rooms in the Vatican, decorated largely by Raphael, suggest Victor's house, while some of the specific frescoes adumbrate scenes within it. Sally holding the open volume of Diaghilev's magazine, for example, is plainly a component of a modern 'School of Athens'. Frescoed corridors, common in the Vatican, are echoed in the text's system of decorated tunnels – the Underground that takes Lancelot down to his death. Raphael painted Bramante's corridor which led to the Belvedere but collapsed during the reign of Clement VII. Near the end of his life, for his friend and protector Cardinal Bibbiena, he also painted the 'Stufetta', the Cardinal's bathroom in the Vatican. The decor, not shown to ordinary visitors, consists mainly of a series of arousing Venuses: Venus Anadyomene, Venus on the Dolphin, Venus wounded by Amor, Venus and Adonis. This is without doubt the binding concept under the subsequent parade of Venuses – by Botticelli, Velázquez and Boucher – who appear during Lancelot's vision of Samantha at the moment of his death. At the opposite extreme but within the same tonal spectrum, Raphael's Madonnas, along with those of several Flemish masters, are to be recalled when Charlotte reads beneath the driftwood shelter.

'You know Vladimir?' asked Victor   But Victor himself would know many another Ashkenazy, or Ashkenazi – the generic name distinguishing all non-Mediterranean Jews from 'Sephardi'. The Hebrew press established at Naples in 1486 by German Ashkenazis was destroyed by the French in 1492 and all the Jewish master printers were put either to the sword or to flight, a bleak datum for a book-collector like Victor, since among their number was probably Joshua Solomon Soncino, prime mover of the Soncino family, who gave the world the first complete printed edition of the Hebrew Bible. For the Jewish bibliophile there is little comfort in the history of his field. It is not just a case of manuscripts destroyed, but of whole printed editions wiped out. Of the 1487 Soncini Pentateuch but a single copy survives.

feminist epic called 'The Woman Lieutenant's Frenchman'   It is hard to know what film is being referred to here. Possible candidates are *The Woman in White*, *Woman of the Year*, *The Lieutenant Wore Skirts* and *The French Connection*.

a Troubetzkoy 'grande dame' about two feet high   The material sounds as if it might be plaster or terracotta, but the model is most probably the small seated bronze figure of Mrs Hoernheimer, marked *Paolo Troubetzkoy, Milano 1897*. There are three known copies (at Pallanza, Paris and Moscow) but Victor might possibly own a fourth. Her *grande robe de soirée* is as likely to be by Worth as by Doucet, a house which at the end of the nineteenth century was already dressing Duse and Réjane but whose international renown was still some years away.

six

Lancelot felt that it had been raining continuously since the fall of the Attlee government   The Conservatives were returned to power in 1951. Lancelot could not really feel that it had been raining uninterruptedly for thirty years, so this must be an authorial hyperbole.

Charlotte would be a good Virgil for him, if you can have a female Virgil   You can, in the sense that a *virgilio* is the generic name for a guide, and that Virgil's job as Dante's guide through the regions beyond the tomb is eventually taken over by Beatrice. Charlotte is not only Dante's Beatrice Portinari but the beautiful and cultivated Beatrice d'Este, who had the misfortune to be married to Ludovico il Moro, duke of Milan. Leonardo watched Ludovico's downfall and sketched the smoke that rose from the burning city. Allusions to *The Divine Comedy* are everywhere in Lancelot's text, whose geography may be likened to a Dantesque spiral flattened into the form of a video disc, with consequent prismatic halation.

seven

those very large establishments with names like Castle This, That or The Other   Here the obeisance is obvious towards the Firbank who created Her Gaudiness the Mistress of the Robes, Count Cabinet and Queen Thleenouhee of the Land of Dates. Firbank and Peacock are the presiding spirits of Elena's and Charlotte's jointly ruled region, which may be most briefly characterised as Headlong Hall *en pantoufles*, or a glass-domed excerpt from that strange country in *The Flower Beneath the Foot*, where Her Dreaminess the Queen's handmaidens hum the melodies of Reynaldo Hahn. Elena and Charlotte, two different versions of Lady Parvula de Panzoust or Lady Georgia Blueharnis ('the Isabella d'Este of her day'), extend their bounty to a various troupe of Peacockian zanies. Ian Cuthbert, for example, is a clear echo of Mr Panscope, the Coleridge figure from *Headlong Hall* – who also turns up as Mr Flosky in *Nightmare Abbey* and as Mr Skionar in *Crotchet Castle*. As is later revealed, Charlotte is a devout Peacockian and thus a fitting hostess for David, whose radical convictions ally him closely to Mr Scythrop, the Shelley figure in *Nightmare Abbey*. When Shelley fainted from vegetarian excesses, Peacock would revive him with a large steak. Peacock's brilliant daughter Mary Ellen, an obvious precursor of Charlotte, married Meredith, who was several years younger than herself. Meredith made her the subject of his important poem-sequence *Modern Love* – the only good thing that came out of the marriage. Meredith presented a copy of his last book of poems to Lady Diana Manners, who as Lady Diana Cooper appears *in propria persona* at Elena's opera ball.

every twenty minutes a Boeing KC-135 Stratotanker   Powered by four 13,750 lb thrust Pratt & Whitney J57-P-59W engines, it is a much noisier aircraft than the later turbo-fan variant, the C-135A Stratolifter. Each Stratotanker carries 31,200 US gallons of jet fuel. Doubtless we are meant to think, as the idyllic scene is painted, of its potential destruction by divine fire three times an hour.

Mrs Hermeneutics left him a piece of steak and kidney pie   That the constantly renamed Mrs Hermesetas should at this point be called Mrs Hermeneutics is no accident. Hermeneutics had, or have, to do with interpretation, from the Greek word *hermeneutikos*. All Mrs Hermesetas's sobriquets derive from Greek roots (Hermes himself was a self-transforming messenger) and all interpret the action, even at this point, where the mention of the *Iliad* is scarcely fortuitous. One of Lancelot's governing myth-patterns is the *Odyssey* but the Trojan war had to be fought first. Samantha is the Helen of Lancelot's *Iliad*. He is Paris not just in the sense of having a memory peopled by that city's literary heroes, but in his being the thief of Helen. (His involvement with the Three Graces, of course, is traceable to the *Cypria* rather than to the *Odyssey*, in which Paris makes no judgment and in which his death is not even mentioned, only implied.) Paris's other name was Alexander. Later in the text Lancelot's mind is compared to the burning library of Alexandria – i.e., to Paris, the hero having once again become the city. The burning books theme is stated in Lancelot's accident with the pie, an evocation of King Alfred which reminds us how a preoccupation with book-learning can be intrinsically pyrophoric.

and the fate of Herculaneum   Not, it should be noted, of Pompeii. Herculaneum was the more elegant town. Both Victor's house and Elena's are in different proportions derived from Herculaneum's Villa of the Papyri, with its inner court, Epicurean library and sculpture collection. The Stratotankers full of jet fuel threaten Elena's Arcadia with an air-burst version of Vesuvius's behaviour in AD 79.

eight

by George Hoyningen-Huene at his most fastidious   Baron George Hoyningen-Huene, whose name probably not even he could pronounce, built the first of his many reputations in Paris, but his background was Russian – here, as at many other points, Lancelot's and Victor's frames of reference overlap. Hoyningen-Huene's unpublished memoirs of his experiences in south Russia in 1919–1920 forecast the Nazi era Holocaust at its most obscene. Like Victor he escaped from his memories into a dream of comfort, style and artistic achievement, but unlike Victor he was a direct creator in his own right. Although his portraits of fashionable women were as hieratic as those of any other great photographer of the period – long exposure times inhibited spontaneity – his thirst for real life led him to seek the moment of sensual relaxation within a given pose. His 'Miss Agnela Fischer' of 1931, recumbent like a reversed Rokeby Venus in a Schiaparelli one-piece swimsuit, could be a model for Samantha. The successor to de Mayer and Steichen at *Vogue*, Hoyningen-Huene was close friends with Gide, Cocteau, Mirò, Chanel, Visconti and Janet (*Paris Was Yesterday*) Flanner. Like Lancelot he set great store by personal elegance. The first and greatest of all Style Consultants, Hoyningen-Huene was colour coordinator on the best of Cukor's colour films, culminating in the sumptuous *Heller in Pink Tights*, which is itself a festival of visual echoes and reflections, with compositions based on Corot, Velázquez and the photographs of Weegee. But he was at his most colourful in black and white, in which his technique was characterised by back and cross lighting that gave an intricate yet always cleanly articulated play of shadows – linear shadows on curved forms, curved shadows on rectangular forms. Sally is most often seen through Hoyningen-Huene's camera.

still called Foscari's   Yet another preliminary invocation of Verdi, who does not emerge as a presiding spirit until the opera ball, but whose benign influence casts itself forward. *I due Foscari* of 1844 was the immediate successor to *Ernani*. Byron wrote a play on the same subject – a relevant consideration, because Lancelot sees himself as a Byronic figure and can be thought of, after his disastrous squash game, as having transformed his whole body into a Byronic club foot. Indeed the squash game is played at a club.

between Benjamin Constant and Madame de Staël   Thus conjuring the relationship between David and Charlotte, which Lancelot-as-character must already be rationalising at a subconscious level, even before it happens. Constant himself, as is well known, sublimated his predicament by writing *Adolphe*. Lancelot-as-author, with himself and Victor in mind, knows that Constant called his heroine Ellénore and that when he finally broke free – or, rather, just before he broke free – of Madame de Staël he married Charlotte von Hardenberg.

The soul of this man is his clothes   Lafeu says it of Parolles in *All's Well That Ends Well*, II, v. Nicholas is almost certainly planning a novel about Lancelot, on whom Lafeu's speech ('There can be no kernel in this light nut') is a judgment – although we must remember that it is Lancelot who writes what we read. 'Trust him not in a matter of heavy consequence,' says Lafeu to Bertram. Lancelot's nature, divided between the innocent Bertram and the sinister Parolles, is, of course, unified in his love for Helena, the stolen Helen of Paris – i.e., Samantha, whose original name has in turn been stolen by Lancelot and given to Elena.

the halls of Dis, the inane regions   From the *Aeneid*, VI: *perque domos Ditis vacuas et inania regna*. Virgil, already present in the text as a guide, is here invoked as a poet, the specific allusion being to that moment when Aeneas goes down into the underworld after having left the antrum of the Sibyl (Janice) whose answers rush as many voices through a hundred wide mouths. In the Land of Shadows, on the far bank of the Styx, he comes to the Broken-hearted Fields, where those consumed by Love are hidden in secret walks. Here Aeneas sees the forsaken Dido, as Lancelot sees Charlotte at the moment of his death. High among countless other relevant Virgilian instances must be reckoned *Georgics* IV, 467, in which Orpheus enters the lofty portals of Dis to go down into the underworld in search of Eurydice.

the Korean translation of 'You'll Never Walk Alone' Mentions of Lancelot's signature tune are not casual. No epic hero was ever unaccompanied in Hell.

nine

'The young in one another's arms,' said Victor The Yeatsian adduction is not happenstance. 'Sailing to Byzantium' announced the theme for *The Tower*, Yeats's most extended cry of pain against old age. As the title poem 'The Tower' goes on to reveal, the tragedy began with Helen. 'Does the imagination dwell the most/Upon a woman won or woman lost?' This is Victor's dilemma more than it is Lancelot's, whose obsession with his Helen/Samantha Homerically blinds him to Charlotte, whereas Victor's commitment to his Helen/Elena can only increase. Victor's treasure-filled house is a repository for what the narrator has lost in 'Nineteen Hundred and Nineteen': all the golden grasshoppers and bees. Sally, in her brief New York episode with Victor, becomes Leda, putting on his knowledge with his power. Elena's opera ball is an All Souls' Night, where the blessed dance.

ten

the only one I could think of was Delacroix It is hard to credit that Serena, if she could think of only one, should think of him. But Delacroix is a species of Nemesis for Lancelot, who is identified with Gautier as a poet attuned to the visual arts. Gautier's capacities as an art critic were rated very low by Delacroix, as his *Journal* reveals.

those little drawings of Rimbaud that bring out the whole business of their relationship Few drawings by Verlaine show him and Rimbaud together: certainly there are none comparable to Félix Regamey's 'Verlaine et Rimbaud à Londres' of October 1872. But most of Verlaine's drawings of Rimbaud by himself are, in their fond regard, revealing enough. The 'Départ de Rimbaud pour Vienne' of April 1876 is a good example. It can be seen in the *Album Rimbaud*, which Lancelot, undoubtedly a subscriber to the Bibliothèque de la Pléiade, would have on his shelves. The *Albums*, supplied gratis to subscribers and not otherwise ordinarily available, have by now become collector's items in their turn.

' . . . *Lermontov would be your most gifted case of the lot.*'   He would, but Lancelot is wrong in calling him a Decembrist, although to the young men of Lermontov's generation Decembrism was undoubtedly still a living force. As the relevant entry in the useful *Lermontovskaya Entsiklopedia* (Moscow, 1981) recounts, Lermontov made personal contact with some surviving Decembrists in the Caucasus from 1837 onwards and formed several close friendships among them in the few years remaining to him. Their influence on his writings was profound. A superb volume of Lermontov's cartoons, watercolours and drawings (*Lermontov: Kartuni, Akvareli, Risunki*) was published in Moscow in 1980. Much as Lancelot would like to think of himself as the Hero of Our Time, the Pechorin figure in this text is unmistakably Brian Hutchings.

' . . . *Apollinaire's "calligrammes" count as a kind of drawing* . . . ' Only if you stretch a point. And why do that, if you are leaving out Dürrenmatt, or Thomas Mann? But Lancelot is determined to count Apollinaire in, probably because of Apollinaire's love for Madeleine (that name again) Pagès, to whom his letters became progressively more desperately erotic throughout the bitter trench warfare of 1915–1916. Some of them were considered too pornographic to be included in *Tendre comme le souvenir*, since they contained 'secret poems' in which he celebrated the various zones of her body. He also told her that he had named one of the trenches after her – a relevant fact, considering the zone of Samantha's body which Lancelot celebrates in Los Angeles. Madeleine's predecessor in Apollinaire's affections, Annie Playden, emigrated to California after she left him, and there, perhaps fortunately, dropped out of literary history.

eleven

Elena was rather proud of Cleopatra's Dinghy   And probably of Cleopatra's nose. 'Le nez de Cléopâtre,' said Pascal: 's'il eût été plus court, toute la face de la terre aurait changé'. As we know from the reference to Madame X, Elena is blessed with a chiselled profile, but this and subsequent Cleopatra allusions are less oblique. Elena/Victor is an obvious Cleopatra/Antony pairing, with Victor's Antony 'marrying' Sally's Octavia, to the rage of the Serpent of Old Nile. In this brief but crowded sequence of rapidly transmogrifying imagery, Cleopatra's Dinghy becomes the Venetian *Bucintoro*, the state barge which plays a key role at the regatta (made musical in Act One of *La Gioconda*) when the city marries the sea. Venice (Venus) is one of Elena's name cities. The Ovidian metamorphosis by which the fleeing marble Daphne enters the laurel tree is there to remind us both of Bernini's fructive Daphne and of Yeats's custom and ceremony. At home in her *Schifanoia* of a country seat, Elena is Lady Gregory at Coole Park: hence the Ledean swan in the prow of her boat. She is also, as she counts the flowers, Dante's Matilda and – supremely – the Flora (Florence is another of her name cities) in Botticelli's 'Primavera', whose central figure is in her turn twin to his Venus. The two Botticellian masterpieces, both of them commissioned by the same Lorenzino de' Medici who assigned Botticelli to the task of illustrating *The Divine Comedy*, are at the trunk of our text's visual ramifications, as later becomes more apparent. Charlotte, too, is a green-fingered Matilda. Her book-lined mill house is the contemplative cell of the Arcadia over which she and Elena jointly preside. Mistress of the intellectual component of *Arcadia*, she is the Countess of Pembroke to David's Sir Philip Sidney. But her most important twinning with Elena is Dantesque. They are both Beatrices. Elena has already shown her Dante into Paradise and now gives instruction to Charlotte, whose own Dante has only just begun his journey.

recurred like the 'petite phrase' in Proust   But it doesn't recur in Proust: only the evocation of it does. In the same way, Keats doesn't say that beauty is truth and truth beauty, he only says that the Grecian urn says that. The very syntax of Lancelot's literary memory has become a fluctuating plasma. As Painter demonstrates in the first volume of his magisterial *Marcel Proust*, Reynaldo Hahn did not originate the 'little phrase'; but by focusing Proust's unwilling attention on Saint-Saëns he helped ensure that Proust would be captivated by the chief theme of the first movement of the Sonata in D Minor for violin and piano. Proust first heard the work played, by Ysaye, at Madeleine Lemaire's salon. Saint-Saëns's 'little phrase' became the theme tune of his affair with Hahn and later, as Vinteuil's, of Swann's with Odette. At Madeleine Lemaire's country house, Réveillon, Proust and Hahn walked together in the rose garden in a way of which Elena's and Sally's *tournée* at the opera ball is an obvious echo.

twelve

mirrors leading into other mirrors   The whole text, as we explicitly hear in the last paragraph, is a hall of mirrors. Here Elena's drawing room, probably modelled on the Amalienburg in Nymphenburg, serves as a vitreous echo-chamber. But the text's mirrors distort images as they transmit them. It is sounds that they reflect intact, in a kind of sonic *Spiegelsaal*: both Nicholas *and* Victor talk about Nicholas's Christmases all coming at once, while both Elena *and* Charlotte talk about the beneficial effects of muesli and yoghurt on the younger generation. Each character's language is replicated in his *Doppelgänger*, while the lovers catch phrases from each other as a mirrored dining room distributes candlelight.

from the 1978 Chloë 'prêt-à-porter' collection   Lancelot-as-author is being over-explanatory. For the house of Chloë, Karl Lagerfeld has never done a *couture* collection, so 'prêt' the suit must necessarily be. Saint-Laurent is the only major designer to do both *prêt-à-porter* and *couture*. Sally would spot Elena's YSL *couture* original by the quality of the fabrics.

The poor man made it for me   Unlikely. The older generation of couturiers, typified by Balenciaga and Balmain, would occasionally lend clothes to women prominent in the fashionable world, but the house of Saint-Laurent, with a gigantic volume of *prêt-à-porter* business providing the solid base of its finances, has rarely felt obliged to give anything away.

her Brontë sisters look   Yet another triad of women is conjured, with Charlotte representing them not just through her look but through, of course, her name. Lancelot, needless to add, is exactly cast as Branwell Brontë. The three sisters and their brother when young devised a saga about a city of glass.

talking about Pfitzner or Kulenkampff   In the strict classicism of the music-teaching atmosphere of post-WWII Vienna, Hans Pfitzner's pamphlet *Futuristengefahr* (*The Futurist Danger*) attacked Busoni, who wrote a reply which impressed, among others, the young Alfred Brendel (*Musical Thoughts and After-Thoughts*, London, 1976). Georg Kulenkampff was a founder member of the famous trio headed by Edwin Fischer.

hummed Siegfried's Funeral March to appropriate effect   One of Lancelot's many symbolic deaths is here underscored (or, the Verdian would probably suggest, overscored) by the music which accompanied Goebbels's announcement of the fall of Stalingrad. In a text which itself aspires to operatic form, all other operas are atomised. The Wagnerian epics, in particular, are raided indiscriminately, with characters and properties detached from their original meanings and ruthlessly redistributed. Samantha is Kundry, just as Lancelot is Parsifal, but where is the Lohengrin for Elena's swan-boat? It is important to remember that Siefgried's funeral takes place, not in *Siegfried*, but in *Götterdämmerung*. The text is a *Totentanz*, a fact driven home by the centrally important invocation of Holbein at the moment when Victor and Sally begin their doomed affair in New York. The Dance of Death was one of Holbein's great themes.

thirteen

'Windhover,' said the immigration officer   It is no accident that Lancelot's surname, the title of Gerard Manley Hopkins's most famous single poem, becomes prominent at this point. Lancelot's is an essentially Hopkinsian metaphysical agony, for what else is Samantha if not his Andromeda — an Andromeda who is her own dragon, rife in her

wrongs, more lawless and more lewd? And so Lancelot/Perseus has come flying to redeem her. *Pillowing air he treads a time, and hangs/His thoughts on her.* The airborne associations of his name having been brought alive by flight, more than one of his name-poem's phrases now beg to be attached to Samantha's body: gash-gold vermilion, for example.

fourteen

'*. . . It's what Rimbaud called it . . .*' The poem 'Obscur et froncé' is one of the erotic sonnets grouped together under the general title *Les Stupra* (*Defilements*). Lancelot is perhaps generous in attributing his own sacred wonder to Rimbaud, whose true tastes are probably conveyed in 'Nos Fesses ne sont pas les leurs' ('Our Behinds are not Theirs'). Lancelot's invocation of Rimbaud, whose creative life was over at nineteen, is a conscious justification of his own sterility. Unconsciously, Lancelot is Verlaine, and Samantha is Rimbaud, who threatened Verlaine's marriage with Mathilde. The final show-down between Lancelot and Samantha parallels the break-up of Verlaine and Rimbaud in Paris, after which Rimbaud went on to complete *Une Saison en enfer* – for which Lancelot dreams the equivalent in his hour of death.

'*Cost you a groaning to take off my edge.*'   Samantha takes Hamlet's role while Lancelot submits, as a potentially suicidal Ophelia. But it is the celebrated, never-named actor who floats until his clothes pull him under. Samantha has Hamlet's *Schadenfreude*. In her basement flat she conceals Nicholas behind the arras so that Lancelot can run him through with a glance.

like a female mythological protagonist trying to shake off a shirt of intermittent fire   But Herakles, the afflicted wearer of the shirt of Nessus, was male. Once again Samantha has taken on the dominant role, this time incandescently. Gautier, prominent among Lancelot's model poets, in *Mademoiselle de Maupin* wrote the textbook for the reasonable male enslaved by the role-playing female.

their hands were ever at their lips, bidding adieu   The allusion to Keats establishes Charlotte, in her own wishes, as David's Fanny Brawne, or rather as the Fanny Brawne of Keats's ideal imaginings. But of course Charlotte is also the Contessa Maffei to his Verdi, the Gräfin Trautmannsdorff to his Joseph Roth, and potentially – an outcome she fears, hence her choice of ode – Madame de Staël to his Benjamin Constant.

'*. . . Like the Cherenkov effect . . .*'   Most commonly seen in a nuclear reactor, when high-energy particles, exceeding the local, water-reduced, speed of light, throw back a wake of brilliance. Lancelot thinks of his injured posterior as a fuel rod being inserted into a reactor core. David's appropriating of Lancelot's imagery is a token of usurpation.

Normally she never lent books   But does now, as an earnest of having fallen in love through the mind. It is characteristic in such relationships for the woman to be the more experienced in the ways of the world, drawn to potential rather than fulfilment, and eager to influence that fulfilment by awakening the too narrowly focused prodigy to the finer considerations. Vittoria Colonna played the part for Michelangelo, Princess Marie von Thurn und Taxis-Hohenlohe for Rilke, and the Queen of the Belgians for Einstein. The Contessa Clara Maffei was probably the single most decisive feminine influence on Verdi's life, even if the friendship was Platonic, while Joseph Roth's adoration of the Gräfin Trautmannsdorff was rehearsed at least once earlier, when as a student he was favoured with the impassioned affections of Helena von Szajnocha-Schenk, a bluestocking thirty years older than her protégé. (She told him that she was 300 years younger than Shakespeare.) Roth's *Radetzkymarsch*, with its Last Post for a lost Elysium, is omnipresent in the background of our text. George Sand's importance for Chopin is also relevant, since it left him open to the accusation that comfort had won him away from his political obligations as a Polish citizen, and thus forced him to redefine his commitment in terms of a higher reality – his music.

'Chap called Kreisky.'   Thus Victor, by closeting himself with Franz-Josef's modern equivalent, compensates for the Viennese past which for him never took place. He embraces the new Europe through the erstwhile capital city of the Austro-Hungarian Empire, which for its Jews, despite social discrimination, represented the concrete possibility of world citizenship. The textual evidence suggests that Victor's father was a German Jew rather than an Austrian one, and indeed there is no Viennese component among the art-works he left his son, but on the imaginative level Vienna is Victor's soul-city, an impression reinforced by his reference to Count Razumovsky and Beethoven. By eliding this reference from the televised conversation between Victor and Sally, Speed Blair symbolically reinforces Victor's cultural isolation as a cosmopolitan.

and 'Randall Hoyle's Wallenstein' from Schiller's or Golo Mann's   A carbuncle of relevant allusions. Wallenstein's unaccountable transformation into what Machiavelli, referring to Cesare Borgia, called a *profeta disarmata*, is closely germane to Lancelot's fate; Schiller's distinction between the naive and the sentimental is at issue throughout the text; and the Mann family are continually adduced. We have already seen how Victor is a counter-figure to Klaus Mann's Mephisto. Thomas Mann will be called up when Lancelot becomes Aschenbach. His son Golo's first book was a biography of Friedrich von Gentz, who, even more than Metternich, was the first fully European-minded diplomatic thinker of the type Victor so approves. Gentz spent much of his free time at the Berlin salon of Rahel Varnhagen, probably one of the models for both Elena and Charlotte, and herself the subject of a monograph by Hannah Arendt – certainly a model for Charlotte. The Jewish blood of Mann's mother and his wife Katja would have been enough to doom the whole family if they had not escaped.

fifteen

dogs barked far away   As they would at the gates of Hell. Lancelot is once again rehearsing his death voyage, by which the London tube system becomes the tunnel to the Underworld.

but that Mrs Hammerklavier would cook him something for his dinner   A prime instance of how Mrs Hermesetas's variable name comments on the action. The Hammerklavier sonata, like the Ninth Symphony and the C Sharp Minor quartet, is a massive musical structure in which Beethoven's death is implicit, no further development being conceivable.

sixteen

'... *a paratrooper from the Mount Olympus Defence Regiment,' said Victor.*   Victor immediately states the theme in terms of affronting the court of Jupiter, among whose ranks he enrols Sally. On the peak of Olympus it was always Spring, the season which has now been reached in the time-frame of the text, and which indeed is already giving way to Summer – time to leave Olympus.

'*That's what Karl Kraus thought about Schnitzler ...* '   Kraus's attacks were a disappointment not only for Schnitzler but for anyone who saw the Austro-Hungarian Empire, and later the Austrian nation-state, as the hope for Jewish dignity within a liberal European country. But Victor, who identifies heavily with Schnitzler, is also being defensive about Schnitzler's personal position as a man who, advanced in years, fell in love with several young women, of whom the last and most notable was Vilma Lichtenstern. The theme of the proud man of the world who sacrifices his equilibrium for a young woman is common in his plays and forms the pivot of his masterpiece *Das Weite Land*. Schnitzler, like Victor, lost a beloved daughter and was ridden by guilt. Victor shares Schnitzler's world view but his remorse along with it. Kraus, secure in his long friendship with the Baroness Sidonie Nádherny von Borutin, was able to view Schnitzler's truth-telling themes as the merest bourgeois self-indulgence. His assaults on Schnitzler are hard to distinguish from anti-Semitic virulence, but it should be remembered that Kraus, like Schnitzler, believed in a Jew's right to dislike Jews individually. Not even Kraus, prophetic in so many other ways, was quite able to imagine that a time would come when racial solidarity would be imposed by decree, with the specific aim of extermination. For Victor the quarrel between Kraus and Schnitzler, which lasted all their lives, is thus at the centre of the modern tragedy.

' ... Freud used to say ... '   He said it in his 1927 article Der Zukunft einer Illusion. I translate: ' ... but if all one can do is to reduce the anticultural majority to a minority, one has still done a lot, perhaps all that can be done.' Freud thought that if cultural restrictions were bad the state of nature was even worse. He reserved judgment, at that time, about what might happen in the Soviet Union, but otherwise insisted that the transformation of a whole people was impossible. Obviously Victor shares that Jansenist view. 'It is the highest task of culture, its characteristic reason for being,' wrote Freud in the same essay, 'to guard us against nature (uns gegen die Natur zu verteidigen).' Anti-Rousseau and therefore anti-Marx, Victor's social democracy goes back through Bernstein to Lassalle.

' ... There's an excellent eighteenth-century translation ...' Victor's Thucydides must be the great 1760 rendition of Geschichte des Peloponnesischen Krieges by Johann David Hellmann, Professor of Theology at Göttingen. Composed in bitterly austere German, it is one of the best ways of reading The Peloponnesian War for those who would avoid the conversational amble of English prose, although Rex Warner's Penguin translation is acerbic enough. Victor is probably drawing David's attention to Thucydides' account, in Book VII, of the first extermination camp recorded in literature. After the defeat of the Sicilian expedition the Syracusans put the Athenian and allied prisoners into stone quarries for eight months. Mauthausen, referred to by Elena, had a stone quarry.

with Modigliani in Paris   Victor is giving his blessing to David and Charlotte, whose friendship was presaged by the Parisian love affair of Modigliani and Akhmatova

for being caught out about Picasso   Victor's disapproval of the painter's political hypocrisy masks a deeper aversion to the ruthless honesty with which he was successively monogamous.

seventeen

Nicholas's novels, argued Bartelski, were multicentred   The author's touch falters when it comes to parodying modern critical techniques, with which he is clearly not familiar. It would be a smugly conventional critic who spent much time looking for even unconscious intentions, let alone conscious ones. The deconstructionist is after more elusive game than that! But since no novels by 'Nicholas Crane' exist, the discussion is – our author might say quintessentially so – academic.

Dinner that night was hilarious   With the Stratotankers threatening fire and brimstone outside the glass bubble of Elena's pleasure-dome, the tale-telling by her guests recalls the *Decameron*. After each day and night, one of the men or women assembled in Boccaccio's idyllic country retreat is appointed King or Queen and reigns over the conversation, in which the men habitually attempt, always unsuccessfully, to shock the women. Pampinea, the first Queen, who gives the example to all the others, is one of Elena's more obvious models. 'This fullness of physical and emotional life,' comments the scholar Bosco, 'confers on Pampinea the tranquil serenity, the peaceful wisdom, the love for everything noble and rich and intelligent – i.e., fully alive – which are her characteristics.'

a small book of Disraeli's letters   Disraeli's letters to his sister are full of the naive delight he took in social climbing, so David's reading of them is necessarily self-referential. If he is seeking justification for the course on which he is embarked, Disraeli makes a strange role-model. In the case of Victor it would be a different matter: he would find Disraeli's untroubled enthusiasm very recognisable. As Joseph Roth said to his admired Gräfin Trautmannsdorff, assimilation is just another way to flee. But here it is Charlotte who represents the well-mannered world into which David is drawn against his convictions yet according to his tastes, and doubly troubled to find that the latter are more powerful than the former. Disraeli was especially partial to 'the great fancy ball', as witness his letter for 20 July 1835. 'Lady Londonderry, as Cleopatra, was in a dress literally embroidered with emeralds and diamonds from top to toe. Castlereagh introduced me to her by her desire, and I was with her a great deal.'

by knowing as much as he did about Büchner   Sally might have impressed the ambassador, but not as much as she would have impressed Victor, who would be well aware that Büchner's Danton was robbed of his sense of reality by physical passion. But passion was the higher reality and Danton was right, Büchner suggests, to embrace it. The women of Danton and Camille Desmoulins are true to the end: Julia takes poison and Lucile, in a great last dramatic moment, cries 'Es lebe der König!' ('Long live the King!') as the night watch passes. Büchner, like Beardsley, Radiguet and Schubert, is for Lancelot yet another galling example of an artist cut down young yet full of lasting achievement.

eighteen

'Sadat, Sadat, Sadat,' said the wheels of the 'Shinkansen'   Victor's position on the Middle East must have been severely shaken by the assassination of the Egyptian leader, whose name haunts him. He is *sad at* it.

the moss was at its best in the temple   The Zen temple Ryuan-ji is probably meant, since it is the sole Kyoto temple to feature gardens both of moss and of raked sand. The temple was founded by one of the Bumei Shogun Yoshimasa's generals, Hosokawa Katsumoto, who might be described as the Victor Ludlow of the Japanese fifteenth century.

had once done Kipling the same favour   A not entirely fanciful suggestion. Kipling was in Kyoto during his Far Eastern trip c. 1888, as is recorded in *From Sea to Sea*, vol. one. The temple he visited, however, was not the Ryuan-ji but the Chion-in, where he saw the Cherry Blossom procession. His description of the priests' brocade robes can be particularly recommended to students of 'jewelled' travel writing.

nineteen

' . . . And they sent one man on to carry two . . . '   But Lancelot has failed to notice how accurately his own position is exemplified by the helpless supernumerary crucified while attempting to carry two spears.

twenty

Elena knew that there was no point fixing on any well-known character for herself   Or rather, the author knew. Elena is not one of the 23 Feldmarschallins because the danger she faces, and overcomes, is radically different: Victor, far from being the young Octavian, would be Baron Ochs if he were more boorish. Nor is she the Queen of the Night in any other sense beyond that of her permanent role as Boccaccio's Reina, queen of both night and day. She is Magda de Cuivry from *La Rondine* (*The Swallow*) honoured, although it was Magda and not her protector Rambaldo Fernandez who strayed, nevertheless her alliance with Rambaldo is similar to Elena's with Victor. Puccini regularly fell in love with his sopranos, to the chagrin of his wife Elvira, who, after the initial dust-up about the too-beautiful housemaid Doria Manfredi, became as patient as Mrs Yeats. She was rightly concerned about Corinna 'the Piemontese' but showed no hostility at all towards Puccini's young soul companion, the banker's wife Sybil Seligman – probably because of Sybil's diplomatic gifts, which enabled her to befriend the family even while playing the same role in Puccini's life as Vilma Lichtenstern played in Schnitzler's. The First World War broke out while Puccini was working on *La Rondine*, which makes that small opera a symbol of unity in a disintegrating world picture. Puccini, in his letters to Sybil, pronounced the libretto trivial, but Victor would be able to see the significance of a pseudo-Viennese masterpiece being composed by a genius at the moment of suicide for the old order. Elvira was griefstricken when Toscanini brought her the news of Puccini's death.

They went as Aubrey Beardsley and Salome   When Sally dances with Victor, Salome dances before Herod. Wilde was appalled when the publisher, John Lane, put the book out in a fancy binding (coarse blue canvas for the ordinary edition, green silk for the *édition de luxe*) instead of giving it the plain treatment appropriate to Beardsley's simplifying, space-massing gift. Nicholas would like to emulate Beardsley's feat of remaining forever twenty-six years old. Beardsley's sister was the subject of Yeats's poem-sequence 'Upon a Dying Lady' in *The Wild Swans at Coole.*

finally settled for being Jimmy Mahoney from 'Mahagonny'   More correctly, Jim Mahoney from the Brecht/Weill *Aufstieg und Fall der Stadt Mahagonny*. Jim Mahoney shares with the soprano (inevitably called Jenny) one of Kurt Weill's most effective duets, the Crane Song, a number which in itself would be enough to put Brecht's theories about opera under strain, and whose invocation at this point sets the seal on the alliance between David and Charlotte. A friend of Mahoney's dies in the boxing ring, just as David's fellow musician dies on the wet stage, before David, unlike Mahoney, escapes the City of Nets. Or does he? Perhaps Charlotte is his Lulu, as Brecht becomes Berg – a *Zauberberg*, if Lancelot will forgive the pun! Brecht, troubled by the attractiveness of Weill's music, said that if society found *Mahagonny* appetising, it would only serve to sharpen discussion about the kind of society which found such works necessary.

she did not feel particularly faithful to her Florestan   Although Charlotte/Fidelio has not yet been unfaithful to Lancelot/Florestan, she has already abandoned hope of rescuing him from his prison, which is of the mind. She puts on his cavalry twills as a token of wishing to wear the trousers in the family, but quickly takes them off again, rejecting the idea of role-reversal. So she becomes Donizetti's Lucia, with David her Edgar of Ravenwood. The sextet from *Lucia di Lammermoor* should remind us, incidentally, that the six main characters of our story combine and recombine during the opera ball, with the other revellers providing the chorus.

He had decided to be André Chénier.   The crucial words being 'he had decided': a death-wish. As with Danton at the opposite social extreme, there was something self-willed about Chénier's destruction. He could have escaped arrest with ease. Also Lancelot is attempting, by association, to spiritualise his passion for Samantha. Chénier's love for Françoise Le Coulteux was on a high plane of devotion, and not only because her husband himself faced death. The poems Chénier dedicated to her are the most delicate in his *oeuvre*. He called her 'Fanny' – an interesting parallel with Keats, and a connection which would intrigue Lancelot, since Chénier's apostrophising of 'Fanny' uncannily forecasts, as a classical signal of the forthcoming modernity, Rimbaud's hymn to female anatomy, ('Viens, Fanny ... ') Chénier sailed to Byzantium before Yeats. ('Liberty which flees from us, you do not flee from Byzantium/You fly above its minarets.') Above all, Chénier resembles Lancelot in having, *a fortiori*, written all his poems young. Yet what binds Lancelot closest to the author of the opera *Andrea Chenier* is that Giordano never repeated his early success. In the opera, Chénier's great love is called Madeleine, which would remind Lancelot of Proust, his *bête noire* because Proust in later life was more creative instead of less.

persuaded her to go as Manon Samantha and Delilah between them offer two possible variations of Manon, reflecting the fact that there are two main Manons in the operatic repertory – Puccini's and Massenet's. Subconsciously Lancelot would approve of Puccini's later but more powerful interpretation, by which Manon is given the emotional resources to love two men. Consciously he must know himself to be Des Grieux, drawn forward to destruction, but with the hope of an aesthetically satisfying apotheosis in a last duet. No such supreme considerations govern the Massenet version, to which Puccini gave credit for its 'powder and minuets', but whose Manon hardly promises divinity. The first night of *Manon Lescaut* in Turin was the only unmixed triumph of Puccini's career, just as Massenet's *Manon* had been that composer's greatest success. Massenet's Manon, of course, dies at Le Havre before being deported, but Delilah would not want to miss out on the mortification of the flesh which Puccini arranged for his version. That Delilah is also the Delilah of Saint-Saëns's *Samson et Dalila* should go without saying, although it is Lancelot whose strength she steals, not Dick Toole's. Saint-Saëns's librettist, Ferdinand Lemaire, was a Creole from Martinique – one of the several indirect invocations which the text affords of the ball in Saint-Pierre on the eve of Mont Pelée's eruption in 1902.

There is not a woman in the world, Proust had said Proust said it, but it might equally have been Pascal, La Rochefoucauld, La Bruyère or Vauvenargues. Lancelot's head full of aphorisms necessarily depends on an authorial capacity to remember everything except precisely who said what. This particular aperçu, however, may be found in vol. 3, p. 496, of the Pléiade *A la recherche* ...

the scarlet velvet choker which Samantha had rather wittily given him It was a standard dressing-up joke among *demi-mondaines* during the Terror. At a ball in *The Red and the Black*, the sadistic Mathilde de la Mole – with whom Samantha has obvious affinities – is interested only in a picturesque Spanish conspirator who is under sentence of death. 'I can see nothing but a sentence of death that distinguishes a man,' she remarks. 'It is the only thing that cannot be bought.'

the air was shattered by the sound of a jet aircraft   Thus the Arcadian scene is threatened, in its finest hour, with destruction by fire from the air. In this respect, Elena's opera ball has clear affinities with the grand occasion in *The Violins of St Jacques* and the dinner dance by candlelight at the end of Joseph Roth's *Radetzkymarsch*, which is interrupted by the news from Sarajevo.

They all had little jokes and clever quotations ready   The quotations are, respectively, from *Le Nozze di Figaro, Tosca, Der Rosenkavalier, Parsifal, Pelléas et Mélisande, Boris Godunov* and *Otello*. Each has a role for Lancelot, but it is no accident that the suicidally jealous Othello is placed last, and that the words are from his dying aria.

obviously meant to be Helen of Troy   From Offenbach's *La Belle Hélène*. David, confronted like Lancelot with the opportunity of stealing Helen, does not do so. For him, the Trojan war does not take place.

Gramsci's idea of culturally defined objectivity   A stumbling block for Gramsci's admirers, who are forced to wonder how Gramsci himself could have arrived at a valid view of events if the truth of his view was culturally determined. The matter is discussed by Leszek Kolakowski in vol. 3 of his monumental *Main Currents of Marxism*.

'. . . in the vicinity of Carinthia'   Holy ground for Sally. The first Porsche sports cars were built there, at Gmünd, before the firm moved to Stuttgart.

twenty-one

Lancelot could not think of any operas about Aztecs   Nor can I, but the man, instead of being a well-dressed Aztec, might have been a badly dressed high priest from *Aida* or *Die Zauberflöte*.

like stars being born in Orion's sword   The source of new stars in our galaxy lies in the direction of that constellation but is obscured by dust clouds from observation in the range of visible light.

while improbably impersonating Adriana Lecouvreur   The improbability probably resides in the exquisite economy with which Adriana deploys fragments of her only but enchanting melody. Cilea, who had a solitary success and then languished, would be another name congenial to Lancelot.

So of all the Cherubinos   Farfalla is *Figaro*'s Cherubino, rather than *Rosenkavalier*'s Octavian, because Octavian married a bourgeois girl. No Cherubino could or should be dressed so richly, but as a page to the Countess Almaviva Cherubino would certainly not be dressed poorly. With the name 'Almaviva' da Ponte would have flattered Mozart's bump for word games. The garden geography of the last act of *Figaro* is incorporated into the opera ball as a whole, with discoveries, alarums, flights and denunciations.

It isn't the what, it's the how   By quoting the Feldmarschallin in *Der Rosenkavalier*, Elena shows that the character's situation is relevant to her even if she has rejected the persona. As if to confirm this, Farfalla's grandfather also quotes from the same opera, but we should remember that although the Feldmarschallin constantly laments the onset of old age she is in fact thought of by both Strauss and Hofmannsthal as being in her middle thirties at the very most. A possible element of self-dramatisation in the Feldmarschallin's character is often ignored by the singer, who by the time she is ready for the role is unlikely to belittle it.

twenty-two

It had been dawn now for some time   The Felliniesque morning after prepares us, as in *La Dolce Vita*, for an eventual symbolic death. But Renoir's *La Règle du jeu* is equally being drawn upon, except that here nobody except Lancelot has been mortally wounded. Renoir's film is never more lyrical than in the tragic morning.

'The Millers couldn't make it!'   The Miller who would be most relevant to Lancelot is named first. Glenn Miller disappeared without trace.

'The Berlins couldn't make it!'   Isaiah Berlin, in his essay on Verdi, refers to Schiller's distinction between the naive and the sentimental. (Tietze, in his book on Tintoretto, avails himself of the same distinction.) The naive Verdi triumphs over the sentimental Wagner at numerous points during the opera ball chapters. Lancelot, wholly sentimental in the Schillerian sense that he must always think about the purpose of his art, has for lack of naivety ceased to be fruitful.

' . . . The Russells couldn't make it . . . '   Bertrand Russell's name is yet another reproach to Lancelot. When Russell realised that he no longer loved Ottoline Morrell he cycled home and told her. Later on, Lancelot adopts Russell's means of locomotion, but not his honesty.

'The Lawrences couldn't make it'   D. H. Lawrence, a connoisseur of death dances, called Baden-Baden 'a *Totentanz* out of Holbein'. T. E. Lawrence is present at the ball in the person of 'Zoom' Beispiel, who thought it was an OPEC ball and came as a sheik. Gertrude Lawrence was a prototype Sally Draycott.

One of the Farinata degli Uberti Montefeltro Cavalcanti boys   All the components of this polygenetic surname are taken from Dante. Lancelot's journey beyond the tomb is already being prepared.

such titles as 'Yeats and Embezzlement'   A mocking reference, I
fear, to my own small monograph *Keynes and Embellishment*, in
which I discuss the economist's marginal doodlings. (Cambridge and
Yale, 1977.) But Charlotte is also casting aspersions on Yeats's marital
behaviour. Yeats expected his wife George to be thankful for the
privilege of managing his life while he idealised other women. Maud
and Iseult Gonne are the women celebrated in most of the poems he
wrote in the tower, but the tower itself, his solid base, he dedicated to
her.

twenty-three

Holbein's drawing of Thomas More's family   The 1527 group
drawing would appeal to Victor not just because of the connection with
Erasmus but because Holbein himself was a cosmopolitan with a
knack for making himself at home, especially with the More family.
The finished painting long ago vanished and the copies are too weak to
convey the full outpouring of creative energy which Holbein ex-
perienced in the More household, but the Basle museum possesses the
preparatory sketch, which Holbein brought back with him and gave to
Erasmus, who was delighted. Margaret Roper sits on the floor with
More looking down at her – the same disposition of figures as occurs
when Sally and Victor meet. The father/daughter relationship is thus
underlined, to the point of hinting at an Electra complex, since Sally
has a missing father to match Victor's missing daughter. Margaret's
fluent Latin astonished Erasmus, who gladly exchanged letters with
her. The preparatory drawings for the individual heads are in Windsor
Castle and would by themselves be enough to show how Holbein's
spirit, like Victor's, fulfilled itself in England.

strong toils of grace   A nervous acknowledgment by Victor/Antony
of the power wielded by Sally/Cleopatra.

She had seen 'Otto e mezzo' only once   Victor has seen it eight and a
half times because to a large extent it is his story, with Anouk Aimée as
the Elena figure, Luisa. (Only in *Giulietta degli spiriti* does Fellini's
real-life wife, Giulietta Masina, actually play the distaff role.) The Sally
Draycott figure is represented directly by Claudia Cardinale and
indirectly by all the other inhabitants of the dream seraglio, an
extended wish-fulfilment for which Fellini, while attempting to
condemn himself, courts forgiveness by making Guido Anselmi
(Marcello Mastroianni) such an artist. When Mastroianni returns to
confront a similar phantasmagoria in *Città di donne*, he has no excuses
and the harem is a horror story from which he can take away nothing,
not even a wry smile: there is no *Entführung* from the *Serail*. Fellini's
Casanova must die in harness. But Victor will have taken some
consolation from the fact that Fellini, by submitting himself to the full

despair of his recurring theme, produced steadily more intense works of art.

if you play the ASA NISI MASA game　　A version of pig Latin, used by the children and the idealised, Vermeeresque nurses in the barn sequence of *Otto e mezzo*. Each vowel of what you want to say is followed by 's' and the same vowel again, asand soso oson. Mozart and his gifted sister Maria Anna habitually employed codes. Mozart was a copybook example of how the musical and ciphering mentalities go together – he filled endless pages with rows of numbers.

Did you know that Casanova in his old age fell in love with a ... mathematician?　　Only in Schnitzler's novella *Casanovas Heimfahrt*. By the time of his death in exile at Dux, Casanova had brought his *History of My Life* only as far as the summer of 1774, the very time when he was pardoned by the Inquisition and allowed to return home, as a paid spy, to Venice, the spy Elena's city of mirrors. (The glass mirror was invented and first used extensively in Venice.) Schnitzler took the opportunity of conjecturing what the homeward journey might have been like. Marcolina, the young mathematician/mistress he provided for Casanova, is a composite homage to Schnitzler's two great young soul mates, encountered thirty years apart during his life, Olga Waissnix and Vilma Lichtenstern. But Schnitzler worked out his guilt by making Casanova possess Marcolina through a trick and murder her young lover while escaping. In alluding to the story, Victor is thus acknowledging his own culpability.

twenty-four

digging her hard bare breasts into that man　　As the wind goddess does to the wind god in the left-hand grouping of Botticelli's 'Birth of Venus'. The two of them are locked together as they skim the small-waved water towards Venus in her shell. All the visual resonances set up by Samantha in this passage are ironically heroic.

the rippling shallow water　　As it is in the 'Birth of Venus', so it is in *Death in Venice*, both in the novella and in the Visconti film. Visconti pervades the text almost as thoroughly as Fellini: the dancing at the opera ball could be from his film *The Leopard*, the opera ball's processional groupings from his stage production of *Don Carlo*, and Randall Hoyle's costume from *The Damned*.

to keep the young girl – his picture of innocence – in focus　　In *La Dolce Vita*, Mastroianni, playing the authorial Fellini-figure for the first time, encounters desolation in the eye of the dead sun-fish on the beach at dawn, but regains the possibility of life by contemplating the untainted visage of the girl Paola. Lancelot, unable to believe in Samantha's innocence, loses his chance for redemption.

as once Nausikaa must have walked towards Odysseus   She does it in the *Odyssey*, VI, although Odysseus is not lying down and does more walking towards her than she towards him. The scholar Bentley, Mario Praz tells us, said that the *Iliad* was written for men and the *Odyssey* for women. Shelley said that the *Iliad* was strong and the *Odyssey* sweet. Samuel Butler suggested that the *Odyssey* had actually been written by a woman. Most informatively, Gladstone maintained that the poem of Ulysses is the story of family life. Matisse's illustration for the 1935 edition of Joyce's *Ulysses* has Nausikaa's handmaidens arranged as Three Graces. It is clear throughout the text that Lancelot, in choosing Samantha, has made the judgment of Paris. Samantha, Serena and Sally form a triad whose connection is indicated by the initial letter as surely as Botticelli's three maidens join hands in the *Primavera*. Nor should the fact be neglected that the demon Mara sent his three lovely daughters to dance seductively before Buddha as he sat under the pippala tree. Lancelot's Parisian apple, of course, appears in the box-file at the beginning of the text – already eaten because his choice is already made, and a withered core because he has made it wrongly.

for the first night of 'La Clemenza di Tito'   Since Mozart's *opera seria* is mainly concerned with a man being generously forgiving to a woman rather than vice versa, Elena would scarcely be pleased to see it: hence her flight. It is notable that the operas mentioned – *La Clemenza, Die Zauberflöte* and *Arabella* – are twilight works, faintly echoing the vigorous upheaval of the opera ball. No Salzburg season has ever featured these operas all at once. Lancelot-as-author plays fast and loose with time.

But when they were alone together she fell silent   Despite Elena's belief that *Les Liaisons dangereuses* is the governing book of her life, a more plausible candidate is *La Princesse de Clèves*. She and Victor are less inclined to speak frankly than to fall silent. Madame de La Fayette, rather than Laclos, sets the tone. Madame de Sévigné is another stylistic ancestor, believing that Castiglione's unperturbed and courtly images must be preserved whatever the provocation. Elena and Victor would exchange regular letters if there were no telephone. As it is, *Briefkultur* is replaced by *Telefonkultur*. The telephone is the instrument of Elena's rule. Ortega y Gasset told the Argentine Dante scholar Victoria Ocampo that history was to a large extent the story of women realising male ideals.

The villas in that area are set within stuccoed walls   At Poggio a Caiano still stands one of the chief villas of the Medici, the family which commissioned most of the Uccello, Botticelli and Raphael paintings used in the text. The bronze fountain-piece in Elena's garden which 'might or might not be by Giambologna' is probably a small copy from the large Giambologna Triton standing shivering in one of the garden pools at the Poggio Villa Medici.

twenty-seven

David was sitting up in bed reading 'The English Comic Writers' Yet another reference to Hazlitt, whose bad judgment in love Lancelot would have been painfully aware of. *Liber Amoris* would have rubbed in the same point.

'These lovers fled away into the storm,' said Victor Madeline (that name *again*) and Porphyro do so in the last stanza of 'The Eve of St Agnes'. Victor's punning references to the Proustian *madeleine* are more benign than Lancelot's. Victor will be content with his memory.

It took an age to get the dogs out into the garden The guardian (garden) dogs must be placated before Odysseus/Aeneas enters the Underworld. In this, the second epicentre of the text, Lancelot achieves brain-death by emptying his mind of imagery.

He had always admired Chénier's bravery Chénier's bravery probably sealed his fate, as Camille Desmoulins's fate was sealed by his joke about Saint-Just. Sainte-Beuve later published the *procès-verbal* of Chénier's interrogation, which showed him to be justifiably but unwisely contemptuous of the proceedings. He called the Revolutionary Tribunal miserable assassins, whereupon Jean-Antoine Rouche, condemned on the same day, and who had spent his time in prison translating Virgil, reminded him that there were others who might complain as well. (*Allons, mon ami, du calme. Ils sont plus à plaindre que nous.*) They died together on 25 July 1794, three days before the fall of Robespierre brought the Terror to an end.

'Déjà ce corps pesant se détache de moi' The line is from 'Enthousiasme, enfant de la nuit', a fragment of Chénier's projected *L'Amérique*. Almost any line from the *Iambes*, written while he was imprisoned in St Lazare, would have been more appropriate, but Lancelot is avoiding, even here, the sense of blasted hopes. 'Suddenly on my lips the rhyme is stopped,' wrote Chénier bitterly. But on Lancelot's lips the rhyme stopped by itself.

a dead spot in the centre of each eye, like Degas In later life Degas was forced by damaged retinas to look askance at the object of his vision. Degas worshipped Ingres and used his example as a stick with which to beat Renoir, who, convinced of his own inadequacies as a draughtsman, was misled into developing his *manière aigre*. Degas was not just an anti-Dreyfusard but anti-Semitic in general; Renoir was the epitome of tolerant sanity; the two are reconciled in the all-encompassing spirit of Jean Renoir's book about his father. 'Look back in, Ingres,' is a very relevant pun for Lancelot, since Ingres struggled all his life to spiritualise his natural concupiscence. In even his most serene paintings it is always there, and towards the end of his life, as at the start, it overwhelmed him.

Which was full of people, like a circle in Hell   The ninth circle of Dante's *Inferno*, Cantos XXXIII–IV, where the treacherous are buried in the ice. 'Why dost thou mirror thyself in us so long?' one of them asks Dante, who can see himself reflected. All the frozen faces are mirrors. Those damned who lie face up have their eyes shut fast by the crystal visors of their frozen tears.

Imagine the sweetness of going down there to live together   From 'Invitation au voyage' by Baudelaire. 'Mon enfant, ma soeur,/Songe à la douceur/D'aller là-bas vivre ensemble!' The two five-syllable lines plus the seven-syllable-line must be read as a single, swaying, curved unit, like Samantha's figure – a not fanciful comparison, since the invocation of Baudelaire's name at this key point prepares us for the onset of synaesthesia. Lancelot, like Baudelaire in the sonnet 'Correspondances', is now subject to the *longs échos* by which odours, sounds and colours change places to construct a deep unity. *Les parfums, les couleurs et les sons se répondent.*

You need a drunken boat   Rimbaud's 'Bateau ivre'. Once again Rimbaud is invoked as a saving grace, so that Lancelot, even at the eleventh hour, may persuade himself he gave up writing voluntarily. When inventing Farfalla's name, Lancelot-as-author drew on this poem's dream of the essential *eau d'Europe*, the pond on which the sad child sails a boat as frail as a butterfly in May.

Malraux told his wife that   But only a small proportion of Malraux's lies became truths later. A mythomaniac on the grand scale, Malraux, like T. E. Lawrence and Hemingway, was never able to include this propensity among his themes. Faulkner, invoked early in the text, allowed people to believe that he had flown in combat, but never made the mistake of actually claiming that he had, so that when the time came to back down he was able to do so with reasonable grace. Yet he was not able to examine, in fiction, his gift for embellishing truth. Joseph Roth encouraged the twin false notions that he had been both an officer and a prisoner of war in Russia. He gave both these attributes to the hero of his short novel *Die Flucht ohne Ende* (*The Flight Without End*) but afterwards, apparently unpurged, went on retaining them for himself until his death. It was said that Roth gave a different account of his life story to every woman he ever loved. Fellini was the only man honest enough to study his own dishonesty – one of the main reasons why Lancelot, both as author and character, is fascinated with him. Guido Anselmi in *Otto e mezzo* wears a false nose to confess his kinship with Pinocchio. Lancelot would like to share Fellini's capacity to make material out of the worst in his own psyche, but even in death can only project his neurosis, into the 'idea' of a book about liars.

It matched the curve of Botticelli's Venus   Samantha has already adopted this pose, when standing in the shallow water between the beaches of Biarritz. The very seductiveness of Botticelli's line has been a standing reproach to Lancelot throughout the text. So decisive an outline contains the pressure of temptation in a way he cannot hope to emulate.

it reminded him of Velázquez's Venus   The Rokeby Venus, naturally. Velázquez was chary about painting nude women but felt justified by the exalted precedent of Titian. The cupid holds the mirror – in which the Venus sees herself reflected and we see her face – at almost the exact point which would be occupied by Lancelot's own face when doting on Samantha in the Casa Perdida.

Boucher's Venus. Venus O'Murphy   Miss O'Murphy was one of Boucher's favourite models. Lancelot almost certainly means the 'Girl on a Couch' in the Älte Pinakothek in Munich. The Paris 'Girl on a Couch' adopts the same pose but is covered with a sheet. It was a standard angle for Boucher, as the Stockholm 'Leda and the Swan' (another Yeatsian connection) further reveals.

Leonardo's lady caressing the ermine in Cracow   The lady, painted circa 1483, is probably Cecilia Gallerani, mistress to Ludovico il Moro and thus, technically, the usurper of Beatrice d'Este's rightful position. Beatrice was the perfect wife but Ludovico was not a perfect man, although Leonardo's Cecilia would have made a saint stray. The caressed ermine is an assertive, not to say potentially explosive, Freudian property, especially since it is by far the best preserved section of the picture. The girl is fading but the ermine becomes ever more clearly defined, in keeping with the orgasmic sequence of Lancelot's demise.

They were both reading from the one book   Paolo and Francesca, in Canto V of the *Inferno*, read from the one book before they kiss. It is a book about Lancelot. 'We were reading one day for delight/About Lancelot, how love bound him.' Lancelot's final humiliation is to imagine these two lovers brought together by their mutual contemplation of his folly.

One can acquire anything in solitude, except character. Who said that?   Stendhal said it, in *De l'amour*. Conceptually, this is the fulcrum of the text. Lancelot, unable to escape the trap of his solipsism, has paid the price. But at the very instant of dissolution, Lancelot-as-character reveals the strategy of Lancelot-as-author. Stendhal had at least 160 pseudonyms and 30 separate disguises, one of them as a woman of quality. As Stendhal was all his characters – even Mathilde de la Mole in *The Red and the Black*, even Madame de Sanseverina in *The Charterhouse of Parma* – so Lancelot is all his. Stendhal, who devised cryptograms for the initials of his loves, wrote his own initials in the dust. Like Lancelot he abhorred the mob and yet desired the happiness of the people, as if they were two different groups. In adopting the persona of Chénier, Lancelot stopped one step short of identifying himself with Stendhal's Julien Sorel, whose severed head, in the last scene of *The Red and the Black*, is placed on a marble table to be kissed by Mathilde. Samantha, the real Salome of the opera ball – Sally stole her clothes – intuitively guillotined Lancelot in advance, by making him wear the scarlet choker. He was like the legendary victim of the Saracen's sword, who did not know his head had been cut off until he shook it. It was, of course, Stendhal who defined the novel as a mirror going down a road.

twenty-eight

'Klee! Clouet! Klimt! Braque! Cranach!'   All painters. Lancelot's derivative vision reasserts itself, beginning with the child-like Klee and ending with the sensual Cranach the Elder, a powerful student of long-stemmed beauties. Our hero is himself again.

'He gave me a book.'   The same book Elena had given Lancelot: *Les Liaisons dangereuses*. But Elena and Victor are not the Marquise de Merteuil and the Viscomte de Valmont. Sally is right when she says that she and Nicholas are better than that. So are the rest of their friends. Certainly Elena herself would not dream of emulating the clinical frankness which binds Laclos's people in their desolate intimacy. So she gives the book away. And by declining to keep it, Lancelot states his preference, not entirely unjustified, for a life of deception. Radiguet in *Le Bal du comte d'Orgel* called *Les Liaisons dangereuses* a bad book in a bad tradition. Laclos's frigid influence pervades all the literature to come. He is the origin of that element in Proust which caused E. M. Forster to say that Proust's analytical knife cut so deep it came out the other side. But Stendhal, an emotional anarchist in love with love, founded a tradition too, and when forced to the choice, Lancelot chooses that, although typically he would rather choose both. He wants the style *and* the fever. Dreaming of a poised frenzy, he can attain it in one way only – by writing it down. Where can he hide except in candour? How can he conceal himself except by calling out? Hence the first word of the first chapter.

© The Peter C. Bartelski Organisation

~ INDEX ~

at Victor Ludorum (*see also* Gillian Jackson project; London, literary; *Short, A World History of the*; writers-who-could-draw project), 21, 23, 69; secretary at, *see* Janice

women, desire for (*see also under individual women*), 52

Windhover, Tessa, 16

Windhover, Toby, 20, 167

Windsor, Duchess of, 98

Wingate, Orde, 24

Wittgenstein, Princesses Butsi, Futsi and Tutsi, 239

Woman Lieutenant's Frenchman, The, 62, 278

Wood, Block (*see also* actor, celebrated), 69

Wotan, 202

Wright, Frank Lloyd, 25

writers-who-could-draw project: information from Ian Cuthbert on, 74, 137–40, 232; Serena as researcher for, 31, 50, 61, 101, 105–7, 232; success, 268

X, Madame, 53, 275–6

Yamani, Sheik, 'Zoom' Beispiel dressed as, 200

Yeats and Embezzlement, 219

Yeats, W. B., 7, 282, 283

Yezhov, Nikolai, 24

'You'll Never Walk Alone', 93, 115, 263, 282

Zinoviev, Alexander, 106

Clive James
Unreliable Memoirs £1.95

The Kid from Kogarah tells all — at last in paperback after months in the bestseller lists.

'You had better not read the book on a train, unless you are unselfconscious about shrieking and snorting in public' OBSERVER

'The public's favourite wit and pundit, reduced in imagination to short-trouser size, wrestling with snakes and aunties and mutual-masturbators in the bush-bordering suburbs of postwar Sydney ... called up in the familiar two-fisted prose. The old boy may be 40, but he times a punchline disgustingly well' RUSSELL DAVIES, LISTENER

Glued to the Box £2.50

'Those who recall the standard set by the two previous volumes, *Visions Before Midnight* and *The Crystal Bucket* will not fail to be impressed by the undimmed vigour and panache of the writing' BRITISH BOOK NEWS

'Clive James founded a column on the principles that humour, intelligence and style were the inalienable rights of his readers. He is as funny as ever' BOOKS AND BOOKMEN

'Along with its two predecessors, it will stand as a once only critical phenomenon: ten years' worth of high intelligence and wit' LONDON REVIEW OF BOOKS

Picador

☐ **Burning Leaves**	Don Bannister	£2.50p
☐ **Making Love: The Picador Book of Erotic Verse**	edited by Alan Bold	£1.95p
☐ **The Tokyo-Montana Express**	Richard Brautigan	£2.50p
☐ **Bury My Heart at Wounded Knee**	Dee Brown	£3.95p
☐ **Cities of the Red Night**	William Burroughs	£2.50p
☐ **The Road to Oxiana**	Robert Byron	£2.50p
☐ **If on a Winter's Night a Traveller**	Italo Calvino	£2.50p
☐ **Auto Da Fé**	Elias Canetti	£3.95p
☐ **Exotic Pleasures**	Peter Carey	£1.95p
☐ **Chandler Collection Vol. 1**	Raymond Chandler	£2.95p
☐ **In Patagonia**	Bruce Chatwin	£2.50p
☐ **Sweet Freedom**	Anna Coote and Beatrix Campbell	£1.95p
☐ **Crown Jewel**	Ralph de Boissiere	£2.75p
☐ **Letters from Africa**	Isak Dinesen (Karen Blixen)	£3.95p
☐ **The Book of Daniel**	E. L. Doctorow	£2.50p
☐ **Debts of Honour**	Michael Foot	£2.50p
☐ **One Hundred Years of Solitude**	Gabriel García Márquez	£2.95p
☐ **Nothing, Doting, Blindness**	Henry Green	£2.95p
☐ **The Obstacle Race**	Germaine Greer	£5.95p
☐ **Meetings with Remarkable Men**	Gurdjieff	£2.95p
☐ **Roots**	Alex Haley	£3.50p
☐ **The Four Great Novels**	Dashiel Hammett	£3.95p
☐ **Growth of the Soil**	Knut Hamsun	£2.95p
☐ **When the Tree Sings**	Stratis Haviaras	£1.95p
☐ **Dispatches**	Michael Herr	£2.50p
☐ **Riddley Walker**	Russell Hoban	£2.50p
☐ **Stories**	Desmond Hogan	£2.50p
☐ **Three Trapped Tigers**	C. Cabrera Infante	£2.95p
☐ **Unreliable Memoirs**	Clive James	£1.95p
☐ **Man and His Symbols**	Carl Jung	£3.95p
☐ **China Men**	Maxine Hong Kingston	£2.50p
☐ **Janus: A Summing Up**	Arthur Koestler	£3.50p
☐ **Memoirs of a Survivor**	Doris Lessing	£2.50p
☐ **Albert Camus**	Herbert Lottman	£3.95p
☐ **The Road to Xanadu**	John Livingston Lowes	£1.95p
☐ **Zany Afternoons**	Bruce McCall	£4.95p
☐ **The Cement Garden**	Ian McEwan	£1.95p
☐ **The Serial**	Cyra McFadden	£1.75p
☐ **McCarthy's List**	Mary Mackey	£1.95p
☐ **Psychoanalysis: The Impossible Profession**	Janet Malcolm	£1.95p
☐ **Daddyji/Mamaji**	Ved Mehta	£2.95p
☐ **Slowly Down the Ganges**	Eric Newby	£2.95p
☐ **The Snow Leopard**	Peter Matthiessen	£2.95p

☐	**History of Rock and Roll**	ed. Jim Miller	£4.95p
☐	**Lectures on Literature**	Vladimir Nabokov	£3.95p
☐	**The Best of Myles**	Flann O' Brien	£2.95p
☑	**Autobiography**	John Cowper Powys	£3.50p
☐	**Hadrian the Seventh**	Fr. Rolfe (Baron Corvo)	£1.25p
☐	**On Broadway**	Damon Runyon	£3.50p
☐	**Midnight's Children**	Salman Rushdie	£3.50p
☐	**Snowblind**	Robert Sabbag	£1.95p
☐	**Awakenings**	Oliver Sacks	£3.95p
☐	**The Fate of the Earth**	Jonathan Schell	£1.95p
☐	**Street of Crocodiles**	Bruno Schultz	£1.25p
☐	**Poets in their Youth**	Eileen Simpson	£2.95p
☐	**Miss Silver's Past**	Josef Skvorecky	£2.50p
☐	**A Flag for Sunrise**	Robert Stone	£2.50p
☐	**Visitants**	Randolph Stow	£2.50p
☐	**Alice Fell**	Emma Tennant	£1.95p
☐	**The Flute-Player**	D. M. Thomas	£2.25p
☐	**The Great Shark Hunt**	Hunter S. Thompson	£3.50p
☐	**The Longest War**	Jacob Timerman	£2.50p
☐	**Aunt Julia and the Scriptwriter**	Mario Vargas Llosa	£2.95p
☐	**Female Friends**	Fay Weldon	£2.50p
☐	**No Particular Place To Go**	Hugo Williams	£1.95p
☐	**The Outsider**	Colin Wilson	£2.50p
☐	**Kandy-Kolored Tangerine-Flake Streamline Baby**	Tom Wolfe	£2.25p
☐	**Mars**	Fritz Zorn	£1.95p

All these books are available at your local bookshop or newsagent, or can be ordered direct from the publisher. Indicate the number of copies required and fill in the form below

11

....

Name_____
(Block letters please)

Address_____

_____

Send to CS Department, Pan Books Ltd, PO Box 40, Basingstoke, Hants
Please enclose remittance to the value of the cover price plus:
35p for the first book plus 15p per copy for each additional book ordered
to a maximum charge of £1.25 to cover postage and packing
Applicable only in the UK

While every effort is made to keep prices low, it is sometimes
necessary to increase prices at short notice. Pan Books reserve
the right to show on covers and charge new retail prices which
may differ from those advertised in the text or elsewhere